#Masterpiece

What you would do with all the time and money in the world

–

By extreme artist and founder of the Masterpiece Movement
Alexander Inchbald

First published 2020
Alexander Inchbald

www.alexander-inchbald.com
Title: #Masterpiece
"The Legacy Diamond" including the Inward, Outward and Upward Journey are registered Trademarks of The (artist) inside.
First published in Switzerland by The (artist) inside, Geneva
ISBN: 978-2-8399-3187-8
Printed on paper from sustainable sources.

Category: self-help/art/business

The author has tried to recreate events, locales and conversations from his memories of them. In order to maintain anonymity of certain individuals in some instances names, occupations and places have been changed to protect individuals. Certain identifying characteristics and details such as physical properties, occupations and places of residence may have changed.
This book is a personal memoir and not intended as a substitute for the medical advice of physicians. The reader should regularly consult a physician in matters relating to his/ her health and particularly with respect to any symptoms that may require diagnosis or medical attention. This is not intended for medical purposes or to promote any particular type of treatment than that recommended to the individual from their own medical team - each person is different.
The views and opinions expressed in this book are those of the authors and do not necessarily reflect the official policy or position of any other agency, publisher, organization, medical team, employer or company. Assumptions made in the analysis are not reflective of the position of any entity other than the author—and, these views are always subject to change, revision, and rethinking at any time.
The author is not to be held responsible for misuse, reuse, recycled and cited and/or uncited copies of content within this book by others.

DEDICATION
To Anna, Sasha and Daniel—let it snow.

Don't read this book... if you don't like being challenged. Don't read this book... if you don't want to change. Don't read this book... how you might normally read a book—in between one thing and another thing, while you're rushing around, trying to do ten things at once. Resist the temptation to try to read it too quickly. Instead, if you do decide to read it, despite these warnings, I encourage you to read it like you would sip a glass of vintage champagne—remove any distraction, savor the moment, drink it in bit by bit, then share it. This isn't a normal book, it's an experience—one I'd like to share with you. I'm extending my hand to you now and inviting you to step over the threshold. Join me and let's go on a journey to create your Masterpiece.

With love

Alexander Inchbald

The Swiss Alps, November 2020
alexander-inchbald.com

Praise for #Masterpiece

"The tools in #Masterpiece helped me translate the work I'd done in my personal life into my professional life and in the process move from CMO of a major fashion brand to CEO of an exclusive fashion brand. By the time I met Alexander, I already had a coach and had attended many courses. What makes this approach and Alexander special is it provides exactly what I need when I need it."

Riccardo Bellini
CEO, Chloé, Richemont Group

"I love Alexander and his work—what he describes in #Masterpiece has changed my life. These tools helped me stop, regenerate myself, then generate the funding my Masterpiece, United Cities, needed to change our world. I imagine a world in which all of us realize we can do this."

Kari Aina Eik
Founder United Cities—the world's most innovative partnership based program at the local level to achieve the UN's SDGs

"Read this book—and it is a game changer. #Masterpiece inspires individuals and teams on how to stay true to personal and team missions. Alexander has a unique ability to get to the heart of the matter and intuitively see what few others can—each individual's personal contribution to the collective goal—and then help them become aware of whatever is stopping them from doing that. I brought this book for my team. I encourage you to do the same."

Michelle Crossan-Matos
SVP Corporate Strategy & Transformation, Samsung Electronics America

"If change starts within, then the framework in this book is desperately needed for companies to become sustainable. With Alexander's guidance, I had my team work on finding their Personal Purpose, sharing them with one another was one of the most meaningful team exercises I have ever done, it allowed us to understand each other's passions and unite our energy to create a new team mission that everyone saw themselves in. Together, this team helped to change the company."

Nate Hurst
President of Wells Fargo Foundation, Chief Social Impact & Sustainability Officer at Wells Fargo

"The core ideas within #Masterpiece bring joy to so many people. I've seen it with my own eyes. It is a real privilege to be Alexander's partner in Japan. I imagine a world in which we all live on Purpose, so I'm looking forward to seeing him back here for more sushi in the years to come."

Tamami Ushiki
Founder and CEO, Japan Wealth Dynamics Association

"These tools helped me to transform my life... moving from Director of one communications agency to Managing Director of another. I realized I was trying to make others happy and that was impossible. Now, I'm freer, happier and healthier. You can do the same."

Mark Harrison
leading advertising executive

"Alexander is a genuine Changemaker. #Masterpiece explains how you can become one too by freeing your true self. Alexander's support has been invaluable to me in my journey and it's been a privilege collaborating with him over the last four years. I look forward to many more years to come."

Jason Bernhardt-Lanier
Acting Director of Fellowship, Ashoka

Contents

Foreword

As Alexander's colleague and friend, I feel honored that he invited me to write the foreword of this book. I'm still learning many things from him, but one of them is that authors of successful Masterpieces usually leave a legacy that lasts long after they have died. So, anticipating that many readers of this book will be from the business realm, I set out on a search to see if I could find the oldest example from this field. Not sure I've been successful, but one of the longest lasting must surely be that of Luca Pacioli, a close friend of Leonardo Da Vinci. In 1494 Pacioli codified accounting and double-entry bookkeeping and effectively created his Masterpiece: the Balance Sheet. I select this example with pleasure, not just for the association with Alexander—as an artist with a business background—but also related to the theme of "balance," which was not just the title of his first book, but I believe also remains at the heart of this one.

The balancing in a balance sheet was not specifically intended by Pacioli to be more than artistic mathematics, but for nigh on five centuries what the balance sheet offered was a semblance of balance for the enterprises it served, for the business world in industrial society and for the world in general. It is still today, of course, in ubiquitous use.

Yet the life of Masterpieces must also pass someday. So, if you're a CEO, a Founder, or for that matter anyone using a Balance Sheet today, I think you might usefully ask yourself, how useful is it, really? How much practical "balance" does its use realistically bring you and your people, and the world in which you're currently transitioning? I'm aware, of course, how radical this question is! But it's relevant here because when Alexander speaks, I regularly hear him talk about how much our world is now out of balance. And of course, his is far from being a lone voice anymore. Rectors of universities, of business schools and other seats of learning, avid advocates of Milton Friedman and shareholder value in the 1980s and 90s are now castigating the same, finally and earnestly joining in citing the challenges we presently face in environment, health, food, divorce, inequality, civil unrest etc. Or in Alexander's own words "a vicious pandemic of disengagement, depression, disease, inequality and climate change."

Diagnosis alone however doesn't improve anything though. For me, Alexander is a forerunner and pioneer—an artist in the truest sense—in reflecting deeply and using his skills to help us go beyond, not just to diagnose but to create something entirely new. His #Masterpiece programs and this book might well bear the subtitle "How to regain your lost balance" and if you'll permit a short tangent, I'd like to illustrate how perfect I find this from another dimension.

If you study "balancing acts" in careful detail, for example walking a tightrope, or more simply just walking or driving your car, you'll see that it's only in infinitesimal nano-moments that you're really in balance, if at all! You may actually be out of balance almost all the time, but if you offer an outer impression of being in harmony and flow for an extended period, like the tightrope walker, it's because you're continually making a series of seamless minute corrections. I'm indebted for this insight to George Soros who elaborated on this idea with his notions of "Dynamic disequilibrium" and "Reflexivity,"[1] tested and translated into his successful financial strategies. What I gleaned from this understanding, with practical consequences for my own endeavors, is that the very first condition for getting into this flow state is to come to terms with a paradoxical corollary: to relax into the total acceptance of the fact that one is almost all of the time, but possibly even all of all the time, out of balance. The second is the need to be in touch with your *sixth sense*, through body, mind and spirit to a sort of "universal energy"; in order that your perception of reality is actually identical or as close as possible to "reality" itself. Only then are you capable of making this continual series of seamless movements which are perfect corrections to redress what one might call "imbalance." Where you fail to do this, where your approach fails to include fallibility, the inconsistency between your perception of reality and reality itself, i.e. your illusion, leads you to fall off the tightrope. Or in Soros's articulation, it creates disharmonious volatility in the form of a bubble, which at some point, has got to burst. The larger the illusion and bubble, the larger the eventual burst.

This is my best, but perhaps inadequate, explanation of something I find barely explainable in words. Nonetheless, with this in mind, let's return now to Pacioli and balance sheets. These, and the associated conceptual accounting tools we use every day as a matter of course in business, undoubtedly "mapped the territory" very well until half-a-century ago, but do they still do so now? We must ask ourselves; I think, have we not become so mesmerized by their

1 Soros, George. *Soros on Soros—Staying Ahead of the Curve*. John Wiley and Sons, 1995.

"truths" that we may fail to notice while they're telling us we're in a green oasis, that we're actually in a desert (i.e. we're confusing the map with the territory)—and that this unwittingly contributes via an enormous "Soros-type bubble" to the forms of symptoms that Alexander expresses? I suspect so.

Moreover, if we do so realize and decide these Masterpieces have seen their day, where should we now turn for guidance? The ancients used the stars, homing pigeons use their instincts, monarch butterflies pass through four generations before returning to the same trees, and the best business entrepreneurs—Richard Branson, George Soros, Warren Buffett and Steve Jobs have always used "gut feeling" rather than narrow metrics to guide them. But, with the development of the rational, scientific intellect in the last 300 years of industrial society, together with the corresponding educational and career models which still prevail so strongly, we have let this innate ability, which we all possess, to become dull. I find there's a hopeful trend of reawakening in progress, for example through meditation, yoga and other body-mind practices, but are the results of these practices yet strong enough to encourage those of us in business to enter the scary vacuum of giving up our existing traditional tools, once we recognize they may be inaccurate or misleading? Not yet, it seems.

As I see it, Alexander's *#Masterpiece* is a deeply reflected and meticulously structured guide, which offers solid ground for anyone who finds themselves at such a point of embarkation. Paraphrased as simply as possible, it's a step-by-step process of doing successively more of what you love in your life, of being and living more and more your essential quality, which culminates in your life becoming an expression of your Masterpiece. Once you're on this path you don't, of course, have to give up the traditional tools you've been using in particular situations where they may still be useful, but as you grow, they lose their universal dominance over you.

This book is a wonderful introduction to this journey.

Enjoy it!

Peter Koenig
Founder of "Moneywork" and "Sourcework," and author of *30 Lies About Money: liberating your life, liberating your money.*

November 2020

Introduction

What would you do if you had all the money and time in the world and you didn't care what others thought about you?

You'd create the Masterpiece you were born to create—the greatest contribution you can make to yourself, your family and society. It could be a painting, a book, or even a relationship; it could be a program, retreat, initiative, or a new business that changes your world for good.

Of course, you may already be in the process of creating your Masterpiece. If so, how is it going? Is it all plain sailing or are you facing some resistance? Does it feel like one moment you're flowing serenely with the current and the next you're facing into a gale force wind? Or, do you have a game-changing idea, but you feel like you're all alone—some people appear to get it, but not enough—and those that do seem to be on the boat with you one moment, and then they've abandoned ship the next—or worse, you've had to ask them to get off? If so, you're not alone. Or perhaps, you're feeling the opposite—your boat is full and more people are joining you every moment. You're amazed by what you've unleashed, but you're feeling overwhelmed that they all depend on you. What would happen if you broke down? Or do you sometimes wonder if your ship is heading in the right direction—whether you're doing enough for your family and the planet as well as your company?

Wherever you are on your journey to create your Masterpiece doesn't matter. What stops us from creating it and bringing it to life is always the same thing: ourselves—or more specifically the fear within us. The fear that we won't make enough money, we won't have enough time, we're not good enough, or others won't accept what we're creating. Clients often tell me, "my boss or my partner needs me to do this or that first." Does this sound familiar? In my experience, these are excuses we use to play small, to stay within our comfort zone, to suppress the voice inside us that calls us to do something different, to be someone different.

Let's stop making excuses. You are more than this. You are not a body with a spirit. You are a spirit with a body. When we were born, we were connected to the entire universe. There was no separation between us and it—whatever you call *it*.

This is what I discovered painting in extreme locations all over the world. When I stopped resisting the elements, they stopped resisting me. I realized I was *it*—I saw how every thought influenced *it*. *I* shaped *it* without even knowing it.

I often describe it like one of those boxes you find yourself in endlessly, on Zoom or Microsoft Teams, or whatever video app you're currently using to connect with colleagues, clients and family around the world. At birth, our little brain produces primarily delta brainwaves: we are in a state of connection, deep in our unconscious, connected to that entire box. Then, at the age of two, our ego starts to form. As we become mobile, our brain shifts to producing primarily theta brainwaves and we start to separate. We are no longer connected to the entire box. We reduce our world. We throw a tantrum, not because we need more food or because we didn't get the toy we saw in the shop. These are just triggers that remind us that we are no longer connected to all of *it*. Then, at the age of seven, we shift again to producing primarily alpha brainwaves. We are no longer in our unconscious mind. We start to introduce rules—I can't do this or I can't do that—and we separate further. Finally, at the age of twelve, just before we become a teenager, we shift a third time. We start producing primarily beta brainwaves and the disconnection is almost complete. Now, we live in just a tiny square within our Zoom window—a fraction of who we were born to be.

At each stage along this journey, our energy attracts experiences to us that cause little traumas, and we interpret each little trauma as a sign we aren't good enough or we won't make enough money if we have fun. Each trauma separates us from us. If this sounds familiar, this isn't your fault. Nor is it your parents or your grandparents' fault. It dates back to the dawn of civilization when our ancestors created the first systems to measure time, hierarchies and slavery, that placed one of us above the other; and marriage and money that inadvertently bound us in chains. These systems introduced inequality. They introduced structures that put you above or below your fellow human being, and all men above all women. In the process, our ancestors disconnected from themselves. Then, they passed this disconnection down through their genes, from one generation to the next. A continuous thread of intergenerational trauma.

Now, we spend all our time trying harder and harder to experience this state of connection again, without even knowing it. We push ourselves to the limits. Then, we push ourselves over the edge. Do you do this? If so, stop! The only person who is impacted by you pushing is yourself and your health.

You are more than this. You are the entire ecosystem. You're not separate from it. This book is designed to help you reconnect again—to become who you were born to be. Of course, this ecosystem goes way beyond the imaginary Zoom box I described above; it is infinite. You are infinite. We all are. As the poet Rumi said, "you are not a drop in the ocean, you are the entire ocean in a drop."

When we realize we are the ecosystem, we see how our thoughts create our reality. So, if you dislike what you do—even a tiny part of it—you will create a reality where you are surrounded by resistance, where it feels like you're swimming against the current or sailing into a gale force wind. This resistance will slowly reduce your world until you become a fraction of who you are. On the other hand, if you love what you do, you will create a reality where you are surrounded by love—constantly expanding outwards, in all directions.

Which reality do you want to live in?

When we don't love what we do, we compromise our mental health and eventually our physical health. Over time, one little compromise will lead to another and depression, disease, divorce, addiction or debt arrives at the door. Perhaps this is what's happening in your world? Maybe you're not depressed, but are you totally fulfilled? Imagine what would happen if everyone around you wasn't fulfilled? Too few of us would care enough to make the right decisions—not just for ourselves, but for our families and society. We'd all make decisions out of harmony with the system. It would lead to extraordinary inequalities between us and irreversible impacts on the environment around us.

This is the world we live in. Too few of us love what we do, and yet we keep taking the same path again, and again, and again—hoping that if we try harder or we work faster something will change. It won't.

The good news is we are living through the greatest transition in the history of humanity—greater than the cognitive revolution fifty years ago, greater than the Renaissance almost 500 years ago, and greater than the first civilization in Sumer 5,000 years ago. We have the greatest opportunity right now to free ourselves from the manmade system and become the entire ecosystem again. For humanity to survive and thrive, each of us must make this choice for ourselves. But will you?

I made my choice a decade ago. I'm grateful I did—I love what I do, I wake up next to a woman I love, with a family I love, in a place I love, and work with people I love. My wish is for you to do the same. Maybe not for you to wake up next to my wife, that could get a little crowded, but for you to wake up next to a partner you love, and love what you do, not just some of the time—all of the time.

So, what do you choose? You will not change your world by what you do, you will change it by who you are and who you become. Doing follows being. Matter follows energy. We think people change the world by what they do. They don't. It is the energy behind their actions that changes the world. We obsess over what we do, because our first five senses create the illusion this is what matters. It doesn't. What attracted thousands of Indians to follow Mahatma Gandhi during his Salt March across India wasn't what he did—it was who he became. What stopped civil war in South Africa at the end of Apartheid wasn't the Truth and Reconciliation Commission that Nelson Mandela enacted—it was who he became while he was in jail. Inside, often in solitary confinement, he freed himself from the constraints of the box. He burst the iron shackles society imposed on him. He became who he is, and others saw themselves in Mandela's struggle.

So, who are you going to become? We don't have much time. The temperature is increasing. Species are going extinct, and so will we if we don't change. Inequality is getting worse. People are dying of preventable diseases or starving when mountains of food are thrown away. We will not change any of these things through our actions, no matter how hard we try. We will change them through who we become.

For the last few years, I have been working with Kari—the founder of United Cities. When I first started working with her, she was struggling to generate sufficient money to pay herself and her team. Now, her initiative to bring business and cities together to achieve the United Nations Sustainable Development Goals is the world's most innovative partnership based program at the local level to achieve the SDGs. It is attracting millions of dollars from banks and entrepreneurs, and support from governments all around the world.

The transition was simple: she stopped pushing and became who she is.

When I first started working with Nate, he was the Chief Sustainability Officer of HP Inc. He worked for a company and in an industry—printers and computers—that was unsustainable. I helped him and his team articulate their Personal Purpose and develop a roadmap to bring multiple Masterpieces to life. He did, and HP was recognized recently by *Newsweek* as the most responsible company in America.[2] Nate changed himself. The by-product was he changed his world.

Your Masterpiece may not be quite as grand as these examples: Garth joined my #Masterpiece program to write a memoir about his relationship to time. He did, and changed his relationship with his family. Erika was PA to the Creative Director of a major technology company. She joined the program to become a coach and has now embarked on a new exciting chapter of her life. Sonia joined the program to regain the sense of connection she had before she joined one of the world's most respected consulting companies—now, she is training 40,000 people in Southern Africa to prevent the region's wildlife from going extinct.

You can do the same. How do I know? Because you have exactly the same access to the infinite world as they do. In the process you come alive. You become who you were born to be. And because everyone else is connected to the same infinite world, no matter where they are on their journey, or how suppressed they are, your Masterpiece reminds them of who they were born to be. However, your responsibility isn't to change them—it is to change yourself. By changing yourself, you change your world—and the fastest way to do that is to create your Masterpiece.

I imagine a world in which I can ski with my grandchildren regularly in The Alps in 2050. Why? Because my children love to ski—it is their favorite thing in the whole world. And I know, for us to ski in 2050, we will have solved climate changes and inequality—and to do this you would have to love what you do. To many this sounds crazy—the snow level rises as the temperature climbs. But I know it's possible. I've seen it happen, again and again and again—every time I paint, I observe the relationship between me and the entire ecosystem. I would love you to have a similar experience.

2 Cooper, Nancy. "America's Most Responsible Companies 2020." *Newsweek.com* https://www.newsweek.com/americas-most-responsible-companies-2020 (accessed September 26, 2020).

So, what is your Masterpiece? It is a self-portrait of the entire ecosystem seen through your eyes, expressed through you. Your Masterpiece is part of your legacy. The world needs you to create it for without your contribution the rest of us are missing out.

Let's stop hoping the future will be different and instead, start creating a different future. We have the ability—the time is NOW.

So, the ultimate question is: how do you create your Masterpiece? That's what this entire book is all about. Are you ready to create your Masterpiece?

1 The Journey of Transition

There is only one thing that makes a dream impossible to achieve: the fear of failure.

Paulo Coelho

Do you feel you were born to create something greater? Is there more to you than most people see? An inspirational dream that you haven't managed to turn into reality? Is there a voice, deep down, that is calling you to do something different, to be someone different?

I hear you; I felt that too. That calling. That not-quite-right feeling. A disconnect between my vision and my actions within it. Not having aligned my thinking, my words or my actions with a greater purpose. Ending up frustrated, fighting myself or others and not always in a state of flow. Something always getting in the way of what I actually wanted—a person, project, or priority. Not to mention fear—the fear both of failing, yet of how great I could be if only I got out of my own way.

Sound familiar? It's not your fault. Like each of us, you grew up in a man-made system that does not value true creation. A system that has shifted us away from our true creative nature, our deepest and most soulful calling. A system that has encouraged you to program your body and mind to sabotage you. A system that has nurtured your fear, hindered your confidence, and fed you distraction after distraction, leading you down a path of disconnection. A system of hierarchies, imposed rules and gross inequalities. A system that has quashed your deeper intuitive *sixth sense* so you become a hostage to society's customs, rules and regulations. The good news is you can transcend this engineered man-made system and create the Masterpiece you were born to create.

Everyone is Creative

Everyone is born creative. Everyone is born with infinite potential—but often, sadly, it gets suppressed over time. Picasso said, "Every child is born an artist, the problem is how to remain one as you grow up."

Every great artist, scientist, inventor, and athlete goes on their own epic journey to discover how to fully express their creativity. We only have to look at the journeys Steve Jobs, Nelson Mandela, Gandhi, Michelangelo, Mother Teresa and Vincent van Gogh took in their lives to see how they too suffered: beaten by parents, impoverished living, fired from jobs, imprisoned, and even suicide. And yet, something drove each of them on: an inner voice, a calling, a greater purpose. Each had a vision for how their world could be. Each contributed something greater than themselves. Each reclaimed the artist inside them. They took the road less traveled and transitioned from suffering to joy along the way. Of course, you might say, "Well that's sounds lovely Alexander, but I'm not Steve or Nelson or Vincent"—and I would agree. But you are just as unique as them. You are different.

You are an artist. We all are. Your art is unique as you are. You might not be the artist that creates paintings or sculptures, composes music or writes books. Instead, your art may be uniting people behind a greater purpose or developing sustainable solutions to address humanity's greatest challenges such as climate change, wellbeing or inequality. Or, your art might simply being, the best husband, wife, father or mother you can be.

It's never too late or too early to transition and unleash the artist inside you.

Paulo Coelho was thirty when he first started writing: his second book *The Alchemist* shot him to worldwide fame. J.K. Rowling was twenty-seven when she started writing her Masterpiece, *Harry Potter and the Philosopher's Stone*. In 1985, Steve Jobs was fired by the board of the company he created only to return in 1997, and inspire it to create two new Masterpieces: the iPhone and the iPad. These Masterpieces made Apple the most valuable company in the world. Mahatma Gandhi was sixty when he trekked 240 miles to the Arabian Sea to protest against the Salt Tax in India, then went on a hunger strike and was at death's door before the British colonial powers relented. His greatest Masterpiece was overcoming the most powerful empire the world had ever seen without firing a single shot. Nelson Mandela was imprisoned in 1962, a convicted terrorist, only to come out twenty-seven years later, at the age of sixty-nine, as a presidential candidate and create his Masterpiece: preventing a country from descending into civil war and inspiring the world with his vision.

Why does this matter? Because you can do the same.

How do I know? Because I've done it—and so have many of my clients.

Let me share my journey with you...

The False Summit and The Endless Abyss

When I was sixteen, two things happened in quick succession. But it took twenty-four years to fully realize their significance. The first incident happened in late Spring at school. To start with, I was hiding at school more than creating. Initially, I used the art department as a refuge to escape relentless bullying. I missed home and felt safe in the art department, knowing bullies felt as vulnerable in this space as I did in their presence.

However, what happened that Spring was a breakthrough. A few months earlier, I'd visited the Monet exhibition at The National Gallery in London and been blown away. Monet's use of light and depiction of water, was beyond anything I'd seen before. It was the first time I'd seen *Impression, Sunrise*—the painting that gave its name to the movement. In fact, it was the first time I had seen any Impressionist pieces in person, and they inspired me to paint. It left such a lasting impression, I realized I could become an artist who influenced millions.

So, there I was in the art department, the sun streaming through the window, working on a piece that was inspired by Monet's *Bridge at Argenteuil*. Suddenly, a pink mist appeared on the canvas. A few minutes later, I felt called to balance it with strokes of turquoise. Now, I'd never used either of these colors before, but as I let go, the whole canvas started to resonate on a different level. The colors started to play off each other and I was lost in the flow of creation. Time disappeared. When I eventually stood back from the canvas, transfixed, I realized it was the best piece I had ever created. Captivating. *Where had this sudden rush of creativity come from? And how could I replicate it?* Whatever it was, I wanted more of it.

The second incident happened shortly after. I was offered £200 for the painting. It felt amazing! My dream of going to art college and becoming an artist was one step closer. But within two weeks, this feeling—and my dream—was crushed. My dad told me that he, my mother and my art teacher had concluded that I would never make money as a professional artist. I believed him more than myself. I brought his story, and agreed to study business instead. In that moment, I suppressed the artist inside me and fell into the Endless Abyss—a dark, downward, bottomless spiral which I wasn't sure I could ever get out of.

Faith in oneself is the best and safest course.

Michelangelo

The next few years were the darkest of my life. In my final year of school, the bright vibrant, post-impressionist colors I used on the canvas, reverted to Rembrandtesque shades of darkness without the divine light. It wasn't just the light that had gone out, I was told that art examiners didn't want original, intuitive art. They wanted an intellectual demonstration of technique. While others in my class, who had chosen to go to art college, explored their intuition and grew, I practiced my technique and stagnated.

Rather than paint nature, I painted cityscapes. It was only years later, when I tried painting in the heart of Paris and Basel, that I realized cities stop the natural flow of energy. The vast majority of buildings in cities aren't designed to channel energy organically through and around them. They stop it in its tracks. And that's what happened. I stopped creating what my heart told me to create. Everything stopped flowing through me, and I descended into the darkness.

I experienced drinking and eating problems and became dependent on liquidized food. I couldn't eat in public from severe anxiety. The only way to calm myself was to get drunk. I abused alcohol. I created a drinking game with a 'friend'—Tequila mixed with Tabasco—to escape my restless mind. I experimented with drugs, and ended up in hospital twice from excessive drinking. The second time, the doctor told me I had torn my stomach lining and it could take years to heal. I didn't need anyone else to abuse me, I was doing it myself. I remember looking up at the Salisbury Crags, a series of cliffs I could see from my halls of residence at university in Edinburgh, and wondering what it would be like to jump off them. What would it feel like to end the torment and pain? Fortunately, I never jumped.

Six years later, I was made redundant from my first job as a management trainee at Unilever, in part, because one of my appraisals said I wasn't creative enough. *Me? Not creative enough?* While the irony is now laughable, I was devastated. The news reopened my wound. I walked out of the building in complete shock, and sat on a nearby bench—I felt like the world had opened up underneath me. I phoned the only person I could think of—my father—the second irony of the day. The one person who'd suggested I follow the path of business was now the one hearing my sobs as I promptly burst into tears the moment I explained what had happened. I felt that I had let him down. I felt like I had let everyone down. The truth was more painful—I'd let myself down ten years before when I didn't stand up to him and say, "I'm an artist. I was born to be an artist. This is who I am."

Rock bottom was a long way down.

> *Bless you prison, bless you for being in my life. For there, lying upon the rotting prison straw, I came to realize that the object of life is not prosperity as we are made to believe, but the maturity of the human soul.*[3]
>
> **Aleksandr Solzhenitsyn**

Your World Reflects You

As humans, we are always looking for answers; something to help make sense of our experiences, to give meaning, to help us understand why. So, I asked myself: *Was my father to blame for me losing my job? Or my art teacher for not having faith in me? Was it the school and their lack of support? Or the education system?*

On reflection, I realized my descent into this darkness had started many years earlier; in fact, much earlier than I was even aware of it. While my dad had "crushed my dream"—all he was doing was reflecting my own self-doubt back to me. Many years later, I realized that if you look into a mirror and don't like what you see, you don't blame the mirror or attempt to break it, you change yourself.

The system which I grew up in didn't encourage creativity. At school, I didn't learn to create intuitively, I learned to draw intellectually. Rather than go into nature to be inspired, I learned how to copy photos inside. And I'm not alone. This happens in almost every classroom all over the world. It's not the fault of the teacher or the school or even the parents. We become victims of the system. From primary school to business school, our education system is designed to focus on strengthening our conscious mind, rather than our unconscious mind, our intellect rather than our intuition. As a result, we strengthen the neural networks in our brain that support intellect over intuition. And, according to epigenetics, this influences which genes our bodies express. We then allow

3 Solzhenitsyn, Aleksandr Isaevich. *The Gulag Archipelago, 1918-1956: An Experiment in Literary Investigation*. New York; Toronto: Harper Perennial Modern Classics, 2007.

ourselves to be abused, stop believing we are artists and our genes do the rest, reinforcing this belief—it's a vicious self-reinforcing cycle.

The good news? You can't kill creativity. No one can. It is the essence of who you are, of who we are. It is your life-force. Which means you can turn the "artistic" genes back on again by changing your beliefs and unlocking the creativity within.

Four months after sitting on that bench crying my eyes out, I was back working for Unilever, in their head office, in a more exciting role, earning fifty percent more money. It was 1999, and the internet was exploding. My role was to catalogue all of Unilever's websites in Europe and help write the first internet guidelines for Unilever marketers. From there I went into communications—first to help create a digital agency inside the oldest advertising agency in the world, J. Walter Thompson—and then, I moved to Geneva, eventually setting up a communications agency with the former partners of Saatchi & Saatchi.

What changed? I had. I had taken a good hard look at myself in the mirror and worked out what I wanted to do with my life. I negotiated a leaving package which included sessions with a work psychologist and an outplacement advisor. The first helped me understand who I am and why I am here—what I call my **Inner Game**. The second helped me understand my strengths and how to describe them in my CV and interviews—what I call my **Outer Game**. I attended my first self-development course and faced many of my greatest fears. So much so, I felt as if I was standing on the edge of a new cliff—one that would lead to an alternative reality. I was ready to jump off... almost.

Despite all my self-work, something still wasn't quite right. That voice, deep inside me was yearning to express itself. The artist inside, desperate to create my Masterpiece. But working as a strategist in communications wouldn't allow me to do it. I was continually climbing the False Summit: the place where I searched for materialistic success within the system, constantly suppressing the artist inside me. And I kept on falling into the Endless Abyss—every exogenous shock triggered my self-doubt my world continued to wobble.

There was only one thing to do. I started painting again—fourteen years after I stopped. But it took work. I didn't just pick up the brush and begin a frenzy of brushstrokes; it took me six months after my decision to paint again, to pluck up the courage to do it.

Then over the coming years, my travels bought me into contact with people—creatives, intuitives, visionaries—who offered words of advice, shared wisdom, and told me what I needed to hear: *You're stuck in your head. Listen to your true calling. Climb back up your mountain. Do the thing you fear most. You know exactly what it is. And you need to do it. Listen to your heart.*

As I started to listen to my intuition again and follow my heart, I became more inspired and courageous. The pivotal movement was when I faced my fears in front of that first canvas on a mountain above Geneva, in Switzerland. Inspired by a line in Paulo Coelho's book, *Eleven Minutes*: "If she had looked more deeply into herself, she would have realized that what had thrilled her about the bird was his freedom, the energy of his wings in motion, not his physical body."4 I started to paint. Creativity flowed out of me, along with a flood of tears, like a dam bursting open.

WooWoo Mountain and Codependent Chasm

Sometimes we don't like what we hear; and for me, being told I was a "drama queen" by a woman I broke-up with, was enough for me to fall into the Endless Abyss again. It turns out she was correct. Our relationship and all of my previous relationships had been codependent. I depended on this woman for love, because I didn't love myself. When she pulled back, I pushed forward. When she pulled back further, I started to manipulate more. When she lost interest, I played the victim. She thought I was the drama queen and I thought she was.

Looking in the mirror and seeing myself reflected in this woman wasn't easy. It was very uncomfortable. In hindsight, I can see every time I experienced a serious bout of self-doubt or an exogenous shock like this, whether it be a break-up, losing my job or even a recession, I tumbled into the Endless Abyss. This time, I knew I had to change something within me. I just didn't know what.

Four months later, after increasing my breathwork practice and attending a retreat in Turkey, I was on another retreat in South Africa, where I finally leapt off the "cliff" and into an alternative reality. This time I didn't fall into the Endless Abyss. I realized I had been living a false life: scared of being accepted for who I was, and hiding in plain view. I had created a mask—an identity that

4 Coelho, Paulo, and Margaret Jull Costa. 2004. *Eleven minutes.* HarperOne; Reprint Edition, 13 October 2009, p230.

hid the real me from the world. I didn't believe that anyone would accept the real me. So, I pretended to be someone different, hoping that someone, anyone would like the fabricated version of me. Of course, they didn't. I just attracted jobs and partners who were living the same inauthentic lie.

On this South African retreat, in the beautiful Drakensberg mountains, I reclaimed the masculine part of me by accepting I had been abusing myself all along. I stopped blaming everyone else and took responsibility. I had abused my body with alcohol, my girlfriends with words, my father with thoughts, and the artist within me with neglect and suppression. I finally accepted who I am and stopped projecting it onto others.

As an important aside, Peter Koenig, who you may remember from the Foreword, coined the term "reclamation." He uses it to refer to the process of reclaiming aspects of "one's identity which we have disidentified from and then projected" onto other people (as in this case) or other things (such as money or time) as we shall discover later in the book. Koenig's work is based in turn on the Swiss psychologist Carl Gustav Jung's hypothesis that we must become consciously aware of the unquestioned assumptions we make about each other in order to resolve any resistance and conflict between us. Koenig's experiments, which started in the 1980s, demonstrated "removal" of these assumption was "a start, but too weak to have a really significant effect." Trial and error led him to conclude the key was to reclaim both the projection *and* its polarity or opposite. Long before I met Peter or had even heard of the term reclamation, this is exactly what I was doing in the Drakensberg mountains.

After reclaiming the masculine aspects of me, I reclaimed the feminine part of me by articulating my Purpose for the first time. For me, Purpose is not what you do, it is but who you are. It articulates your essence, your spirit, your life-force, the artist inside you: your Inner Game.

Your Masterpiece is what you create to bring your Purpose to life. It is your Purpose expressed in the world outside you.

Masterpieces emerge through us when we take action on Purpose—when we hold the opposing masculine and feminine forces within us in balance. Each force has its role to play—**the masculine holds the space for the feminine to create**.

When I paint, the masculine, art director in me, organizes the date, the time, sets up the easel, ties the canvas to it, lays out the brushes and paints. This enables the feminine part of me, the artist, to feels safe enough to create. Creation emerges in the dance between the two forces: masculine and feminine. The art director guides and the artist paints. Just like the relationship between the petals of a flower and its stem. The stem holds up the petals, so the flower can blossom and become all that it is.

On this retreat, I let go of the "old me." No more victimhood. I literally stepped through a portal into a different world. It was both exhilarating and terrifying at first. Everything appeared to be brighter and lighter, and that included my paintings. They resonated on an entirely different level, because I was resonating on an entirely different level. I had shifted my energy. And a new more complete me was beginning to emerge.

One week later, I met Ashoke—one of the world's leading Ayurvedic healers. He taught me to meditate and helped me master my craft. Two weeks after that, I met my future wife, Anna. Transitions accelerated. Within five years, I went from living alone and being director of a communications agency to living with four others (my wife, our two children, Sasha and Daniel. and my mother-in-law), creating my own coaching company and self-publishing my first book *#Balance*. However, ironically something was still off-balance.

I moved from having a previous masculine imbalance to having a feminine imbalance. I pulled myself out of the masculine imbalance—the Endless Abyss—only to find myself stuck in a feminine imbalance. This time with my head in the clouds where I couldn't see the ground, I didn't realize I was climbing another mountain of illusion: WooWoo Mountain—a place where you can get lost for years living on lofty, head-in-the-clouds dreams. But there was no actual mountain, it was just thin air. I was throwing myself headlong into multiple ideas all at the same time—more and more extreme painting, coaching individuals, running workshops for companies, unleashing creativity in schools. And then, I launched a second company. While all of them were connected to my Purpose, none of them were my Masterpiece. They weren't generating sufficient income for us to live.

I was focused, but lacked focus on my Masterpiece. Why? It turns out the drama queen was still running my life. I had misinterpreted what had happened in South Africa. I told myself and Anna I had buried the drama queen in a coffin and walked away—and while I had initially used the masculine part of me to attract Anna, I rejected this part of me too. However, as Koenig and Jung point out, you can't kill any aspect of yourself. Whether you call these aspects of yourself the artist, the art director, and their opposites—or shadow sides—the abuser and the drama queen, it doesn't matter. These are just labels.

Labels don't matter. What really matters is that you accept and reclaim these aspects, or parts, that exist within you. You were born whole, complete, connected to all that is. As we shall see in Chapter 3, your ancestors created a system, that we called civilization, that separated you from you—and this is why we need to reclaim ourselves again. This is a 5,000-year-old problem that your parents, grandparents and great grandparents inherited.

Your responsibility is to reclaim these parts of yourself so you transcend the system.

The alternative is human history ends with us. Humanity goes extinct. Everything your ancestors fought and died for stops.

Not only can you not kill these different aspects of yourself, but each aspect has a role to play. You can suppress them or accept them. If you suppress them, they will find a role for themselves. In my case, the drama queen resurrected herself to buy the artist within me time to create art. It's just I wasn't aware of it at the time. She went to any extreme to push other priorities away so I could just create. In that space, I was at peace, but because I wasn't aware of it, my finances were in a mess, I wasn't looking after my health and I was constantly running out of time.

I had solved codependency in my intimate relationships. But I hadn't solved my relationship to money, time, power or my body. I saw opportunities everywhere and was terrified of missing out. So I seized every opportunity. I created opportunities from thin air. I ran round and round in circles chasing illusions. I believed my responsibility was to provide for my family and others including Anna, who valued the feminine, caring aspect of me more than the strong masculine.

And the result? My relationship, children, body and bank account all suffered. My body was utterly exhausted from trying to do everything. It kept on giving me warning signs to stop. And I ignored them. I wasn't climbing a mountain. I was stuck in a chasm. I hit rock bottom for the third time when a big marketing promotion I worked on for six months failed. We were relying on it for the deposit for our dream home. We missed by a mile. No dream home.

I stopped, took a long hard look at myself and realized I am more than this. I traced each dependency back to its roots: I recalled my mother being stressed counting the pennies to pay for the weekly groceries; her sense of powerlessness around anything related to money; my father's single-minded pursuit to provide for us financially; and my birth—I was almost born outside the post office in our local town, because my mother refused to waste a moment more than necessary in the maternity wards. What my parents modeled I followed.

Step by step, I unwound each dependency and with the help of Koenig and other phenomenal coaches, I gave each aspect of myself a role to play. I detoxed my body and started to care for it; stopped competing with others and started to partner; removed the money blocks and focused on generating true wealth; and I said no to some opportunities and focused on one Masterpiece at a time, not one hundred.

The result? My coaching, partnerships and relationships are soaring to new heights. I feel healthier and wealthier. I see each coaching session, painting, workshop, relationship and program as an opportunity to see where I am in or out of flow. I understand everything that occurs outside me is a reflection of my current state of mind. Life itself is the ultimate teacher, and the faster I learn the lesson and integrate it, the less I suffer.

Breaking the Cycles

You may have noticed two vicious cycles stopped me from transitioning to my new world—one masculine, the other feminine.

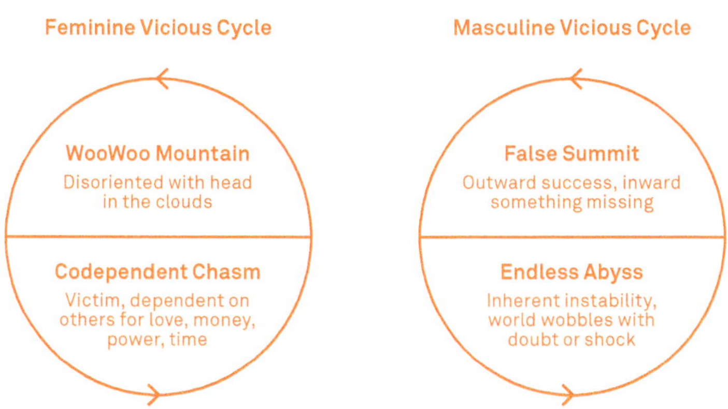

The Masculine Vicious Cycle: False Summit and Endless Abyss

When we suppress and abuse the feminine (the artist within) we climb a False Summit: the place where you search for materialistic success within the system. This false, frantic search can lead us to fall into the Endless Abyss, only to try to climb the same summit again in an endless vicious cycle. I did this after my father told me I would never make money as a professional artist. I stopped painting for fourteen years and lived as a business man for twenty years. I built my life on sand. Any exogenous shock or bout of doubt exposed my inherent instability. I would panic and descend into the depths of the Endless Abyss. This was what happened at university, when I lost my job at Unilever and when the woman told me I was a "drama queen." I lived in constant fear of the next shock and didn't even know it. However, the seeds of this suppression were planted long before the conversation with my father. The system I grew up in reinforced the value of masculine intellect over feminine intuition. So every time I fell off, I thought I'd done something wrong, pulled myself up and promptly tried to climb up the same mountain again. I felt I was better prepared, but something was missing. I felt hollow. I had enough when I realized I had built my entire life on sand and had been living a lie.

The Feminine Vicious Cycle - WooWoo Mountain to Codependent Chasm

When we suppress the masculine, (the art director within) we climb WooWoo Mountain: the place where we have our head in the clouds. This often leads to feeling lost and we wander aimlessly into a Codependent Chasm. I did this when I perceived Anna and others valuing the more feminine, creative, caring aspect of myself over the directive masculine aspect. Unconsciously, I allowed the drama queen to re-emerge and bully the masculine. Falling into the Codependent Chasm exposed my dependency on power, money and time. I started working on multiple different projects with multiple different partners, all at the same time. I wasn't ruthless enough either with myself or them. I didn't focus on only one Masterpiece, because I didn't value myself enough. I didn't believe my partners were good enough, because I didn't believe I was good enough. I was scared there wasn't enough, because I was scared I wasn't enough. And I believed we were running out of time, so rather than wait for others to contribute, I would do it for them. The drama queen was running the show. I ended up running round in tight circles, putting my body, bank account and family under increasing pressure. I had enough when I realized I had built my entire life on thin air (again) and we were running out of money: the "dream house" moment. I came down to earth with a thud.

Life is an Art

I have just described this journey as though it is a linear, logical series of separate events. And of course, we know life is not like that. Life is an art. It is one continual opportunity to stop resisting what is both inside and outside you. It is a perpetual experiment to explore what it takes to be creative everywhere.

A few years ago, I went on a painting expedition with a poet friend and experienced this infinite journey first-hand. The idea was to create art from different points around Mont Blanc, the tallest mountain in Western Europe, to illustrate the concept of diversity—how a different viewing point gives a different perspective. Our intention was to make a film that showed me painting and my friend writing poetry.

When we planned the trip, we imagined we would have sunny, blue skies and a perfect view of the mountains. On the first day, we hiked up to Lac Blanc, from where you can see a perfect reflection of Mont Blanc in the lake—only to find the cloud hadn't lifted—and during the six hours we were there, we probably only saw the mountains for thirty minutes in total.

So, the following day, we went over to Les Grand Montets, a famous peak, on the other side of the valley from where you can get a perfect view of Mont Blanc on a clear day. Just after we arrived at the top of the mountain, the cloud lifted and we thought we would be able to create art. However, after thirty minutes, the cloud descended again. And then, it started to rain softly. After fifteen minutes, the canvas was so wet, I couldn't add any more paint without it running straight off and my friend couldn't write. So, we decided to take a break.

When we came back, the rain had turned to ice and it had started to snow. The canvas was frozen. I was faced with a difficult decision: do we abandon painting for the day and head over to the Italian side where we had planned to paint the following day, or do we battle on in the rain and snow? The decision was complicated by the fact that I knew if we left I would have to do something I had never done before—remove all the paint from the canvas. Otherwise, it would either melt in the cable car and run off or melt in my car and run off. I decided to stop. And so, for the first time ever, I took the paint off the canvas. In other words, I went up the mountain with a blank canvas and I came back down again with a blank canvas as well. The artist in me was upset. The drama queen was even more upset. It wanted to be seen. But, the art director in me knew the biggest opportunity was on the following day.

So, that's how I found myself on the third day, with one blank canvas and one rushed canvas. We woke up to find it was minus 5°C, the wind was blowing at 60mph, and we couldn't see the mountain. The wind was blowing so hard I struggled to attach the canvas to the railing. I was literally on WooWoo Mountain. My friend said to me, "just paint the wind."

I responded, "I can't paint the wind. I can't even see it."

"Feel the wind," she said. "Listen to what it wants to tell you. And paint that."

So, I got up and walked to the canvas, picked up a painting knife and started to paint the wind. As I did, I broke down into floods of tears. I cried because I heard the wind. It told me, "*I am more powerful than the mountain and the clouds because I can make both come and go.*" The wind continued, "*but no one likes me, no one accepts me, no one sees me. Everyone believes I am cold and heartless. Paint me. And I will show you how powerful I am.*" So, I painted. And as I did, the wind started to reveal the mountain, first one part, then another, then the glacier. Over the next five hours, the wind revealed every aspect of the mountain. And finally, it revealed the stunning peak of Mont Blanc.

Ten minutes after I stopped painting, exhausted from the effort, the wind stopped too and revealed the entire mountain range in front of us. And then it struck me, the wind wanted to be seen, so did the fog and the rain and the ice. All of them wanted to be included. Diversity and inclusion isn't about including what you like, it is about seeing what you don't like and including it as well—and the key to this is reclaiming what we have suppressed.

What I resist in the external world—the wind, fog, snow, rain—resists me. The more I resist *it*, the more *it* resists me. And *it* grows. When I stop fighting *it*, *it* stops fighting me. I accept *it*. I integrate *it*. And then I become *it*. When I become it, I can change any aspect of *it*. Because there is no separation between me and *it*. I am *it*.

I have had similar experiences again and again and again—all over the world, in a blizzard, gale force winds and a tropical storm. These experiences have helped me to understand the united and infinite loop of life—the story of creation—a continuous journey to reclaim the artist inside you and create the Masterpiece you were born to create.

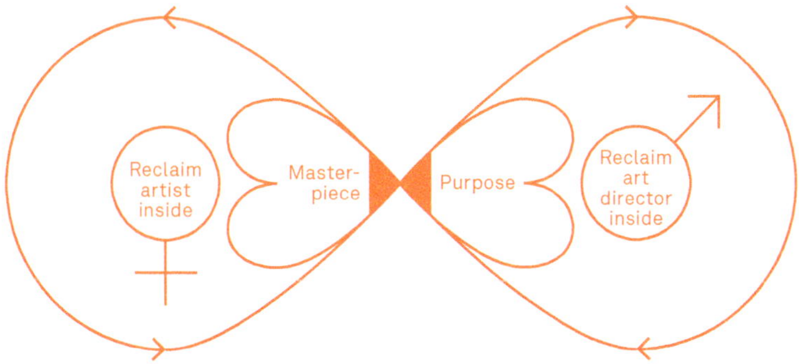

Breaking the Feminine Vicious Cycle

To break the feminine cycle you need to reclaim the masculine, the art director inside you. You can do this by bringing your Masterpiece to life and resolving your relationship to money. However, for the masculine to have a purpose in life, it needs the feminine to animate it. Thus, you also need to reclaim the feminine victim or drama queen who suppressed the masculine in the first place. Otherwise, you end up climbing The False Summit. If you do this, you reconnect to unconditional love, the ability to hear the Masterpiece that wants to emerge through you, and magically everyone you need to bring it to life is drawn to help you.

Breaking the Masculine Vicious Cycle

To break the masculine cycle, you need to reclaim the feminine, the artist inside you. You can do this by acting on Purpose and resolving your relationship to love. However, for the feminine to blossom it needs the masculine to hold it. Thus, you also need to reclaim the masculine abuser, manipulator or bully who suppressed the feminine in the first place. Otherwise, you end up climbing WooWoo Mountain. If you do this, you reconnect to true power, the ability to act on Purpose. And the entire Universe, including the wind, the snow and the rain will conspire to help you.

***

This journey is no fairy tale. Don't expect to live happily ever after. Creating your Masterpiece doesn't stop when you place the last brushstroke on the canvas, or type *the end* on your manuscript, or finish the perfect script for your TED Talk.

That's just the beginning of a whole other journey. It never ends. There is no destination. No point at which it stops. We don't arrive. Life doesn't end. Even when we think it ends, it goes on.

It's just one long experiment to align our words, our actions, and our beliefs with our essence in more and more extreme conditions until there is nothing more to align, until there is nothing more to detox, until there are no more tears to release, until we are finally freed from this physical experience, until we integrate all the resistance, until we become one. Until we become ALL of ourselves.

2 Belief: The Pivot Point

If you hear a voice within you say, 'you cannot paint,' then by all means paint, and that voice will be silenced.

Vincent van Gogh

It is the power of belief that causes things to happen in our lives. The power of belief is both the cornerstone and catalyst for our transitions in life. Comparing the lives of Michelangelo and Vincent van Gogh reveal insights about how to create Masterpieces and leave a Legacy for good.

Michelangelo and Van Gogh are two of the most famous artists in the world. The Sistine Chapel in Rome and the Van Gogh Museum house their masterpieces and are two of the most visited attractions in the world. During their lifetimes, both artists created hundreds of Masterpieces of extraordinary quality, which reflected their vision of the world; and both believed their artwork reflected their God-given gifts. They were true innovators; they didn't copy, they created. Rather than reflect society, they inspired society, and they were years ahead of their time. Through their art, they provoke us to think differently about human potential.

Michelangelo's sculptures are magnificent; larger than life portrayals of our brilliance and the divine light within each of us. The centerpiece of the Sistine Chapel *The Creation of Adam* is an example. God gives life to man, and man reflects God's brilliance back to Him. Michelangelo's work depicts the choice we face: to reflect the light or the dark, the beauty or the beast, the courage or the fear. Michelangelo inspires us to create, rather than follow. His art and life encourages us to rise to higher and higher states of consciousness through the exercise of our free will.

Van Gogh's canvases are extraordinary explosions of creativity and color. He challenges us to create with our heart and soul, rather than with our head and ego. Take the *Sunflowers*. They are full of light and passion. They reflect humanity's hopes for a brighter future. Vincent knows from bitter experience we face a choice too. His art encourages us to follow the light within rather than be swallowed up by the darkness, even if his legacy reflects how fragile his grip on life was.

However, despite their talent, both artists experienced very different journeys and legacies. Van Gogh only produced art for ten years before he committed suicide, and his best-known paintings were produced in a flurry of activity in the last two years of his life. Michelangelo produced art for seventy-five years and died of natural causes. His *oeuvres* consisted of hundreds of drawings, paintings, sculptures, murals and poems. His creativity was limitless.

When the artists died, they left very different assets. Michelangelo had a fortune in gold ducats and a number of houses in Florence and Rome, however, he lived like a poor man. When the inventory of the house where he died was made, the only thing of value the authorities found was the gold and a few simple, well-made clothes. Van Gogh also lived like a poor man, although unlike Michelangelo, he didn't have a penny to his name when he died. Throughout his life he depended on either his father or his brother, Theo.

So why did one die penniless and the other die wealthy?

The simple answer is Van Gogh committed suicide before his reputation was established, whereas Michelangelo established his reputation before he died. But why did one take his life and the other live into old age? Why did one have his legacy created and the other create it? What separated these artists, and their individual journeys, was one thing: belief. One believed in himself, while the other didn't. Why does it matter? Because belief is the catalyst to creating a Masterpiece in your lifetime. And when we analyze both artists, it becomes apparent how important belief is to them, and us.

> *I feel like such a failure.*
>
> **Vincent Van Gogh**

Fathers

At the beginning of their journeys, both artists had fathers who disagreed with their artistic ambitions and tried to prevent them from pursuing them. Michelangelo's father beat him horribly, whereas Van Gogh's father encouraged him to do anything but paint, including paying for him to go into the ministry. Both fathers encouraged their sons to pursue intellect rather than intuition, and study Latin rather than art. What differed is the way in which the young artists responded to their fathers' demands, and this is where their two journeys diverge.

At the age of fifteen, Michelangelo ran off to an atelier and started producing art. Van Gogh followed his father's advice and tried his hand at selling art in Holland and England, then practiced as a lay preacher and later trained to become a pastor. He failed at each job. This fruitless journey took him ten years, by which time, he was twenty-seven years old. By the same age, Michelangelo was well on his way to becoming one of the most famous artists of all time.

Power

These different reactions to similar paternal resistance led each to have a different relationship to power. One believed power arose inside him, the other believed power arose outside him. And this belief influenced their lives and art. Michelangelo integrated his power within himself. His art inspires us to do the same. Van Gogh projected his power onto others. His art suggests power is in nature.

During his life, Van Gogh was dependent on others. He depended on money from his brother and love from other women. All of his relationships were codependent—with women (who he tried to save), with his brother (who gave him a monthly stipend), and Paul Gauguin, with whom he lived in Arles (and with whom he had a dream to start a community of artists in the South). The women who Van Gogh was attracted to were either "fallen angels"—women who had suffered and Vincent wanted to try and save, or older women who would mother him. He never reclaimed the masculine "abuser" within so he abused himself, over and over again. The ultimate abuse was killing himself.

Conversely, Michelangelo was independent of others. He faced the fear of being beaten by his father and painted anyway. He claimed not to have a master who taught him to sculpt or paint. He left the patronage of the Medici family, the most powerful family in Florence, when he felt it was best for him. He told Popes what to do rather than wait for their call. And he never depended on anyone else for love—he was never married or had a long-term relationship. His sole purpose was serving God. Not only did Michelangelo reclaim the feminine artist inside him, he reclaimed the masculine art director and used "him" ruthlessly to protect "her."

Strengths

The power of belief changes the journey of life. It is the catalyst that helps us transcend the resistance we face in the infinite loop I described in the previous chapter. It emerges from the inward feminine loop and is tested in the outward masculine loop.

Michelangelo passed the test. Van Gogh didn't. Van Gogh doubted himself, while Michelangelo didn't. Michelangelo mastered both journeys, Van Gogh didn't.

Think of the **inward feminine journey** like the roots of a tree. The deeper the roots, the higher the tree can grow, and the more stable it is when the wind blows or a storm picks up. This part of the journey helps you to embody your Purpose to such an extent that what you create is the clearest possible reflection of your Purpose. It removes deadwood. Like a sculpture, it is about reduction—removing something from the stone. This loop generates the belief or nourishment the tree needs to grow.

Think of the **outward masculine journey** like the branches of the tree. The healthier the tree, the broader its branches and the more bounteous its leaves and fruit. This part of the journey tests your belief to such an extent you master the skills to produce a Masterpiece with impact (or, like Van Gogh, you allow your inner "drama queen" to sabotage your inner art director). It generates fruit. Like a painting, it is about creation—adding another layer to the canvas. This loop produces the shade for others to shelter under and bounteous fruit.

There are four dimensions to the Outward Journey:

> **The Creator** who creates ideas.
> **The Collaborator** who connects those ideas to communities.
> **The Calculator** who harvests those ideas to generate value.
> **The Choreographer** who organizes and regenerates so the organism is ready to bear fruit again.

I call the combination of these strengths your *Artist Profile* (and will describe them in more detail later). The more you master these strengths, or partner with others who do, the broader the canopy of your tree grows.

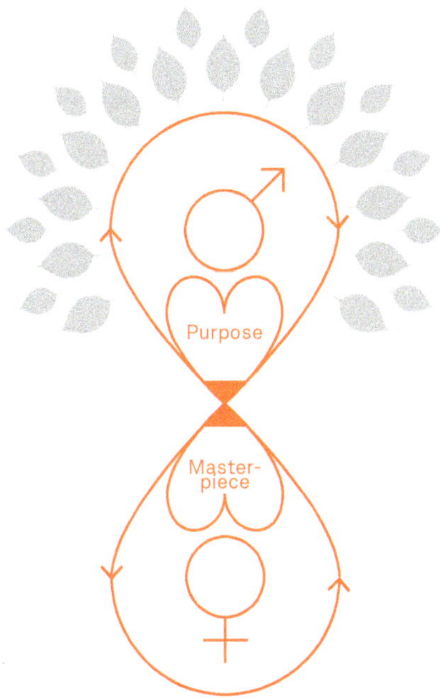

Michelangelo mastered all four of these strengths on the Outward Journey, because he discovered sufficient belief on the Inward Journey. You can too. He was both a Creator and a Collaborator. While he could create Masterpiece after Masterpiece, he also knew how to connect them to other people. He accepted his doubt and communicated his brilliance. At the age of sixteen, he was invited to join the Medici court, where he was surrounded by a network of the leading philosophers and thinkers in Europe. He learned from all of them. This network would serve him well later. Michelangelo also mastered the ability to Choreograph ambitious building projects such as St. Peter's Basilica, the Laurentian Library and the Medici Chapel, and the ability to Calculate how to invest profit to create more wealth and transform the entire environment around him.

Van Gogh was a Creator, but when it came to the Outward Journey, he lacked the belief required to transcend the resistance. He was driven to create painting after painting after painting. But self-doubt plagued him. Rather than stop and regenerate as Michelangelo did, Van Gogh drove himself on and on, constantly searching for external validation.

***

It takes enormous courage to create something original rather than copy. Doing something that has never been done before isn't easy. Others almost always reject you to start with. And, even if you succeed, the results are rarely immediate.

> *First they ignore you. Then they ridicule you. And then they attack you and want to burn you. And then they build monuments to you.*
>
> **Nicholas Klein**

Love

Perhaps more importantly, unlike Michelangelo, Van Gogh was a terrible communicator. Not only was he a Dutchman living in France with a strong accent, but his poor communication led him to fight Paul Gauguin and even his brother, both of whom were key to realizing his vision of creating an artist community. Interestingly, his vision—a network of artists supporting each other—exposed his greatest limitation, his inability to connect. To establish any network requires an individual to master the art of connection. Van Gogh didn't.

This inability is probably best illustrated through his relationship to women. Take the incident for which he became famous: he cut off his ear and gave it to a maid at a brothel, in a manner reminiscent of Christ's last supper, saying, "take this part of me, and look after it safely." According to Bernadette Murphy in her ground-breaking book *Van Gogh's Ear*,[5] it was an act of misguided generosity, an attempt to heal the maid who had been savagely bitten by a rabid dog the year before and was still badly scarred from the incident. She suggests that Vincent desired to go beyond what a normal person may attempt to do for a friend. That he was driven to exceed simple "helping" and become their savior and salvation.

This is codependency in action. It demonstrates Van Gogh's failure to truly connect and communicate with others. He flipped from a God-like ability to create Masterpieces to acting like he was God in his relationship with others.

Murphy claims there were mitigating circumstances that affected Van Gogh's state of mind. The same day the extraordinary ear incident occurred,

5 Murphy, Bernadette. *Van Gogh's Ear*. Chatto & Windus, London. Vintage Digital; 01 Edition (12 July 2016)

Van Gogh's vision for an artist community of the South all but died. Paul Gauguin who had been living with him in the Yellow House in Arles announced that Sunday morning that he was going to return to Paris for good; and his brother announced his engagement to Jo Bonger, which in Van Gogh's mind meant any funding for his future venture would be severely reduced if not entirely cut-off.

These circumstances weren't a coincidence. They were an opportunity for Van Gogh to do what he needed most, to find the faith in himself, the self-belief and courage to continue fighting for his vision and to learn how to connect. But rather than focus on finding that belief and courage inside himself, he went to try and save someone else in the vain hope that this poor unsuspecting woman would end up compensating for his own lack of self-belief and inability to connect. He projected his own shortcomings onto another person and tried to save her rather than himself.

Van Gogh could channel divine energy into his paintings, but not into his conversations. He could create brilliance with his heart and soul, but not with his thoughts or mouth. He could turn his essence into brushstrokes, but not into spoken words. Without the ability to partner with someone who did have these skills, he failed to turn his brilliance into a legacy during his lifetime.

Time

Van Gogh never solved his relationship to time either. He was addicted to creation. In one period, he produced sixty paintings in sixty days. His art emerged in a half-crazy frenzy of activity. His drama queen was running the show, and he had no idea. In the act of creation, Van Gogh found solace. In a state of flow, the problems he faced in the world outside him receded. They didn't matter. All that mattered was creating, creating, creating. But there was no time to regenerate his body or to generate the finances to sustain himself. He became a victim of the feminine vicious cycle. And so, his body burned out too soon.

Michelangelo on the other hand paced himself. He created an upwards virtuous circle. He used his "drama queen" to buy his inner artist the time to create. And he used his inner art director to focus his time on Masterpieces that generated the money needed to buy him more time. His first Masterpiece, *David*, took him four years to complete. It was the most polished piece he ever created. This breakthrough attracted other clients, including his first Pope. His second Masterpiece, The Sistine Chapel, took him another four years to complete. Michelangelo must have doubted himself during these periods, but rather than let himself become a victim of doubt, he used his inner bully to negotiate more money from his benefactors. This helped him live to the age of eighty-nine.

Van Gogh had the same courage when it came to painting, but not when it came to being. He shied away from that moment, hoping beyond hope someone—Theo, or Gauguin, or a woman, or God would take care of him.

***

No one will take care of you. No one will find you. No one can realize your vision for you. No one but you. The catalyst is faith in yourself. You cannot project your lack of belief onto anyone else. Nor can you depend on someone else to believe in you. Belief is something that emerges from within. You are born with everything you need to create what you are born to create. All you have to do is reclaim this ability. That's the journey. It's the same journey for artists, athletes, scientists, social entrepreneurs and spiritual seekers. It's a lonely journey, which exposes any shred of doubt.

And that's exactly what Michelangelo did. His mastery had nothing to do with looks or genes or anything else. Neither he nor Vincent were particularly good looking. Nor did it have anything to do with a lucky break.

You create your own luck. You create your own reality. Do you believe in you?

Growth

Your relationship to the four elements I have just described—Power, Others, Money and Time—define your ability to grow. They constitute a third Upward Journey. In our analogy, they define the height of the tree. The higher the tree the more light it receives and the longer its lifespan. Again Michelangelo mastered all of them and Van Gogh didn't.

I will explore each of these elements in more detail later and illustrate how they form **The Cycle of Life**. For now, here is a brief summary:

True impact comes from changing your relationship to power. You stop abusing and start partnering.

True love comes from changing your relationship to others. You stop depending on them for something and start loving independently of anything.

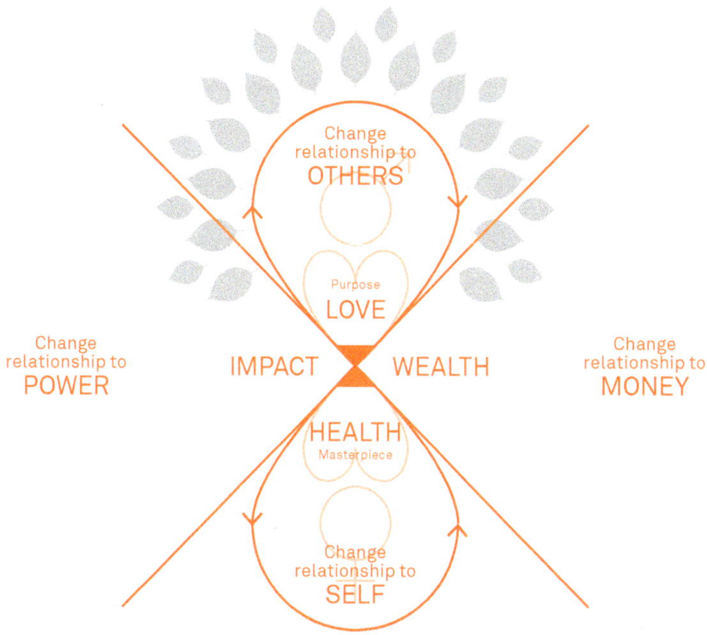

True wealth comes from changing your relationship to money. You stop devaluing yourself by associating money with self-worth and start re-evaluating what you're worth independently of money.

True health comes from changing your relationship to time. You stop pushing yourself to the limit and start caring for your body, mind and soul.

Michelangelo exerted true power in his relationship with the Popes and the Medici family; true love by not allowing a love affair to distract him; true wealth by living within his means; and true health by living more than twice the average age in the 1500s. Van Gogh on the other hand abused himself, was codependent on others, died penniless and lived significantly less than the average age in the 1890—failing to master these elements.

Mindset

Michelangelo had one master, God. Van Gogh was dependent on many, none of whom were masters. As a result, one spiraled downwards in the vicious feminine cycle into the darkness, exacerbated by his doubt and dependence on others, eventually taking sulphur bromide as medication for his supposed insanity (which incidentally causes hallucinations as a side-effect). The other spiraled upwards in a virtuous circle, accelerated by his belief, independence and ability to unlock all the gifts he needed.

When Michelangelo was buried for the second time in Florence, the representative of the Duke of Florence ordered Michelangelo's coffin to be opened, partly out of curiosity and partly to satisfy the demands of the growing crowd. What greeted them was shocking. The human body starts to decompose within hours of death. Within a month, it starts to liquefy. And yet, according to Giorgio Vasari, his official biographer, who was there, "We found it [his corpse] still perfect in every part and so free from any evil odour that we were tempted to believe he was merely sunk in a sweet and quiet sleep."[6]

This was an extraordinary end to the life of an extraordinary artist. Ancient wisdom traditions claim only the corpses of enlightened souls, saints, Buddhas, or Christs don't decompose. They remain youthful into old age and beyond.

On the other hand, doubt kills us prematurely. It's a disease that eats away at our insides until there is nothing left. It is a poison that suffocates dreams and kills ambition. In Van Gogh's case, he had to die before his legacy took off. He had to stop thinking, to stop doubting, to stop sabotaging himself so someone else could play the role of art director.

There is a gestation period between the act of creation and the recognition of that creation. That gestation period may take weeks, months or years. Take a baby for example it is conceived and arrives only nine months later. There is always a delay between creating and receiving. If there is a single doubt during that time, then the gestation period is extended, sometimes indefinitely. Van Gogh didn't survive the gestation period. It was left to Theo's wife, Jo, to resurrect his legacy by selling Vincent's paintings after both he and Theo died.

Michelangelo accepted self-doubt from the outset. He stood up to the beatings from his father. He faced the fear of what others thought. He found the courage inside himself. He disciplined himself to use his art director to fight for his soul's

6 Vasari, Giorgio, *Lives of the Artists*, translated by George Bull, vol. I, London, 1987, pp. 436-438

greatest ambitions rather than to sabotage it. So, Michelangelo's legacy took off before he died.

Belief in the Modern World

You may be reading these words and thinking—that's great, but how exactly does it relate to me? Wasn't Michelangelo creating art over 500 years ago? Isn't creating a Masterpiece in the 21st century very different from being an artist in Rome or Florence during the 16th century? Yes and no.

Today, we may have the internet, AI, nanotechnology, biotechnology, neurotechnology, and the promise that we can create super humans, but within Michelangelo's lifetime, Copernicus published his theory that the earth was not the center of the universe; Christopher Columbus discovered America; Leonardo Da Vinci designed the first parachute and flying machines; the first scientific journal was published and the telescope was invented.

Just before Michelangelo was born, Johannes Gutenberg invented the printing press and just after he died, Sir Isaac Newton articulated his three physical laws of motion. In other words, breakthroughs in the 16th century were as revolutionary as breakthroughs in the 21st century. They fundamentally changed humanity's understanding of our body, our place in the world and the universe. And Michelangelo played a pivotal role in this revolution.

Belief is at least as relevant today as it was 500 years ago.

Today's greatest artists do exactly what Michelangelo did 500 years ago. They provoke us to think differently by reclaiming both the masculine and feminine aspects of themselves. Their art may be expressed through business, but it is still art. These artists outmaneuver the world's biggest industries by anchoring their Masterpiece in an idea that serves a greater societal purpose and then they put their faith in it.

Steve Jobs believed personal computing could challenge convention. In the 1970s when he and Steve Wozniak launched Apple, computers were dominated by IBM, known back then as "Big Blue." Anyone wanting to run a complex calculation within an organization had to go to the central mainframe computer with their request and invariably wait in a queue until the engineers could run the calculation for them. Jobs, with Wozniak's help, designed everything to do the opposite—he put computer power in the hands of the user. He made using a computer simple, fun and enthralling. Apple was the first company to launch a computer mouse, a windows-type operating system, multiple fonts, and applications which enabled the user to draw and express their creativity. His big idea was best summed up by one of the greatest TV ads of all time which parodied George Orwell's book, *1984*. It featured a young woman escaping from the police to throw a sledgehammer at a big screen on which a Big Brother-like figure is brainwashing a room full of people and ends with the strapline: "Why 1984 won't be like 1984." Jobs believed everyone was an artist. This belief transformed computing and telephony. In the process, he transformed how and who can create and consume music, video, and photography. However, like Van Gogh, he also became a victim of addiction to creation. Rather than buy himself the time to regenerate, he burned himself out and died at the age of fifty-six.

Richard Branson believed affordable travel enabled equality. His breakthrough came when he took on British Airways by looking at the problem of transatlantic travel from the perspective of the customer. At the time, British Airways dominated the marketplace focusing primarily on the wealthy and business travelers. Branson focused on the rest of us. He created Virgin Atlantic, when Virgin was on the verge of bankruptcy, because he believed if he looked after his employees they would look after his customers. And they did.

Elon Musk believes alternative banking, energy and space travel will help humanity survive. At PayPal, he took on the banking system with the intent of enabling its customers to get a better deal. At Tesla, he's taking on the energy industry by designing the world's best car, which happens to be electric, and cutting-edge energy systems for the home. At SpaceX, he's aiming to be the first pioneer to establish a colony on Mars. Musk believed in himself so much that he put everything he earned from PayPal into Tesla and SpaceX, leaving himself begging friends to help him pay the rent. When the first three rockets SpaceX launched crashed on take-off, it cost him $180 million dollars. But each time, he came out of the control room and inspired his team to greater heights. So when the rockets worked, they secured a $1.6 billion-dollar contract from NASA. On 6 February 2018, SpaceX launched the Falcon Heavy, the most powerful operational rocket in the world by a factor of two. With more than five-million pounds of thrust it equals approximately eighteen 747 aircraft at full power. That's belief in action.

Everyone who creates a Masterpiece connects to something greater than themselves and then believes in it. Nelson Mandela was a closet Christian. He had the last rites administered by a Methodist Minister just before he died, but to ensure unity in a country where Afrikaners had used the church to reinforce Apartheid, Mandela kept his faith to himself.

Belief as the Breakthrough

Creating your Masterpiece takes belief. And that's what the common denominator with the successful creators is: they believe. Whether it's in the unlimited potential of people, humanity, the self or a greater God, everyone finds their own way to unleash the artist inside them.

Michelangelo and Vincent van Gogh's breakthroughs have inspired countless generations of artists. Their stories represent how we are all born to create, and can create, albeit different pathways. Fundamentally what their journeys provide us with, are lessons. Of course, we can tell ourselves we don't have enough time, skills, courage, connections, or money, to follow our dreams—but that's simply an excuse to play the victim longer. These artists have shown us that the only thing stopping us from creating the Masterpiece we were born to create, is our own lack of belief and courage to bring our Purpose to life.

3 The Great Transition

Human industry, especially during the past century, wreaks change far more quickly than nature can deal with. Where we tip the balance, we create desert, and at some point we may tip the balance planetwide.

Yvon Chouinard, owner of Patagonia

It has never been more important to create your Masterpiece. The world as it stands right now is more out of balance than ever. COVID-19, climate change, inequality, racial divisions—all symptoms of imbalance; symptoms that highlight the *dis-ease* of humanity. The root cause of these symptoms runs deep. Most of us aren't aware of what the cause is; yet even when we are, all too often we end up using the wrong approach to try to rebalance ourselves.

When I was five years old, I cut my head open so badly, my parents called the doctor. I had climbed up on the linen basket in the bathroom and shouted, "I'm Superman, I can fly," and jumped off. Of course, I wasn't Superman, and I couldn't fly. My head collided with the bidet taps; blood spilled everywhere. The doctor arrived, checked me for concussion and sent me to hospital. The hospital took an x-ray to make sure I was okay and then stitched me up. That's exactly what you would expect them to do. They treated the visible symptoms, patched me up and sent me home.

However, not long afterwards I found myself struggling to sit cross-legged in school assembly. A few years after that, I started to have problems with my knee. Again, I saw the doctor. This time he recommended physiotherapy. The physiotherapist gave some long-winded, technical explanation, which led to many physio sessions. However, deep down, I felt these sessions weren't solving the problem. I didn't know what the cause of the problem was. All I remember was being in agony, just sitting. So, I stopped sitting cross-legged.

It took me more than twenty years to work out what the root cause was. I took up yoga when I moved to work in Switzerland. This helped me to open my hips enough to sit cross-legged again. However, my yoga teacher noted my right knee was much higher off the ground than my left knee. She suggested there was a problem with my hip, because it was out of balance with my sacrum. It turns out she was right. But it took another accident to confirm her diagnosis. A few years later, I dislocated my left shoulder skiing. On exactly the same day, my right hip opened for the first time, with an almighty crack.

When I mentioned the incident with my hip to the doctor who was treating my shoulder, he said this was just a coincidence, and he told me to visit a physiotherapist. This time I listened to my intuition and visited an osteopath instead. The osteopath looked at my body from a different perspective. He explained that the hip had released at the same time the shoulder had released, because I released the tension inside me.

A few years later, another osteopath explained the root cause of my hip problem was related to a trauma as a child. And I connected the two incidents. Hitting the bidet taps headfirst with sufficient force to create a wound that required stitches had also sent a wave down my spine and moved the sacrum out of alignment with the hip. I had spent the next twenty-five years out of balance. But no one noticed. No one checked. The doctors did their job. They treated the symptom. But they ignored the deeper problem. I was out of balance. And even when my yoga teacher identified what it was, other "experts" advised me to take the wrong approach.

Humanity is a global body, and it is out of balance too.
We treat the symptoms, but we ignore the deeper problem.

We don't dig deep enough to get to the root cause. Even when we do, we rely on experts who often advise the wrong approach. Thus, the symptoms continue.

Civilization disconnected us from our true nature

Over the last 10,000 years, we have shifted increasingly from a focus on what was going on inside us to what goes on outside us. In the process, we have slipped out of balance.

Before the agricultural revolution, between 9,000 and 12,000 years ago, a hunter-gatherer lived within the ecosystem and was part of it. For simplicity sake, let's say it was a man, and his survival—both hunting and escaping being hunted—depended on his interaction within the ecosystem. And that required him to be in touch with his intuition or *sixth sense*. After the agricultural revolution, a farmer lived outside the ecosystem. He domesticated it. His survival depended on his mastery of the ecosystem; and that required him to be in touch with his intellect and separate himself from it.

This separation accelerated around 5,000 years ago when the first civilisation, in Sumer, introduced money and began to divide things into boxes. Sumer's growth was predicated on a series of inventions: money, writing, marriage, time measurement and record-keeping.

Money enabled us to exchange what we created for things that other people created. It oiled the market and fueled commerce. It enabled us to acquire what we needed as well as what we desired. Before the agricultural revolution, a hunter-gatherer could only own what he or she could carry. After the agricultural revolution, a single household would own more than an entire tribe of hunter gatherers. And since then, possessions have exploded.

The second, third and fourth Sumerian inventions—writing, data management and the measurement of time, also accelerated the shift from inner to outer. Before Confucius, Shakespeare and Solzhenitsyn wrote their Masterpieces, writing enabled taxation. The original purpose of writing was not to write sonnets, novels or even business books, it was to keep track of who possessed what, so the few could extract capital, in the form of taxes, from the many. If you owned land in Sumer, it would be recorded on a clay tablet. This enabled elites to tax it. And it fueled the bureaucratic mindset. As Sumer expanded and commerce grew, more clerks were trained to produce more tablets. To keep track of these tablets, the Sumerians created the first data management system. There is no point in producing thousands of tablets if you can't find the one you need when you need it. So, the first civilization started organizing tablets into categories. Categorizing led to thinking in boxes. We taught ourselves to put this tablet in one box and label it "land," that one in another box and label it "livestock," and a third one in a third box and label it "crops." Then, they tracked these records over time by dividing it up as well. Sumerian astronomers and mathematicians divided a day, a month and a year into small increments or silos, using base-60. They chose sixty, because at the time, they believed the year consisted of 360 days: sixty divides into 360; and is itself divisible itself by one, two, three, four, five, six, ten, fifteen, twenty and thirty equal parts. This approach led to hours, minutes and seconds, which all subsequent civilizations have inherited and reinforced without question. But more importantly it accelerated separation.

If we still believed we were part of the ecosystem, we wouldn't divide it up. Before civilization began, we believed the ecosystem was indivisible. We were one with it. That's not to say being a hunter-gatherer was an easy life. It wasn't. But at least we didn't have to worry about mortgages, taxes, data management and running out of time. Before these inventions, we followed the natural cycle of each day, each season and each year in one infinite loop. Time was eternal and cyclical. It flowed through us. Today, we attempt to manage time or make the best use of our time as though it is some external force, rather than an innate part of who we are.

Artists don't divide things into boxes. They freely associate between different ideas. If I say think of a baby, what do you think of? Your baby? The most recent baby you saw? When you were a baby? The baby of another species? We freely connect a baby to other thoughts when we think outside the box. But bureaucratic thinking doesn't do this. It disconnects related thoughts and divides them into boxes.

If the last few Sumerian inventions divided things up into silos (horizontally), the next two, slavery and marriage, divided them hierarchically (vertically). Slavery seeded the idea that all men are not created equal. Slaves became the property of their masters—prisoners of war, criminals and children of slaves were bound to their masters so men could control each other. Marriage seeded the idea women are not equal to men. Women became the property of men—women were bound to men, so the man could ensure he was investing his energy into his true biological heir(s). Consecutive civilizations—Egyptian, Greek, Roman—reinforced these power structures. They placed one person above the other, creating an artificial hierarchy, based on history, parents, gender or race. In the process, we created oppressors and oppressed. Today, we may have outlawed slavery and claim everyone is created equal. However, this is simply untrue. Our unbalanced relationship to power is as alive today as it was 5,000 years ago. And it separates us further from who we are.

A thousand years later, one more invention accelerated this separation. Ancient Egyptians introduced branding to identify ownership of livestock. This meant not only did the authorities know who owned what, our neighbours and society did as well. The more we owned, the better our standing in society. Today, a single household may own up to two million possessions. We increasingly associate our identity with these material possessions. If we lose them, we believe we lose ourselves.

Let's recap.

- We divided the inner and outer world, because we separated ourselves from the ecosystem we were part of.
- We used possessions to compensate for our separation.
- We developed innovations which accelerated the division: money, writing, data management, time measurement, slavery, marriage and branding.
- Money fueled markets; markets fueled possessions; slavery, marriage and branding fueled possessiveness; possessions enabled taxes; taxes required writing; writing required organizing; organizing required us to measure time; and that reinforced the separation in one continuous, vicious cycle.

In the process, we slipped out of balance.

> *We don't need more stuff, we need more humanity.*
>
> **Seth Godin**

Changing Time, Power, Love and Money

Together these inventions changed our relationship to the four elements I described in the previous chapter: **Time, Power, Love and Money**. Subsequent transitions have reinforced and accelerated this change.

Take time and love. Between the first civilizations and The Renaissance, The Church turned marriage into a sacrament and introduced the concept of fate. In the process, they radically altered our relationship to time and love. Rather than something cyclical, time became linear. At the end of your life you either went to heaven or hell. Infidelity or divorce was forbidden—either would lead to hell. Love for Christ and God would lead to heaven. Just before the Renaissance, we divorced ourselves further from time with the invention of clocks; and Shakespeare's *Romeo and Juliet* and *Othello* divorced us further from true love.

Then, the Industrial Revolution standardized our relationship to both. Before the Industrial Revolution, there was a proliferation of different time zones, calendars, and perceptions of time. Afterwards everything was standardized. For instance, in the US, there were seventy-five time zones alone. After the invention of a Coordinated Universal Time (based on Greenwich Meantime) there were just three. This helped trains run on time, goods to be delivered on time and factory workers to work to time. In parallel, we standardized our perception of love. The Brothers Grimm developed a system for collating and standardising 200 fairy tales (including the romantic *and-they-lived-happily-ever-after* classics such as *Cinderella*, *Sleeping Beauty* and *Snow White*) to reduce confusion and provide a narrative consistent with the Romantic ideals. Standardization created one consistent, global narrative. We have been chasing time and love ever since.

Today, marketers use the promise of romantic love and sex to sell everything from cosmetics to tires. Our relationship to time shackles our relationship to love. We have turned the search for love into a sixty-second speed date or a "swipe right" on Tinder. Even if we are in a relationship, we run our days according to our calendar making it harder and harder to spend time with the people we love. Steve Jobs died of cancer before his time. Elon Musk almost burnt out from spending too much time at work. Is this really the world we aspire to? Surely, there is an alternative, which reconnects us to our true nature and allows us to experience true love.

Before the agricultural revolution, our ancestors cared for each other because it was essential to their survival and growth. Time and love flowed through them naturally. It was who they were. Love wasn't something they searched for outside themselves, nor was time—love was the glue that connected them to the entire universe and fueled their existence irrespective of time.

When I paint, time and love flow through me. I feel love for everything around me. I think of my children and my wife. I connect to the trees, the mountains and the weather. When I stop resisting them, they stop resisting me. In that moment, there is no separation between me and it. I lose track of time. Six hours feels like an eternity and twenty minutes at the same time. I don't try to manage time. I don't focus on the end-result. I simply focus on the next brushstroke, in one endless loop until the painting is finished.

> *An hour sitting with a pretty girl on a park bench passes like a minute, but a minute sitting on a hot stove seems like an hour.*
>
> **Albert Einstein**

Something similar happened with our relationship to money and power. Power increasingly amassed money. During the Renaissance, European townships produced *Brakteaten* money, slivers of gold and silver leaf. They collected this money two to three times per year. For instance, you would receive three new coins for four old coins. In other words, if you kept the coins you would lose twenty-five percent of their value in the form of a tax. If you spent the coins, you retained the value of what you possessed. Thus, the system encouraged the masses to spend more and those with power amassed more.

Then, as we will explore later in this chapter, the Industrial Revolution strengthened organizations' grip on power. Printing money helped. It radically changed our relationship to money by divorcing money from true value. Goldsmiths in London became bankers by printing banknotes—the value of which amounted to many multiples the value of the metal deposited in their vaults. This practice became known as *fractional reserve banking.* Every financial instrument created since, from bank accounts to credits and loans to interest on those loans to credit cards and now crypto-currencies are based on the same principle. The link between money and true value left hanging by a thread.

Then, fifty years ago, President Nixon cut the last thread. In 1971, he unilaterally left the Bretton Woods exchange, a Gold Standard developed to prevent a repeat of The Great Depression in the 1930s. Now, you don't need gold deposits to create a crypto-currency or a financial instrument. You don't even need to be a bank. Anyone can do it—often with disastrous results: pensions companies and mortgage companies created the pensions crisis and the sub-prime mortgage crisis, which triggered the financial crisis of 2008; now, we have cowboys creating crypto-currencies. Is this really what we aspire to collectively?

Before the agricultural revolution, money did not exist. Wealth would have been measured in terms of our health, our influence, our children and our contribution to our tribe. But it wasn't measured. Because it didn't matter. What mattered was the survival of the tribe. And that depended on everyone collaborating—young and old—talented and untalented. Money wasn't something we searched for outside ourselves, it was the glue that held us together and enabled our existence.

When I paint, the wealth I generate has little to do with the painting that emerges on the canvas. For me, true wealth is connecting to nature and to my true nature. It is growing into the person I was born to be. If I had all the money in the world, I would paint, spend time with my family and launch a foundation to enable everyone in the world to create their Masterpiece starting with the next generation in schools.

Our current relationship to money is passed down unquestioned by generations of economics professors to their students, as a central part of a well-ordered modern economy.

Peter Koenig

Masterpieces help us reconnect

Masterpieces help us reconnect to our true nature by giving form to the paradigm that emerges after the transition—while most of us are still stuck in the midst of that transition. All art, in fact anything we create, reflects the moment when we create it. It gives form to the mindset of its creator in the moment of its creation. Thus, you could say, all art is a self-portrait. It reflects the artist's mindset in that moment in time. A Masterpiece is different, because it is a self-portrait of an artist who has reclaimed what he or she has suppressed to such an extent that they reconnect to who they truly are—outside of space and time, beyond money and marriage, irrespective of bureaucracy or silos. They connect to all that is, before civilization disconnected us. In that moment, they become the ecosystem. There is no separation between them and *it*. A Masterpiece is a self-portrait of the (artist connected to the) entire ecosystem. Others resonate with what the artist has created because they see themselves in it. They long to feel the same sense of connection as the artist again. In other words, the Masterpiece is a self-portrait of what the audience aspires to become after the transition *as well as* who the artist is at that specific moment in time.

Transitions unleash powerful forces. As I described in Chapter 1, these forces lead to two outcomes depending on our mindset: a virtuous upward cycle of creativity and a vicious downward cycle of suppression. Rather than resist these tensions or simply depicting them—for instance, by depicting racism, environmental destruction or lockdown—artists who master their art use these forces to help them reveal and reclaim what they have suppressed. They create Masterpieces amidst the tension of these opposing forces. They use cutting edge mediums that attract the most powerful institutions of the day and provoke them to think differently.

Shaping the next paradigm may not be the artist's original intention. Their original intention is to grow personally through painting. They don't focus on the final product. They focus on the act of creation by reconnecting to their true nature. What emerges may become a Masterpiece. If it does, the influence of this Masterpiece extends way beyond the edge of the canvas. As we will explore in Chapter 7, the act of creation creates ripples that don't follow logical Newtonian science. They appear to shape the paradigm that emerges from this transition in ways we can't explain with logic alone.

> *Life imitates art far more than art imitates life.*
>
> **Oscar Wilde**

For instance, Sumer created the first full-time artists as well as money, bureaucracy, slaves, the measurement of time and marriage. In other words, the first civilisation both enabled us to become artists and stopped us from becoming artists. These artists worked for the state. They used their art to establish the state and enhance the reputation of its rulers by producing statues and vases made of rare materials like alabaster that linked their rulers to their Gods. Other artists created ziggurats, enormous terraced compounds, as places to worship local Gods. These artists shaped the original state and our relationship to God.

One such example is Michelangelo, who may have influenced The Protestant Reformation and at the very least changed our relationship to God. For instance, the centrepiece of The Sistine Chapel, which he finished in 1512, depicts the moment God touches Adam, filling him with the Creative Spirit. It appears Michelangelo interprets the following verse in *The Bible*—"God created man in his own image" to mean God gave us the powers of Creation. However, if we take a closer look at God and the cluster of angels on the right, we see another interpretation. This is an anatomically correct outline of the human brain. Given his experience dissecting human bodies, perhaps what Michelangelo was really saying is "man creates God in his mind" and is provoking us to think differently about our relationship with God. That God isn't an old man out there sitting on a cloud, but rather each of us has the power of creation inside us.

Six years later, Martin Luther posted his *95 Theses* on a church in Wittenberg and kicked off The Protestant Reformation, the greatest schism in a single religion humanity has ever seen. On one side of the schism was the corrupt Catholic Church which was perceived to be separating its congregation from a direct relationship with God. On the other side was a group who became known as the Protestants. They wanted a direct relationship with God. In other words, the schism was about taking personal responsibility for your relationship to The Creator.

Did Michelangelo influence Luther? Who knows for certain. What we do know is Luther visited Rome while Michelangelo was painting The Sistine Chapel. And

Michelangelo was exposed to a movement as a young artist when he lived in the Medici court in Florence, which believed in a more intimate relationship with God.

Since then, master artists have provoked us to think differently about our relationship to God and creation by continuing the tradition Michelangelo started: attracting the most powerful institution—in Michelangelo's case, The Church—the patronage of the most influential leaders—in Michelangelo's case, eight Popes—and the most provocative technology and media of the day—in Michelangelo's case, murals and sculpture. Have these artists inadvertently influenced the transition to future paradigms? Let's look at the evidence.

In the early 1800s, the great English landscape painter, J M W Turner appeared to pick up the baton from Michelangelo and provoked us to think differently about industrialisation. Take one of his most famous pieces, *The Fighting Temeraire*. It depicts an elegant sailboat, *The Temeraire*, which played a pivotal role in The Battle of Trafalgar against Napoleon, being towed into port for the last time by a modern steamship, as the sun sets behind it. Turner evokes the sense of a lost world - modern industrial production destroying romance and beauty, head replacing heart, factories replacing nature, ego replacing essence. His depiction of *The Temeraire* is mysterious, majestic, bold and soulful, and his loose brushstrokes imply there is more to this world than meets the eye.

The Industrial Revolution was a melting pot of opposing forces. It was the precursor to the creation of modern innovation (corporations, factories, production) and the modern nation state (education, media, government departments), while at the same time it also led to the greatest suppression of creativity humanity has ever seen. Farmers became factory workers. They left the fields where they were more connected to nature to become cogs in a machine.

So, what is Turner's influence? The Romantic philosophy Turner visualized and others such as William Wordsworth and Lord Byron pioneered led to a backlash against the mechanisation of humanity. And this counter-philosophy influenced English companies such as Lever Brothers (which eventually became Unilever) and Cadbury's when they established their communities for workers at Port Sunlight and Bourneville fifty years later. Each centered their communities in nature and provided housing and social support to improve employee welfare. Turner (inadvertently) created this influence by exhibiting his Masterpieces at

The Royal Academy of Arts in London, his patrons were nobility—Lords, Dukes and Knights of the Realm—and he integrated innovations in color and pioneered innovations in brushstrokes, which enabled him to bring the mystical to life.

In the late 1800s, Van Gogh picked up the baton from Turner and the Impressionists (who created their art in between), provoking us to think differently about how we create, with our heart and soul rather than our head. Masterpieces emerge when we get out of our mind and into our body as we shall see in Chapter 7. As the impact of the Industrial Revolution accelerated, this was a period of incredible transition—the introduction of the steam train and photography were transforming our relationship to space and time. Rather than reflect these transitions, he transcended them. In addition, he integrated innovations in the form of paint tubes, which allowed him to escape the confines of the artist studio and push the brushstroke even further, turning it into an evocative expression of his deepest emotions. His influence? Van Gogh has inspired all of us to express ourselves whether we consider ourselves artists or not—and he has done this without the same fear of us being called crazy.

In the aftermath of the Second World War, Jackson Pollock, the famous drip-artist, picked up the baton from Van Gogh provoking us to think differently about control. Pollock did away with the brushstroke altogether—replacing it with a drip or a flick, implying in the process that that we create best when we trust the process, stay connected to the Masterpiece and simply allow the energy of what Carl Jung called the "collective unconscious" to flow through us. In his short life, he lived through a period of even greater turmoil than the aforementioned artists: The Great Depression, The Second World War and the start of The Cold War. This was the precursor to the fastest increase in innovation (the rise of corporations, marketing and global supply chains) and collaboration (the welfare state, European Union and United Nations) humanity has ever seen, while at the same time it also led to the greatest conflicts (Second World War, Cold War) humanity has ever seen. His influence? As we shall in the next section, organizations fundamentally changed the way they organized themselves immediately after his death. After millennia of increasingly hierarchical control, they started to enable their employees to contribute their own Masterpieces, albeit a slow journey. Pollock did this by exhibiting his drip-work Masterpieces in super-galleries, with the patronage of philanthropist, Peggy Guggenheim. He built on the pioneering work of Carl Jung and Sigmund Freud and he painted through the night, when it's easier to access the collective unconscious, thanks to the innovation of electric lighting.

Fifty years after that, performance artist Marina Abramovic picked up the baton again, provoking all of us to think differently about creation yet again. She did it without paint. In her 2010 performance, *The Artist is Present*, Abramovich challenged us to consider that we all create, and true creation occurs in the space in between us. Abramovic created her performances in super-galleries, such as The Museum of Modern Art in New York, supported by corporate and philanthropic sponsors. Like Pollock and all the others, she did this in a time of extraordinary turmoil, in the midst of the financial crisis. It was and still is both the greatest period of innovation and collaboration (smartphones, social media, apps) humanity has ever seen, and, as we shall see, a period of incredible transition, to a world where climate change and inequality must disappear for humanity to survive.

Today, the task of rebalancing the world is monumental. The tradition Michelangelo started—using cutting edge media alongside the patronage and support of the most powerful people and institutions—is key. However, we need to unravel thousands of years of history. And this requires us to go one stage further.

Each of these artists provoked the observer (viewer of the art piece) to awaken the artist inside them, but none had the courage to reverse the relationship between observer and artist entirely, to make the observer the artist and the artist the observer. Nor did any of them create their art in today's most powerful institutions—business—let alone attempt to provoke these businesses to change their relationship to power, money, love or time so that the leaders within them create their own Masterpiece.

Today, contemporary art focuses more on profit than purpose. It extracts money from business to pay for it, rather than provoking business to change itself. Yet that's what the world needs today. We are living through what I believe is the greatest transition in the history of humanity. This requires an entirely different type of artist—one who can rebalance, reimagine and recreate our world.

Artists Integrate Opposing Forces to Create Masterpieces

Masterpieces emerge amidst the tension of opposing forces. Notice Michelangelo did not side with either the Roman Catholic Church or the Protestants—he created art that integrated the two. Turner did not ignore the Industrial Revolution—he integrated the steamship and the sailboat in one painting.

Van Gogh did not ignore the world of form entirely—he integrated figurative and abstract elements in one piece. Great Masterpieces integrate opposing forces.

The Impressionists realized opposing hues on the color wheel occur right next to each other in nature and this is what makes nature so vibrant. Shadows aren't black, they are blue, green, and purple. Light isn't white, it is yellow and orange. They saw the opposites and balance in nature at the same time. It was this tension that made their oeuvres shimmer.

Nikola Tesla realized that energy was cyclic. It flowed back and forth. It was neither one way nor the other—it was both at the same time. Direct Current (DC) flows in one direction continuously. Alternating Current (AC) changes direction fifty to sixty times per second and can be stepped up to very high voltages, facilitating long-distance transmission and minimizing energy loss. Tesla harnessed these opposing forces by developing devices that transformed this tension into electricity and in the process won the so-called "War of the Currents" against Edison's DC system.

German philosopher, Georg Friedrich Hegel realized human history evolves from one paradigm to the next through a process of opposites: a *thesis* is developed, which gives rise to a reaction, the *antithesis*, which negates the thesis, and the tension between the two is resolved by means of a *synthesis*. In other words, when a new idea or hypothesis or artist movement emerges, it is often criticized. It is too new or doesn't fully take account of the wisdom of the old, so it faces resistance. If the inventor or artist integrates this knowledge, he or she can refine their invention. The combination of action and reaction leads to resolution and a better outcome.

In Chinese philosophy, the opposing forces are symbolized by the yin, which refers to the negative, dark and feminine, and the yang, which refers to the positive, light and masculine. One cannot exist without the other. Both are required to create. They complement each other. The whole is greater than the sum of the individual parts. In nature, this duality manifests as light and dark, fire and water, expansion and contraction. A baby is the fruit of opposites—masculine and feminine, sperm and egg, yin and yang. New life requires these opposites. So, does existence itself. And yet today, we focus often end up focusing on one or the other as we saw in the first chapter.

Parallel dimensions

Today, we have more paradigms running in parallel than at any time in history, because we haven't resolved the underlying tensions from previous transitions. As we shall see in the next section, this creates an unprecedented level of opposing forces—and an even greater opportunity. For now, let's focus our attention on the transitions in the last 250 years to better understand what these opposing forces are before looking at the symptoms they have amassed.

Since The Industrial Revolution, there have been three major transitions, leading to four different paradigms. I call them the **Control, Compete, Create** and **Collaborate** paradigms. COVID-19, inequality and climate change all help us to see there is a "fifth" meta-paradigm, which underlies or connects all of the others. I call it **Consciousness**.

The rise of **Consciousness** reconnects us to our true nature, taking us full circle. It has the potential to return us to a "pre-civilization world", with the benefits of civilization. We will explore it more in Chapter 7. Before then, let's explore the first four paradigms so we can better understand the context in which this meta-paradigm is emerging.

Business has become the dominant force in the last 250 years, so I will describe each of these four paradigms by exploring how companies have organized and reorganized themselves before explaining how these transitions changed our ability to create a Masterpiece.

Each paradigm builds on the previous one. Rather than discarding a previous paradigm as outdated, we can learn from it. You may find it useful to think of each paradigm as a tool. Organizations operating from more recent paradigms have more tools in their toolkit. It doesn't mean they are better or worse than other organizations which have fewer tools. It just means they are better able to cope with the current tensions. And they are more likely to shape the paradigm and create a Masterpiece, which will address the root cause.

CONTROL

From the start of the Industrial Revolution until the end of the first half of the twentieth century, almost every organization in the world followed the same model, where a few people, usually the top two to three percent, defined the strategy of the organization and the rest followed. Think governments, The

United Nations, the Catholic Church, the military, educational institutions, and factories. Following the principles of Fordism or Taylorism, tasks were divided up into silos to increase productivity. One department focused on engineering, another on production, another on research and development, and another on marketing, sales, or finance. The various departments were coordinated by managers who sat above these departments. Process and bureaucracy were designed to support these managers. This led to the classic top-down pyramid.

This model was extremely effective in rooting out Corruption (the paradigm before Control) and along with the next stage, Compete, has led to the fastest increase in wealth and health humanity has ever seen. The advantage of this paradigm is coordination and standardisation. Control enables organizations to scale, reduce deadlines, and deliver on time.

Think of this paradigm as a hammer. Sometimes the challenge you face is a nail. To iron out the challenge, you need to hit it precisely in the centre with exactly the right amount of force.

The success of this model is predicated on the idea that what is good for the organization is good for the employee. Philosophically, it is paternalistic. Management knows best and will do what is right for the employee. Consequently, Control suffocates creativity and enslaves workers. They are not involved in the development of strategy and processes don't allow individuals to contribute their full potential. They become small cogs in a big wheel.

> *In so many companies, ideas get lost in the process.*
>
> **Jony Ive**, Chief Designer, Apple

Governments, (public) education, health, the military and supra-national bodies like The United Nations operate primarily from this paradigm. Take health. Hospitals divide treatment into departments which focus on individual organs: cardiology focuses on the heart, neurology on the brain, gastroenterology on the gut and liver etc. Yet if you look at our bodies, we are a whole person. Our brain interacts with the gut, our heart with our head, and (for me), my shoulder with my hip. If we divide our health down into silos, we miss these interactions.

The same is true in education. (Public) schools divide learning into subjects: mathematics, science, languages, art. Yet again though, we are a whole person. Even if our artistic capabilities may lead to a breakthrough in science, or speaking another language may expose us to other artists, our education system separates us from us and often forces us to choose between these different aspects of "us," labeling some of us artists, others scientists and yet others linguists. What if we considered these "subjects" were all just different aspects of each of us?

Organizations operating from Control that do this, and expand their toolkit, learn how to involve leaders and employees in the key decisions of their organization. They learn to let go and trust the process, like Pollock, by creating systems that enable creativity to flow again.

COMPETE

Following the Second World War, a new model designed to engage employees started to emerge. It was influenced both by the changing nature of work from predominantly physical, executional work to intellectual, conceptual work, and ironically by the rise of Communism in Eastern Europe and Russia. The Communist "experiment" was anti-industrialist and anti-capitalist. Yet, capitalists also read the manifesto and integrated the opposing force—their employees—into a new design.

This new approach led to the creation of HR departments, engagement surveys, talent management, complex matrix structures, and internal communications. Think international corporations like Procter & Gamble, Nestlé, Pfizer, Exxon, BA, Walmart etc. Organizations still spend millions of dollars attempting to design strategies to engage employees and increase their loyalty based on the principle that the more engaged the individual, the more likely he or she will be productive.

Compete builds on the first model. It accelerated the increase in health and wealth. Think of this paradigm as a screwdriver. Sometimes, the challenge you face requires more subtlety than a hammer. You could use a hammer to knock a screw into a piece of wood, but you would damage both the wood and the screw in the process. In other words, the ends do not justify the means.

The problem with Compete is without other tools, the vision and strategy are still defined predominantly by the top two to three percent of the organization without consistently and coherently ensuring it is realized throughout the organization. A leader, no matter how visionary, cannot impose a vision on another person. That's "Purpose-washing," trying to brainwash another person with your vision for the world. It's akin to a religion. You can only enable another person to find himself or herself in that vision.

> *Growing into a new form of consciousness is always a highly personal, unique, and somewhat mysterious process. It cannot be forced onto somebody.*
>
> **Frédéric Laloux**

In far too many cases HR is employed as a mouthpiece of the CEO to reinforce the vision, a nice way of gift-wrapping the same end-result. But there is no genuine attempt to help the individual grow, because the underlying philosophy remains the same. Consequently, there is a lack of authentic, consistent, coherent alignment across the organization between what it says and what it does. It flips back and forth between attempting to be purposeful and tackling problems which create more problems.

Too many organizations exploit problems without realizing the wider problem they are creating. Reducing the cost of books may make it harder for writers to earn a living. Satisfying our need for sushi may deplete our oceans. Reducing the cost of travel may increase climate change. The matrix structure doesn't help. It's more likely to create confusion and implicit conflict rather than acknowledging the underlying tensions and allowing creativity to emerge amidst these opposing forces. So, we are constantly reorganizing this structure, putting individuals and teams into different boxes and changing the reporting lines, without realizing none of us are designed to fit in boxes. As a result, creativity is still suffocated, and employees feel undervalued and disengaged.

Eighty percent of the world's organizations operate from one of these first two models. And yet, today, too few of us are engaged by the organizations we work for. The result is conflict rather than collaboration, competition rather than creation, and resistance rather than results.

Organizations operating from this level expand their toolkit by learning how to turn the model upside down. If the philosophy of Control and Compete is predicated on the idea that what is good for the business is good for the individual, the next two paradigms are predicated on the idea that what is good for the individual is good for the business. During the last millennia, organizations have predominantly been led top-down, assuming that the head has all the answers. This is a very masculine, ego-led approach. However, the head doesn't have all the answers. Sometimes the gut and the heart do too.

Artists who master their art integrate information received from their bodies. Within organizations they integrate information from the body of their organization to make better decisions. Doing this requires a leap of faith, because you never have all the information you need. There is no GPS, map or compass. It is always a step into the unknown.

CREATE

In the 21st century, new models have started to emerge fueled by the internet and technology in Silicon Valley. Technologies such as the internet, email and AI cut across traditional silos, enabling employees to email senior management in a second and making the original purpose of a hierarchy redundant. This led organizations like Google, Amazon, Tesla and Netflix to flip the hierarchical model upside down, enabling their employees to express their creativity and support a greater purpose. Other companies such as Virgin and Unilever are evolving to operate in this space and others such as Apple, Airbnb, and Uber were born in this paradigm, but flip back and forth between Compete and Create. Today, around 15% of organizations including most of Silicon Valley, the vast majority of NGOs and well-known "self-appointed gurus," operate from this space.

Create builds on the Control and Compete paradigms. Think of this paradigm as a step-ladder. It enables employees to elevate themselves and hands them the hammer and screwdriver so they can unleash their own creativity in line with the organization's Mission or Purpose. It encourages employees to trust their intuition, develop hypotheses, test these hypotheses through experiments, and refine them. To expand the toolkit requires a leap of faith—from "I" to "we" from "self-service" to "service."

In theory, this looks like a simple evolution. In reality, this is the hardest step. Success in the first three paradigms depends on individual brilliance. Success in the next paradigm depends on collective brilliance. This requires the leader to use their ego consciously, rather than it use them unconsciously.

However, Create organizations are by definition overly dependent on their leader. If Elon Musk contracted a virus tomorrow and died a couple of weeks later, both Tesla and SpaceX would revert to a Compete model. This is exactly what happened when Steve Jobs was fired from Apple in the 1980s. The share price collapsed, innovation dried up, and the organization was paralyzed until Jobs returned over a decade later.

As we shall see in the next section on symptoms, all of the organizations mentioned above are overly dependent on their leader. Above ground, they appear to be flourishing. They produce fruit, much of which is a Masterpiece, but if you look carefully, the leader overshadows the rest of the organization. Succession planning is limited, because no one lives up to the leader's standards. The result is everyone's potential is limited by the leader's ego. And that's because below ground, his or her roots are too shallow. The leader has not done the inner work to sustain his or her legacy. More importantly, the Masterpieces they create do not address the root cause of the symptoms of imbalance. They exacerbate these symptoms. These organizations and their leaders may wrap their Masterpieces up in the language of a greater purpose, but this is just a flimsy façade. It is an even more pernicious form of "Purpose-washing."

COLLABORATE

The emergent paradigm of Collaborate doesn't depend on a single iconic leader, although the Founder of the organization has a critical role to play. Peter Koenig, who you met in the Foreword and Chapter 1, refers to the leader or Founder of an organization as the "Source." In any organization, there is only one Source. His or her responsibility is to articulate a (greater) Mission, which inspires others to contribute their talents to it for as long as it helps them further their own Personal Purpose, and then hold the space within which they can do this.

Most of us who have heard of collective organizations misunderstand them. The idea gained popularity and attained almost cult status following the publication of Frédéric Laloux's 2014 book *Reinventing Organizations.*[7] In it, he explains how he moved from "I" to "we" by designing organizations based on a number of principles:

1. An organic structure that enables every individual to contribute;

7 Laloux, Frederic. *Reinventing Organizations: A Guide to Creating Organizations Inspired by the Next Stage of Human Consciousness.* Nelson Parker; Illustrated Edition. Belgium. (20 February 2014).

2. Organic processes that support their individual contribution;
3. A philosophy of wholeness that enables individuals to contribute all of their capabilities.

All of this is true. However, what Laloux missed and Koenig pointed out (to Laloux) is Laloux only interviewed the Source, or CEO, for his book—where the CEO underplayed the importance of their own role in creating the mission and holding the space in which others could create. In other words, neither Laloux nor the Source perceived the role they were playing to enable the collective to collaborate.

I fell into this trap when I founded Creative Leadership Partners with four other partners. I read the book and even saw Laloux speak at CERN—which includes the largest particle physics laboratory in the world. I fell in love with Laloux's concept. I thought it addressed the root cause of the problems we face. So, I helped each of my partners to articulate their Personal Purpose. Then, I helped us to create a Collective Purpose, before I went around the world advocating the same (to all my clients). However, what I discovered is the organization or team becomes aimless unless the Source (in this case me) plays the role of Source and defines the direction of the organization and holds the space for others to fulfill their potential. Other partners can provide input, but it is ultimately the Source who feels what is true and what isn't. He or she becomes the Master Artist who holds the tension of the opposing forces and allows creativity to emerge in their midst. I didn't do that either for me, the others, or the organization. As a result, we lost our way, never became sustainable and eventually closed the company.

Theoretically, it is possible to operate collectively, but practically speaking it doesn't work. I tried a similar experiment with another partner a couple of years later, believing it would work with the right partner. However, after two workshops—one around Mont Blanc and the other with a major healthcare company in Canada, I realized it couldn't work. If two or more people operate at a high enough level of consciousness, to be almost telepathic, it is possible for the model Laloux outlines in his book to work. But practically speaking, all of us have an ego, and we must use our ego to bring our Masterpiece to life. We are not ten Dalai Lamas or ten Buddhas operating in parallel. We are spirits, having a very human and often messy experience. Christ may have had his twelve disciples, but he was the Source—when they collaborated, they did so in support of his Mission.

Special forces, such as the Special Air Service (SAS) in the UK operate from the Collaborate paradigm, organically. They work in four-man "cells." Leadership circulates within these cells depending on the task at hand. Each member of the cell plays a specialist role—the officer (or Source), the sniper, the cook and the radio operator. Each person can do each of the others' tasks in case one is injured or killed—they are interdependent rather than dependent. For certain operations, two or more cells may deploy at the same time. These special forces teams operate in stark contrast to a typical military regiment (which operates from the Control paradigm).

With this important caveat, the seven organizations Laloux describes in his book do operate from this model. Examples include Patagonia, and Buurtzorg, the leading nursing organization in the Netherlands. For instance, Buurtzorg operates just like the SAS—although with a slightly different purpose—by operating in small cells of eight to ten nurses. Each nurse is responsible for their patients and one specialist area—for instance, finance or planning. Before Buurtzorg, the state employed and organized nurses. Each nurse was tasked with one responsibility, for instance dressing a bandage, and given targets within which to complete it. In most cases, this left insufficient time to provide the care that the patient really needed. However, repeated studies demonstrate care is critical to cure. So, rather than increase the effectiveness of care, it decreased it and demotivated nurses in the process. Now, the nurses can provide the level of care both need to feel fulfilled. The results are impressive. Buurtzorg repeatedly wins the Best Employer in The Netherlands award and saves around forty percent for the Dutch health care system by providing better care for the patients.

Treating the symptoms exacerbates them

When we use the wrong approach (or paradigm) to resolve the symptoms of disconnection that have built up over millennia, rather than address them and change our relationship to Time, Power, Love and Money, we create more unintended symptoms. For example, if we see every challenge as a nail or a screw and attempt to hit it with a hammer or drive it inwards with a screwdriver, we will damage the tool, the medium and the environment. Only those consistently using the Collaborate paradigm are reconnecting themselves sufficiently to change their world. Sadly, that's less than five percent of us.

The symptoms have now reached unprecedented levels. We can see these symptoms at three different levels—societal, organizational and individual.

These levels are connected. Each level and each symptom within each level reinforces the others in a complex web of mutual self-destruction.

Disentangling them is hard. This is a ball of string with hundreds of knots, which have developed over thousands of years. Finding the loose end isn't easy, let alone working out how to unravel it. Nonetheless, I believe we can learn from Michelangelo by: starting with the most powerful institution of the day—business, both corporations and start-ups; using the most provocative medium of the day—video and online meetings—to get their attention; picking up the baton from Abramovic and others to help the leaders and founders of these organizations to become artists; helping them change their relationship to Time, Power, Love and Money so they reconnect to themselves and create their Masterpiece; and then, asking them to pay for it. In other words, I believe the loose end of the ball of string is disengagement within organizations. Let me explain.

Disengagement from what we do disconnects us from who we are

Record levels of disengagement within organizations have accelerated a global breakdown in trust, which increases depression and *dis-ease*, exacerbates inequality and fuels climate change. COVID-19 is accelerating these tensions to breaking point. It has triggered the greatest increase in unemployment since The Great Depression in the 1930s. This is devastating for those operating from the Control or Compete paradigms. However, for those operating from Collaborate, it could be a godsend.

According to Gallup's latest State of *The Global Workplace Survey*[8], only fifteen percent of employees globally are engaged in their work. That figure drops to ten percent in Europe and six percent in East Asia. That means, in East Asia, ninety-four percent of employees are disengaged. That's appalling. Employees are disengaged for many different reasons, but the underlying cause is always the same. They are disconnected from their work, because they are disconnected from themselves. Too many of us do something we don't love to support our family, who we end up not loving, because we don't love ourselves enough to change what we do.

8 Gallup.com. *State of the Global Workplace*. Gallup Press, New York 2017. Retrieved October 8, 2020. https://www.gallup.com/workplace/238079/state-global-workplace-2017.aspx

Disconnection and disengagement within organizations creates unintended ripples outside organizations. According to Chief Executive Officer of Edelman, Richard Edelman, "There is a trust crisis that is leading to a systemic meltdown."[9] His 2017 Edelman Trust Barometer report reveals only fifteen percent of us trust the system,[10] we don't believe governments, the media, NGOs and business will address the root cause.

Disconnection has a knock-on effect at the level of society too. We are off balance. The two main symptoms of imbalance at this level are inequality and climate change. They are linked to disengagement. If we remove inequality, by enabling everyone to do what they love, climate change will disappear. I'll explain how in Chapter 7.

Inequality is a parasitic disease

Inequality is getting worse. The wealthy are getting wealthier and the poor are getting poorer (relatively speaking). According to Oxfam, in 2009, the combined wealth of the wealthiest 380 people equalled the poorest 50% of the world. In 2019, it was just 26 people.[11]

The rest of us are either drowning in debt or being devalued. We overextend ourselves by spending more than we earn. At the time of writing (November 2020), global debt is more than sixty trillion and may be as much as seventy-eight trillion dollars.[12, 13] That's more than the global production of goods and services and means every man, woman and child owes on average $10,000.[14] This includes a baby who has just been born, a rice farmer tilling a paddy field in China, and a hunter gatherer in Papua New Guinea. We are living beyond our

9 Koziol, Michael. *Sydney Morning Herald*. "Distrustful nation: Australians lose faith in politics, media and business." Published online January 20, 2017. Retrieved October 2020.

10 Edelman, Richard. 2017 Edelman Trust Barometer report. January 21, 2017. https://www.edelman.com/research/2017-edelman-trust-barometer

11 Lawson, Max et al. Oxfam Briefing Paper "Public Good or Private Wealth," Published online, January 2019.

12 Economist Intelligence Unit, "Global Debt Clock," The Economist. https://www.economist.com/content/global_debt_clock

13 Commodity.com LLC, "World Debt Clock." https://commodity.com/data/debt-clock/

14 Worldometer.com "Current World Population." https://www.worldometers.info/world-population/

means, buying and consuming products we don't have the resources to pay for and in many cases, we don't need.

It's no good saving money either. For instance, the amount of money printed in the six months following the COVID lockdown in March 2020 was the equivalent of what is normally printed by governments in an entire decade—and that's on top of all the money printed by government following the financial crisis in 2008. Central banks act as "the banker of last resort" to save an entire ecosystem or economy from defaulting on payment. But the greater the supply of money in a system, the lower the value of each note or coin within that system—and the higher the level of debt that each of us owes. This is a myopic vicious cycle—vicious, because it's hard to break, and myopic, because if we define the ecosystem as just the economy, we ignore the real banker of last resort—Mother Nature.

We are bankrupting Mother Nature

Mother Nature is paying the bill for our greed. She is balancing the books. We can see the symptoms of her balancing act in the number of endangered species, natural disasters and the extent of deforestation, habitat destruction, degradation and devastation.

Every year we lose 18.7 million acres of forest.[15] That's the equivalent of 82 football pitches since you started reading this chapter. That's more than the number of grounds in the top flight in England, Germany, Spain and Italy. Imagine wiping them out; not just games without spectators, no football games at all—ever again.

In the last fifty years, we have destroyed seventeen percent of The Amazon[16], primarily to feed ourselves steaks. Yet, forests produce forty percent of the world's oxygen and soak up carbon dioxide, which keeps the climate cool.[17] So,

15 World Wildlife Fund. Published in 2015 by WWF—World Wide Fund for Nature (Formerly World Wildlife Fund), Gland, Switzerland. https://www.worldwildlife.org/threats/deforestation-and-forest-degradation

16 Nunez, Christine. Reference article, "Rainforests Explained." *National Geographic*. May 15, 2019. https://www.nationalgeographic.com/environment/habitats/rain-forests/

17 United Nations Forum on Forests, published online 2 March, 2011: http://www.fao.org/forestry/iyf2011/69186/en/

we are producing more meat at the cost of the air we breathe and the climate we live in. That sounds like a very unhealthy balance sheet. The more trees we cut down, the hotter it will get. The hotter it gets, the more the ice-caps will melt, the more carbon is released and the hotter it will get in a vicious cycle. The hottest ten years have occurred in the last fifteen years. This isn't normal.

Mother Nature is getting more extreme in her rebalancing efforts too. According to *The New England Medical Journal*, there were three times as many natural disasters between 2000 and 2009 as between 1980 and 1989.[18] Eighty percent of this increase can be traced to climate-related events such as floods and hurricanes.[19] I see these rebalancing efforts like releasing pressure between two tectonic plates during an earthquake. This pressure builds up over hundreds if not thousands of years. When the pressure gets too great, the plates shift. In the process, they create unintended consequences. Pressure may have been relieved between the plates, but the enormous amount of energy unleashed creates ripples elsewhere within the system. For instance, when it happens under water, as we have seen recently in South East Asia and Japan, it can lead to enormous unintended waves or tsunamis that wreak destruction and in the case of Japan led to the Fukushima nuclear disaster, which degraded the ecosystem further.

I don't need statistics to tell me the climate is changing though. When I first moved to The Alps over seventeen years ago, I lived on a mountain overlooking Geneva, at over 1,000 metres (over 3,000 feet). I was there for two winters. The snow fell in November and stayed until the end of April. Now, we're lucky if it stays for more than two days consecutively.

> *If government, the private sector, and science don't cooperate immediately to address issues of environmental degradation, the earth will lose its ability to regenerate. In other words, life as we know it is toast.*
>
> Yvon Chouinard

18 Leaning, Jennifer M.D. Guha-Sapir, Debarati, Ph.D. "Natural Disasters, Armed Conflict, and Public Health." *The New England Journal of Medicine*. November 7, 2013 DOI: 10.1056/NEJMra1109877.

19 Idem

Disconnection leads to disease

The source of this disconnection is us - each and every one of us. Companies consist of people. We create them. They hire us. If we don't love what we do within them, it impacts us personally. We're more stressed and depressed than ever. According to *The Lancet*, depression is the leading cause of mental health disease.[20] According to the Centre for Disease Control and Prevention (CDC) in the US, the use of antidepressants increased by 400 percent between 1998 and 2008.[21] During the initial phases of COVID-19 in March 2020, the use of antidepressants, sleeping pills and anti-anxiety prescriptions increased by a further twenty percent.[22]

Stress and depression manifest themselves in dis-ease, divorce, poor diet, addiction and sleep deprivation. In 2016, you were five times more likely to die of a heart attack or a stroke than you were of a respiratory disease or Tuberculosis (commonly known as TB, the world's most prevalent communicable diseases).[23] Heart attacks and strokes are caused by stress, and even if you do die from a respiratory disease (including COVID-19) or TB, your immune system, which is designed to protect you from them, was probably compromised because you were stressed or depressed.

Our lifestyle causes stress. We go to work to earn money doing something we don't love—we come home and we compensate by eating poorly, sleeping poorly, and spending our time poorly. Today, you are more likely to die of obesity than starvation—we eat too much sugar and consume too much social media or Netflix. Even if you eat well, you may not sleep enough, and then you spend too much time on your phone or laptop and too little time with your partner,

20 Patel V, Chisholm D, Parikh R, et al. "Addressing the burden of mental, neurological, and substance use disorders: key messages from Disease Control Priorities," 3rd edition [published correction appears in Lancet. 2016 Apr 16;387(10028):1618]. *Lancet*. 2016;387(10028):1672-1685. doi:10.1016/S0140-6736(15)00390-6

21 Lee, S. H., Paz-Filho, G., Mastronardi, C., Licinio, J., & Wong, M. L. (2016). "Is increased antidepressant exposure a contributory factor to the obesity pandemic?" *Translational psychiatry*, 6(3), e759. https://doi.org/10.1038/tp.2016.25

22 Express Scripts. *America's State of Mind*, April 16 2020: https://www.express-scripts.com/corporate/americas-state-of-mind-report

23 World Health Organization, "Global Health Estimates 2016: Deaths by Cause, Age, Sex, by Country and by Region." 2000-2016, published 2018.

your children or in nature. That's the fast track to divorce, which is where half of US marriages end up. I could go on, but this would risk making you more depressed! You get the point. We need to change our lifestyle.

To change our lifestyle requires an entirely different approach. We cannot prevent lifestyle diseases such as heart disease, strokes, cancer, diabetes and depression by popping a pill. Drugs lead to side-effects, because the drug was developed to tackle that specific disease not to increase health or wellness systemically. The body isn't a set of silos that can be treated separately. It is a complex organism which must be treated holistically. The same is true with organizations and the planet. Our home is one ecosystem and everything in it is linked.

Rebalancing it starts with us. Depression is not caused by an imbalance in our serotonin levels. It is caused by a loss of meaning in our jobs. A loss of meaning in our lives. This imbalance will worsen unless we tackle the root cause—disconnection! And we can change that by creating a Masterpiece, so we do what we love.

Racism - a global pandemic

Today, racism illustrates both the consequences of using the wrong paradigm to deal with its underlying cause and the build-up of tension from not resolving it over the last 5,000 years. Racism isn't new. Today, the vast majority of us no longer believe slavery is acceptable. And yet, we haven't resolved the underlying imbalance that led slavery to emerge in the first place so it emerges unconsciously in other forms.

Racism cannot be resolved by changing the law (Control). For example, each time the United States changed the law (the abolition of slavery or The Civil Rights Act), racism re-emerged. Changing the law didn't change anything.

Taking sides doesn't help either. We legitimize racist politicians both by voting for them *and* by resisting them. Some politicians need resistance to justify their existence. So why does racism re-emerge after the law changes? Because it's not outside us—it's inside us. We are the cancer we are trying to heal. And it's been growing for thousands of years.

We fear what we don't understand. Politicians understand this fear, because they are part of the system too. Some of them share the same fears, which they then exploit—either consciously or unconsciously.

How do we change the system? How do we stop reinforcing it? By changing ourselves! And that requires some deep digging. It requires us to articulate our fears—to become consciously aware of them. We fear what we do not understand. We stop fearing when we become consciously aware of the fear. When we shine a light in a dark room, nothing in the room moves, but our *perception* of what is in the room changes. The same is true with our fears.

I grew up in the country which created the greatest empire the world has ever seen. My ancestors enslaved and oppressed. According to UK journalist and author Johann Hari, The British government in India deliberately adopted policies that led to as many as 29 million Indians dying through starvation. That's almost five times more than died during the Holocaust in Nazi Germany. You could argue the latter was intentional genocide in concentration camps. However, The British Empire invented concentration camps during the Boer War in South Africa. In other words, before I can accuse any other person or country of racism, I need to deal with my own. Relying on the law won't do this. We need to change our own humanity.

We are attempting to use old methods in a world that has forever changed

Albert Einstein

Reconnection and rebalance

If big pharma continues to produce pills that create more side-effects, marketers continue to produce stuff that we don't need, politicians continue to exploit racist fears; and all of us continue to produce CO2 that creates a hotter climate, humanity will go extinct. The treatment is to reconnect before it's too late. From the agricultural revolution onwards, we have used each subsequent transition to benefit the few rather than the many, placing personal profit over sustainable growth. We must stop.

Instead, we ignore the truth. We distract ourselves with our mobile phones, Netflix and social media. We don't want to suffer, but we end up suffering more.

We have a unique opportunity to change course now. The global slowdown triggered by COVID-19 and before that—the financial crisis, has helped many of us realize we have created our lives on sand. We realize we are living an illusion, out of touch with ourselves and the planet.

Masterpieces emerge in the silence amidst the tension of opposing forces. And these opposing forces have never been greater. They are the furnace in which you can create your Masterpiece. This is the greatest opportunity you or your ancestors have ever had to break the shackles of slavery and love what you do. Let's stop hoping the future will be different. Let's start creating a different future, together.

4 Finding Balance

Maintain a state of balance between physical acts and inner serenity.

Gautama Buddha

Creating your Masterpiece is a journey to becoming who you truly are—your essence, your spirit, your soul. It doesn't matter what you call it. What matters is you reconnect to it. Not as a theoretical concept in your head, rather as a practical experience in your body. And not just some of the time, but all of the time.

We get so wrapped up in the world outside that we forget who we are in the world inside. Rather than focus on the root cause of the symptoms we get distracted by the symptoms themselves. We patch up the symptoms and go back out into the world. But, because we haven't rebalanced ourselves, we continue to unbalance the world. Even if our intentions are good, unintentionally we create ripples.

This lesson was brought home to me in Japan a few years ago when I painted Mount Fuji. I prepared weeks in advance and worked out exactly where to stand to paint a reflection of this iconic mountain in a lake. I got up early that morning and was delighted to see the lake was flat. So, I rushed to paint it. But, by the time I got there, the wind had escalated, and the reflection had gone.

I tried to "will" the lake to calm down and nothing happened. Instead, the wind got stronger and the waves grew bigger. Waves are much harder to paint than reflections. Each wave is different and they're constantly moving. So, I painted. And painted.

Finally, six hours later, frustrated and exhausted, I stopped. I packed up my gear and a little despondent walked back around the lake, wondering why it hadn't calmed down. Half-way around, I got the answer. I passed a Japanese guy, wearing a t-shirt, which said in English—*Don't create waves!* I was creating "internal waves" and that chaotic energy rippled out from me.

The same is true in life. We create waves all the time without intending to. Our beliefs, thoughts, and actions which aren't aligned with our essence create these unintended consequences. The world outside us then reflects these waves back to us. It's not just some of us who do this, all of us do it.

You are not a body with a spirit. You are a spirit with a body. We conveniently forget this. Everything in the Universe is either energy or matter. Albert Einstein's famous equation, $E=MC^2$, assumes a small change in energy (E) leads to a large change in matter (Mass or M). Matter follows energy. The physical world follows the metaphysical world, yet today, we focus far more on the matter than the energy. The Inner | Outer Game model explains why.

The Inner | Outer Game

Every cultural tradition describes a duality that exists inside us. Most of us flip-flop between these worlds without a consistently balanced mindset that links them: psychologists talk about the conscious and the unconscious; philosophers talk about the personality and the essence; artists talk about the intellect and intuition; and scientists talk about the Newtonian physical world of things and the Einsteinian metaphysical world of ideas.

I call it the *Inner Game* and *Outer Game*, based on Bob Anderson and Bill Adam's research in their book *Mastering Leadership*.[24] Their research with over 250,000 leaders around the world found that those who lead with their Inner Game are up to 1,000 times more effective than those who don't.

Even if we understand this, most of us still use our Outer Game to tackle the symptoms of the problems we face. As we discussed in the previous chapter, we can see these symptoms at a societal, organizational and personal level: we have the highest temperatures and record levels of inequality, debt, natural disasters, ecological destruction, unemployment, distrust, disengagement, divorce, depression, sleep deprivation, poor diet and addiction. Is it a coincidence we see all of these symptoms at the same time? I think not. Everything is connected.

24 Anderson, Robert. Adams, William. *Mastering Leadership: An Integrated Framework for Breakthrough Performance and Extraordinary*, John Wiley & Sons, New Jersey. 20 November 2015.

> *Pollution is not outside us. Pollution is inside us. You are not observing the earth. You are the earth.*
>
> **Thich Nhat Hanh**

The Outer Game

Ever since the agricultural revolution, we have increasingly been using The Outer Game to tackle these challenges. So, what is the Outer Game? It consists of our identity or personality. The doorway into the Outer Game is our first five senses: our sight, hearing, touch, taste and smell. This is how we connect to the world outside us. The key to unlock our Outer Game is our strengths. We can use psychological profiling tools like Myers Briggs Type Indicator (MBTI), Gallup StrengthsFinder, Wealth Dynamics from GeniusU (the largest community of entrepreneurs in the world) to identify our strengths.

Your Outer Game creates influence.

I have developed my own tool, called **The Artist Profile** which explains how each of us creates in one of four different ways. All of these tools are based on the same Source—the *I Ching*, or the *Book of Changes*, a 5,000-year-old book from China. I will explain more about The Artist Profile later in this chapter.

When we unlock our Outer Game, we unlock our ability to influence our world by bringing our Masterpiece to life.

The Inner Game

So, what is the Inner Game? The Inner Game is much harder to describe. Because as soon as I give it a term, I will trigger your belief system, what you believe about the world—in other words, which paradigm you are primarily operating from, and this is influenced by your culture, upbringing and your experiences. So, rather than give it a name, I will let *you* give it a name. What's easier to describe is how you access the Inner Game. The doorway to the Inner Game is yours *sixth sense*, your intuition. The key to unlock it is your Personal Purpose. When we articulate our Purpose, we unlock creativity, collaboration, compassion and courage—all the things that we need today in order to tackle the root cause of the symptoms we talked about, whether they be at a societal, organizational or personal level.

Your Inner Game creates connection

When we align our Outer Game with our Inner Game, by putting our ego and influence (Outer Game) at the service of our essence and inner connection (Inner

Game), we change our behavior rather than attempting to manipulate the world outside us. We create the fertile conditions in which a Masterpiece can emerge. We easily foster a state of flow, in the zone, and in this moment, we can create miracles.

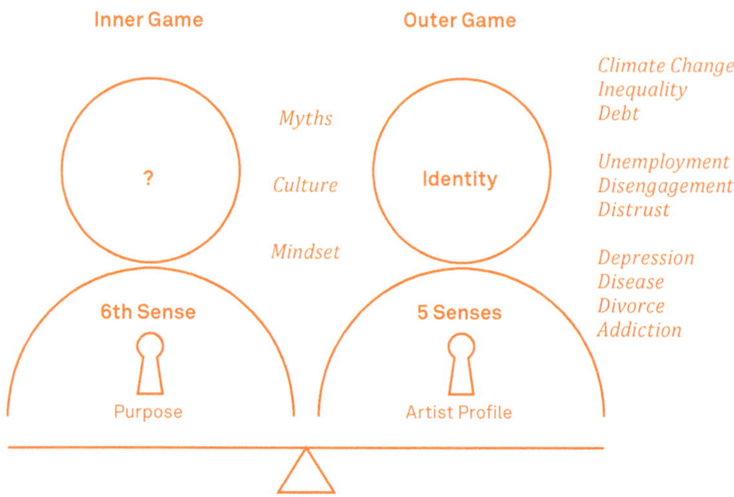

Miracles and Mindset

A few years ago, I ended up painting in a blizzard. I hadn't intended to paint in a blizzard. It just kind of happened. As the snow started to fall more heavily, I started to lose control over the canvas. My ego, my identity, kicked in because the paint was starting to run. But as I started to observe what was happening on the canvas, I started to see something really interesting was occurring. The snow was merging with the paint and creating really interesting patterns.

So, I paused, and stopped painting. I stopped reacting to the snow; stopped resisting it. The palette became covered in so much snow that I could hardly see the paint. But rather than resist, I continued; painting through the snow, rather than against it. I wondered at the time whether it was me or the snow that was panting the picture. It certainly wasn't my ego. That had dissolved into me. Was it my essence? Or was it something greater? Was the entire ecosystem creating in unity?

I didn't care. All I knew was that I felt at one, in total peace. Towards the end of the painting, I turned to Tony, my friend who had been filming me, and asked him if the painting was finished. When he replied "No," I continued for another fifteen minutes and then asked him again. At the exact moment he said "Yes," the sun came out and the snow and ice which had merged with the paint, holding it together, started to melt. Everything dissolved. The paint ran off the canvas, with nothing to hold it together, leaving me with a blank canvas: the same blank canvas I had started with. And a video to show what happened.

The funniest thing is, in that state, I was happy to let it go. The experience had been so mind-altering for me, I didn't care. When we are in total balance, we are in unity with ourselves and everything around us. We feel safe although we may be doing something that would appear incredibly unsafe.

When our Outer Game merges with our Inner Game, we become part of the ecosystem again. There is no separation. We are at one, in unity, at peace. In the process, we see the world outside us is a blank canvas on which we can create anything we choose. It's always a blank canvas. But because we're so wrapped up in our thoughts, we miss this essential truth: that we are the universe and influence everything in it, not just with our actions, but also with our presence. How else can we explain metaphysical phenomena such as healing people without drugs, levitating, talking in tongues, or changing the weather?

> *I am Life. I am the space in which all things happen. I am consciousness. I am.*
>
> **Eckhart Tolle**

You may not paint in a blizzard; however, your environment is changing all the time. And you face challenges all the time. Think of the biggest challenge you have faced in your lifetime. Maybe you lost your job, a partner, a home, a business, a parent or a child...? Whatever your biggest challenge is, just bring it to mind. Now, go right to the moment when you overcame that challenge, what did you do? My guess is you tapped into your Inner Game. If you're still facing that challenge, you may want to try tapping your Inner Game. Whatever you call that greater part of yourself is what we need to tap into today in order to address the symptoms we described in the previous chapter. We need both the Inner in order to find the solution and the Outer to take action on that solution.

We have known this for thousands of years: every wise culture in the world describes a version of this model: Tantra, Tao, *I Ching*, yoga, Shamanism etc... so, why don't we do this? Why don't we put our Outer Game in service of our Inner Game to change the world outside us?

There is something that sits between the Inner Game and the Outer Game, and we call this mindset. Mindset is the collective of beliefs. Often our beliefs stop us from unlocking the Inner Game and allowing our infinite creative energy to flow naturally through us into the Outer Game. In organizations, we call the collective mindset *culture*. Often, it is a company's culture that stops it from fulfilling its potential. The opposite is also true: when a company culture is fully aligned with its Mission, it can perform miracles.

At the level of society, we call the collective of beliefs—*myths*. This is a fascinating word in the English language, because it is one of the few words that is both one thing and the exact opposite. Myths can be both true and false. For instance, commonly held "false" myths include the idea that generating money is hard work, time is linear, power depends on status or love is found outside ourselves, whereas "true" myths include the idea that all men and women are created equal irrespective of skin color, gender or family and are entitled to certain inalienable rights. I find that fascinating because it is the myths or beliefs we hold about ourselves and society that we need to change today if we are to unlock our Inner Game and create influence at any level in the world outside us.

If we place our collective Inner Game and Outer Game on a balance to assess where we focus our attention, the scales would tip towards the Outer Game. This would be fine if the challenges we were facing were simple. Normally our Outer Game would be enough. However, as I explained in the previous chapter, the root cause of these symptoms is disconnection from the Inner Game, so we can't resolve them with the Outer Game. If we attempt to tackle them with the Outer Game, we create unintended ripples no matter how well intended we are or which paradigm we operate from. Using the Outer Game to tackle disconnection from the Inner Game will only make matters worse.

As we discussed in Chapter 1, some of us have made a leap and are more focused on our Inner Game, we escaped the False Summit vicious cycle. But unless we take action in line with our Purpose, we climb WooWoo Mountain and make no more contribution to tackling the root cause of disconnection than those still on False Summit.

Balancing Inner and Outer

Your Outer Game creates influence. Your Inner Game creates connection. You need both in balance to create a Masterpiece and be recognized for it in your lifetime. A comparison between Nikola Tesla and Thomas Edison illustrates this point.

Both were giants of electrical engineering in the nineteenth and early twentieth centuries. Both died in their eighties. Both were prolific inventors. And both could comfortably lay claim to being the greatest inventor of all time.

However, they differed on how they leveraged their Inner and Outer Games. Edison lacked purpose (Inner), but generated profit (Outer). Tesla did the opposite. He was so driven by purpose; he didn't generate enough profit to live. Tesla made poor business decisions and was constantly chasing financing to support his addiction to inventing. Neither approaches alone are sustainable in the long run. Both men were out of balance.

Edison invented the incandescent lightbulb, the first electricity system which runs on Direct Current, the carbon microphone, the kinetoscope (which allowed viewers to watch a short motion picture through a peephole), nickel iron batteries, and the phonograph (to record sound), which earned him the nickname "The Wizard of Menlo Park." Tesla invented the fluorescent lightbulb, the modern electric system which runs on Alternating Current, x-rays, radio, remote control, the electric motor, robotics, laser, and wireless communications.

Tesla's inventions represented greater breakthroughs, and often bore little relationship to what came before, whereas Edison's were more incremental, building on the work of others. Some of Tesla's insights are still inspiring scientists today, whereas many of Edison's have been superseded.

> *Everybody steals in commerce and industry. I've stolen a lot myself. But I know how to steal.*
>
> **Thomas Edison**

On this basis, we might imagine Tesla died the wealthier man. However, he didn't. Edison died with his wife next to him at home on his estate at the age of eighty-three, a multi-millionaire, but Tesla died at the age of eighty-six on his own in room 3327 on the thirty-third floor of the Wyndham New Yorker Hotel in New York, in debt.

Tesla was an originator. Edison was a businessman. Tesla developed broad concepts, which he rarely refined. Edison refined everything so he could make money from it. Tesla almost exclusively used his Inner Game. Edison used both his Inner Game and Outer Game.

What made Edison remarkable was the system he created and the effort he expended to mass manufacture his inventions. He started his first business at the age of twelve, selling newspapers, snacks, and candy on the local railroad. By the age of fourteen, he had developed his own newspaper, *The Weekly Herald*, which had over 300 subscribers. In his lifetime, he accumulated 1,093 patents worldwide compared to Tesla's 278. Edison created the first research and development lab at Menlo Park. He called it his *Invention factory*. This business became the Edison General Electric Company. Today, it's simply known as GE. In 2000, it was the most valuable company in the world with a market capitalization of $480 billion.

Edison's approach to innovation was based on hard graft. He wasn't afraid of hiring the very best and claimed he didn't need to be a great mathematician. He could always hire one. He even hired Tesla when Tesla first came to New York, although this experiment was short-lived. Edison regularly worked an eighteen-hour day and pushed himself to the limit. He claimed to have "constructed 3,000 different theories in connection with the electric light, each one of them reasonable and apparently likely to be true."[25] For Edison, Masterpieces were the outcome of hard graft.

Edison understood what people were willing to pay for. The first invention he patented—an electronic voting system—was rejected, because it was too fast. It didn't allow politicians the time they needed while the vote was being counted to lobby others to their way of thinking. In other words, it didn't solve a problem. From that point onwards, Edison's definition of a great invention was it generated profit rather than serve a greater purpose.

> *I find out what the world needs. Then, I go and invent it.*
>
> **Thomas Edison**

25 *The Humboldt Times*, Volume XXXIIII, Number 61, 13 March 1890. Retrieved from the Center of Bibliographical Studies and Research, November, 2020.

Tesla was different. What made him remarkable was his ability to visualize an invention in graphic detail. He could work out the finest details and ensure everything worked in his head before turning it into something outside his head. Albert Einstein did something similar. He called them his "thought experiments." The difference between Edison and Tesla's approach to invention is summed up in Tesla's criticism of his one-time employer: "If Edison had a needle to find in a haystack, he would proceed at once with the diligence of the bee to examine straw after straw until he found the object of his search."[26]

Tesla would pluck ideas out of thin air. The problem was that he could rarely share his ideas with others. He wasn't very good at sketching, and he rarely produced blueprints. As a result, turning his inventions into reality was largely dependent on himself. He did have a lab and assistants, but nothing on the scale of Edison's Menlo Park, let alone General Electric.

Tesla didn't lack the ability to connect with others. Women, the media, and celebrities adored him. Through his friend, the editor of *Century Magazine*, Robert Underwood Johnson, Tesla befriended Mark Twain, the humorist and writer, and socialized with Anthony Dvorak, the Czech composer, and Rudyard Kipling, the English poet and recipient of the Nobel Prize for literature. Tesla always dressed elegantly and loved to put on a show, regularly inviting his friends to performances in his lab where he would dazzle them with light displays, often conducting high-voltage electricity through his body to light up fluorescent lamps held in his hands. Tesla didn't lack self-belief either. He arrived in America with only four cents in his pocket and a letter of recommendation to introduce him to Edison.

What Tesla lacked and Edison had was business acumen and a system to generate wealth from his inventions. Yes, he did partner with George Westinghouse to bring AC to the world. But when he discovered that the royalties Westinghouse owed him would make Westinghouse's company go bankrupt, rather than see humanity not profit from his invention or renegotiate the contract to make it work for both parties, Tesla tore up the contract and settled for a one-off payment of $60,000 and a monthly salary of $2,000. That's around $50,000 in today's money and a lump sum of somewhere in the region of $1.5 million. In

26 Cheney, Margaret. Tesla: *Man Out of Time*. Touchstone; Illustrated edition, 8 November 2011. (Retrieved from Audiobook 2014).

other words, Tesla had a habit of pushing money away from him, as something dirty, and when he did have money, he spent it. Indeed, $60,000 was not a life-changing amount of money for an inventor with a habit for purchasing expensive lab equipment.

What Tesla lacked was positive cash flow and the mindset to generate and retain it: inventors and entrepreneurs need a retainer from a client or passive income from a product to free them up to invent more. That's where Edison's genius lay. Teams and companies need to generate revenue from their core business. They need to "stick to the knitting" according to Tom Peters and Robert Waterman, authors of the groundbreaking 1980 book, *In Search of Excellence*.[27]

Positive cash flow frees us up to create the Masterpiece we were born to create. Otherwise, we will constantly be distracted. Like Van Gogh, Tesla lacked this throughout his life. He never had a business model that generated sustainable revenue and he was pushed out of two businesses he co-founded. He regularly forgot to patent ideas. And other ideas sat on the sidelines, because he wasn't interested in investing the time to refine them.

Yes, Tesla had a patent expert on his team, but there is no point of having an expert if you don't refine the ideas you generate sufficiently to commercialize them. Take the radio. Marconi is commonly attributed with inventing it. He even shared the Nobel Prize in physics in 1909 in recognition for his *contribution to the development of wireless telegraphy* (commonly known as the radio today). However, Marconi's patent for the radio was registered in 1900. Tesla registered his patent in 1898 and he had worked out how to pass intelligence wirelessly as early as 1893.

Tesla only gained recognition for his contribution to radio six-months after his death. In 1943, the US Supreme Court reversed an earlier ruling, saying, "Tesla had anticipated all other contenders with his fundamental radio patents."[28] As we discussed in Chapter 2, like Van Gogh, Tesla had to stop thinking before the gestation period elapsed and he was properly recognized for his inventions.

27 Peters, Thomas J. Jnr Waterman, Robert H. *In Search of Excellence: Lessons from America's Best-Run Companies* HarperCollins Publishers Inc; Reprint Edition (21 May 2004).

28 Cheney, Margaret. Tesla: *Man Out of Time*. Touchstone; Illustrated edition, 8 November 2011. (Retrieved from Audiobook 2014).

The problem was Tesla didn't refine his ideas sufficiently to be commercialized easily. He invented and moved on. Tesla's radio ideas were left for others to pick up and refine for less ambitious but more practical purposes. Instead, Tesla was addicted to creating and connecting. He couldn't stop. No sooner had he invented one breakthrough than he had moved on to the next. Edison was addicted to calculating how to grow his empire, while Tesla was addicted to inventing new ideas. As soon as he generated profit from one invention, he invested it into the next one.

Seventy-five years later, the world is still trying to catch up with Tesla. But during his lifetime, he didn't master the skills Edison mastered to leave a legacy. He didn't calculate how to generate sustainable revenue, nor did he develop a system that would enable him to scale up his inventions. As a result, like Van Gogh, he died in debt.

Imagine what Tesla and Edison would have created if they had collaborated for longer. Between them, they had the perfect balance of the four Artist Profiles, but their failure to find a common language led to a breakdown rather than a breakthrough. As we shall see, that's why it's so important to create a **Collective Mission** that unites opposing forces.

Intellect and Intuition

If creativity is the raw material, and creation is what's created, creativity without creation is meaningless. What makes this physical dimension special is that we can see, touch, taste, smell, and hear things. We can turn things in our head into things outside our head. It's why we're here. Creation gives purpose to our lives.

Creativity emerges from the world inside us. Innovation occurs in the world outside us. The art of creation links the two. Without creation, there is no Masterpiece. There is nothing. Master artists combine the best of both worlds—intellect and intuition, head and heart, conscious and unconscious mind to produce breakthroughs.

Intellect makes sense of the information you receive from the world outside you through reasoning and logic. It helps you position yourself in space and time. From the moment you wake up to the moment you go to sleep, it is active. Think of your intellect like the latest laptop. Normally, it's super-fast and can process enormous amounts of data within a matter of seconds. However, even the latest laptop has its limits. If you fill the hard-drive with data and then have multiple different applications running at the same time, your short-term memory will overload, and the computer will start to slow down. At a certain point, you may get a warning message, saying something like your hard-drive is full—free up more data. At this point, applications may start crashing, losing our latest thoughts and the connection to the internet may slow down. Our intellect works in exactly the same way. If we overload it, it slows down, our short-term memory may start to malfunction—we forget words or our keys, or where we parked our car—we cease functioning properly and we lose our connection.

Intuition works differently—it is the doorway to creating your Masterpiece. Intuition is an inner wisdom that lies largely untapped inside us. The word intuition comes from the Latin verb *intueri*, which means "to look inside." It connects us to other dimensions outside space and time. When we open the doorway, we access what Carl Jung called the *Collective Unconscious* and Albert Einstein called the *Unified Field*. We will explore the Collective Unconscious in more detail in Chapter 7. For now, think of your intuition like your connection to the internet. It enables you to connect to every other laptop and access their information irrespective of time and space. Using our intuition enables us to cut through vast amounts of information without needing to go through it line by line. Either it feels right, or it doesn't. We just know, one way or the other. It speeds everything up, but only if we slow down sufficiently to hear it. Given the explosion in the quantity of information we receive every day, using our intuition is both harder and more important than ever.

You may say your intuition has let you down in the past, and this is why you don't trust it. According to the definition I have just given, I disagree. Your intuition never lets you down. You have let your intuition down. Intuition is always right. The problem is hearing your intuition above the noise of the enormous amounts of information you are receiving. To make matters worse, your ego will often sneak in and pretend it's your intuition to justify its existence. Distinguishing between the two isn't easy, especially if you're running at a million miles an hour.

Your intellect and intuition play different roles. You would not use a knife to do what a fork does, and vice versa. Each has a specific purpose—one for cutting food, the other for picking it up. On the rare occasions when you don't have a knife, you make do. However, attempting to cut boiled potatoes with a fork or pick up mashed potatoes with a knife compromises the experience. To avoid your ego sneaking in and pretending it's your intuition, give both your intellect and your intuition a role to play. But put your intellect at the service of your intuition.

> *Intellect is a faithful servant. Intuition is a sacred gift.*
>
> **Albert Einstein**

Master artists combine intellect and intuition. Intuition is the key to your Masterpiece. Intellect is how to realize it on time and on budget. Think of LEGO, Patagonia or Buurtzorg. Each one is a crazy, an impossible idea that transformed an industry. Each started with a creative breakthrough based on intuition, a gut-feeling. And then over time, this breakthrough was refined and refined and refined using intellect.

Yet today the majority of the business world and education system focus primarily on intellect, because the Control and Compete paradigms emphasize its importance. The result is we are trying to tackle the challenges we face incrementally without the breakthroughs required to make the difference needed.

Take the iPhone. The first iPhone was a creative breakthrough—what the Japanese call *Kaikaku*: the philosophy of *radical change*. It requires a lot of intuition and a little intellect. The iPhone was the brainchild of Steve Jobs, who famously dropped out of school, experimented with psychedelics and championed intuition. Since its launch, Apple has focused on refining and refining and refining the iPhone—what the Japanese call *Kaizen*: the philosophy of continuous improvement. *Kaizen* promotes hundreds of little changes rather than a few big breakthroughs and was popularized by Toyota's manufacturing department. It was perfect for the industrial age when little changes and new variants, flavors, prices, and pack sizes were sufficient to drive growth. You wouldn't use the first iPhone today; it doesn't have sufficient memory to cope with your current applications or the quantity of information you process on a daily basis.

Without the initial breakthrough—*kaikaku*—the latest iPhone wouldn't exist. Without refining it—*kaizen*—the latest iPhone wouldn't be relevant. Without a greater Purpose or Mission, they won't help us reconnect. In other words, we need a combination of Purpose, *Kaikaku* and *Kaizen* to tackle the underlying cause of the problems we identified in the last chapter.

Intuition is more powerful than intellect.

Steve Jobs

Being and doing

We create Masterpieces with our Outer Game when we connect to our Inner Game by reclaiming our relationship to the four elements: Time, Power, Love and Money, described in Chapter 2. In these moments, we are doing something from a state of being. We connect to all that is—outside of space and time, and in these moments something miraculous appears to happen. Often, these events occur "off the canvas"—in other words, something else in your life changes, while you are creating your Masterpiece. When you connect to the soul of the universe, something will change in your world for good. This can happen when I'm painting, coaching, or playing with my children, Sasha and Daniel.

What I'm doing doesn't matter. Who *I am* does. I am more likely to connect doing the things I love. Thus, I am more likely to manifest miracles in these moments, in other parts of my life. I am less likely to connect doing the things I don't love. Instead, I clutter my mind, stop being me and reduce the likelihood of something miraculous happening. It is why creating your Masterpiece—loving what you do is important.

The purpose of creating anything in the Outer Game, whether it be your Value Proposition, Mission, Artist Profile or Money Flow System (see below) is to give you sufficient confidence and belief when it comes to communicating your Masterpiece. If you believe in your Masterpiece, others will as well. If you don't, others won't. It's that simple.

The balance between being and doing is a tight-rope. When we overbalance towards the Inner Game (being), we climb WooWoo Mountain and get lost in the clouds. When we overbalance towards the Outer Game (doing), we climb False Summit and create unintended waves.

We often climb False Summit when we get over-attached to our Masterpiece. Our doing compromises our ability to be and we sabotage our Masterpiece. If this is you, you may find it useful to think of your Masterpiece as an experiment. Every experiment starts with a hypothesis. You do the experiment to prove or disprove the hypothesis. If you disprove the hypothesis, you refine it. Then, you run another experiment. What is important is not what you do, it is how you feel when you do it—your state of mind will determine the outcome of what you create. If you start to feel too attached to your Masterpiece, it will fail. Remain free, light and committed. This will allow your audience to become free, light and committed—and in the process they may purchase your Masterpiece. The inverse is also true. If you become overly attached to your Masterpiece, for instance, you doubt it will succeed or fear it will be rejected, your Masterpiece will take on these feelings and project these fears to your audience.

Your Masterpiece is not you.
It is something you create when you connect to all that is. It comes through you, but it is not you. You create it, but it does not define you. You are not the thing you do. Indeed, after you have created your Masterpiece, it will take on a life of its own.

Think of one of Jackson Pollock's drip paintings in the Museum of Modern Art in New York. We recognize the creator of the painting, in this case Pollock, independently of the painting he created. We can like one and not the other—reject one and accept the other. Do not define yourself by what you create. Adopting this mindset allows you to experiment, fail and experiment again.

With this in mind, let's explore the relationship between the Inner Game and Outer Game by looking at the key components of each in more detail. Then, in the next chapter, I will explain how you can reclaim your relationship to each of the four elements: Time, Power, Love and Money, so you can bring your Masterpiece to life.

Everyone has their own definition of terms like Purpose, Vision, Values, Mission, Objectives, Strategies and Goals. Your definitions may differ from mine. For instance, you may use Vision or North Star instead of Purpose, or Goals or Objectives instead of Mission. The terms themselves don't matter. The principles behind them do.

Koenig distinguishes between two types of terms: those which are outside of space and time, such as Purpose, Vision, Values, North Star; and those that need to be achieved within a specified space and time, such as Mission, Goals and Objectives. The former are eternal and personal. They relate to our Inner Game. The latter are temporal and can be personal or collective. They relate to the Outer Game.

Personal Purpose (Inner Game)

Your Personal Purpose is the guiding light of your life. It is a single sentence that sums up who you are and why you are here. It articulates your essence, your spirit, your soul. It is eternal, outside of space and time. Everything you create reflects your Purpose. How pure the reflection is depends on your mindset. If your mind is polluted what you create lacks clarity. If you empty the cup, you clear your mind, and create the conditions to create your Masterpiece.

The French term *fil rouge* has no real equivalent in English. Literally it means red thread. In French, it describes a pattern that runs through everything. A film has a *fil rouge*, an organization has a *fil rouge*, and so does your life. Your Personal Purpose is the *fil rouge* of your life. It is how to channel your creativity effectively.

Knowing your *fil rouge* will help you make both the big decisions and little decisions. Should you invest effort here or there? Should you start this project or that project? Should you respond to this person or that person? Think of it as a rudder. It gives direction to your life.

Your Personal Purpose shows up when you make your best decisions and is absent when you make your worst decisions. It connects your biggest breakthroughs to your biggest breakdowns. If you look at them objectively you will see a pattern running through them. This is your fil rouge: the red thread that runs through the heart of everything you think, say, and do.

My Personal Purpose is to *free the world's creativity for good*. When I am fulfilling my potential, I am freeing creativity in myself and others. When I'm not, the resistance I experience physically is an unconscious lack of alignment between my Inner and Outer Game. If I shine light into this resistance and become consciously aware of it, I can uncover an insight which may help me grow and help others to free creativity. Thus, I am always pursuing my Personal Purpose, whether I like it or not. Painting frees creativity in me. Coaching frees creativity in others. When I get stuck, I'm learning a lesson. If I don't learn the lesson, it repeats until I do, again, and again!

In each moment, you have only one Personal Purpose, one *fil rouge*. However, your *fil rouge* has many threads leading towards it. What you think may be your Personal Purpose right now may turn out to be just a thread in a few years!

That's fine so long as it works for you in this moment; it will help you channel your creativity.

Aligning your life with your Personal Purpose creates more meaning and can lead to greater success and fulfilment. We do that by tapping into what motivates us.

Research suggests that there are two types of motivators for engaging in an activity: internal and instrumental. Internal motivators comprise doing an activity because you love it, whereas instrumental motivators mean doing it to become famous or make money. The stronger internal reasons we have, and the more we focus on the meaning and impact of our work, the more likely we are to achieve the rewards.

In a world where we are driven by financial rewards, money, status and technology—rather than what brings us joy—this might seem counterintuitive. In fact, if you spent all your time reading life-science journals or immersed in the world of big data, Artificial Intelligence and machine learning, you could be forgiven for thinking meaning and purpose are dead. According to this perspective (from the Create paradigm), we can simply strap on a device, embed a chip, take a pill, or outsource the problem to AI to help us to tackle the symptoms I described in the previous chapter. But if biotech really was the answer, why do we appear to have record levels of depression and divorce? The solution to overwhelming amounts of information isn't delegating the problem to AI or using biotech to obtain a Zen state of mind, it's creating a vision that focuses AI and biotech on a greater Mission. If we continue to do the opposite, tackling symptoms before balancing ourselves, we will continue to get the same result. In a world where science claims there is no meaning, meaning is more important than ever.

> *People don't buy what you do; they buy why you do it.*
>
> **Simon Sinek**

The Artist Profile (Outer Game)

Your Artist Profile describes the different skills required to create and bring your Masterpiece to life. It describes your Outer Game, whereas your Purpose describes your Inner Game.

As I mentioned earlier, The Artist Profile is based on the *I Ching*, a 5,000-year-old Chinese book which formed the basis for Jung's work on archetypes.

Most personality profile tools claim that the identity is static. It isn't. It is constantly evolving. You are not the same identity you were when you were nineteen as you are now. However, the idea that your identity is constantly changing can be challenging if you associate with your identity. If, on the other hand, you accept you are more than your identity, then you free yourself to create the Masterpiece that emerges from your essence (Inner Game) using your strengths (Outer Game) to bring it to life.

The Artist Profile

Each of us create in different ways.

> **Choreographers** create the *Culture* in which Masterpieces grow.
> **Creators** create and refine the *Idea* behind the Masterpiece.
> **Collaborators** create the *Community* that it serves.
> **Calculators** create the *Money Flow System* that makes it sustainable.

These four profiles also follow the four seasons:

Choreographers cultivate and regenerate the soil (or culture) in winter. **Creators** grow the seed in Spring into flowers that attract others. **Collaborators** invite other species to pollinate and cross-pollinate these flowers, so they become fruit (your Masterpiece). **Calculators** harvest the fruit that is produced. We will explore how to put these into practice in Chapter 8.

You need all four in balance to create and bring your Masterpiece to life. That doesn't necessarily mean you need four different people in your team. It means that you need all four of these profiles represented *within* your team. A Masterpiece may take time to develop, requiring multiple revolutions of this cycle. After each harvest, the Choreographer regenerates in winter and prepares for the next Spring.

The Choreographer

Their Art: Choreographers create the *Culture* in which Masterpieces grow. They focus on the details underground, ensuring the soil is fertile enough for a seed to grow. Their art is to create systems and processes that help Masterpieces to scale. They get their energy from putting things in order and love to solve complex puzzles that enable others to perform at their best. They're constantly looking for consistency and harmony, although creating the idea and connecting to others aren't their strengths.

They tend to be great finishers rather than great starters. And they'll sweat the details and have extraordinarily high standards to ensure what they create works.

Choreographer Traits: They tend to shy away from the stage and are often found in the back room, beavering away as the engine of a team or organization. They tend to see problems others can't see and love trying to fix them. They'll be around long after Creators and Collaborators have moved on to the next idea.

They have the potential to scale Masterpieces profitably so long as they have a Creator and a Collaborator to build it on.

Shadow-side: They'll often get frustrated that others don't share the same concern about the details and need balance either in the team or with the finances. If they're putting on a show, expect the result to be immaculate.

They are often accused of being more interested in what's going on inside a team than outside and can be direct and very critical of those who don't focus sufficiently on details, timing or structure. However, if left unsupervised they tend to make systems that the business or audience they are trying to serve doesn't actually need. They can make great leaders so long as they stop obsessing over the details.

Unlike Creators and Collaborators, they will rarely push themselves to the limit. They are driven by creating systems that enable others to perform to the best of their ability.

Famous Choreographers: Masters who started out as Choreographers include Mark Zuckerberg, Tony Hsieh (CEO of Zappos and bestselling author of *Delivering Happiness*) and Bill Gates.

The Creator

Their Art: Creators focus on the art of creation. They create and refine the *Idea* behind the Masterpiece. It doesn't matter whether it's a project, a product, a discovery, an innovation, a business, a book, a painting, a sculpture, or a poem. They get their energy from creating and simply love to create. Given the opportunity they would focus on that all day, leaving others to make the connections and handle the details.

Creator Traits: They're great starters rather than great finishers. In fact, they are constantly moving from starting one creation to another and are fascinated by what's new and innovative. They simply can't stop themselves. Rather than take what someone else has created, they'll often recreate it themselves.

They tend to see further than others and tend to be visionary even if they can't always explain their vision to others. They'll often get frustrated that others can't see what they see and close themselves down just to focus on creating.

They have the potential to start trends so long as they have a Collaborator who can help spread the word.

Shadow-side: They are often accused of having their head in the clouds or being naïve. And they tend to be very sensitive and take criticism of what they are creating badly. They can make great leaders so long as they enable others to do what they don't master. And that's anything other than creating.

They push themselves to the limit and sometimes over it physically, emotionally, and financially to ensure their creations are seen by others. They create breakthroughs as easily as breakdowns and sometimes both at the same time as a breakdown can be the precursor to a breakthrough.

Famous Creators: Masters who started out as Creators include Michelangelo, Vincent Van Gogh, Nikola Tesla, Albert Einstein, Steve Jobs, Elon Musk, and Richard Branson.

The Collaborator

Their Art: Collaborators focus on people. Their art is to create connections between people and Masterpieces. They create the *Community* that it serves. They get their energy from interacting with others and love to connect people in their network to other people in their network. They're constantly looking for the next deal and can be great at closing it, although finances and systems may not be their forte.

Collaborator Traits: Like Creators, they tend to be great starters rather than great finishers. And they're constantly moving on to the next project, sometimes even faster than Creators. But while Creators love to take to the stage, Collaborators will steal the stage. They tend to make connections others can't see and are brilliant at forming teams although they rarely want to stick around to see the results of their creation. They are already on to the next interaction.

Shadow-side: They have the potential to start movements so long as they have a creation worth starting it around. They'll often get frustrated that others don't work as fast, and they hate being slowed down by ignorance or lack of contribution.

They are often accused of being more interested in what's going on outside the organization than inside. And they tend to make poor leaders unless they appoint a couple of deputies to make sure the team is running smoothly, or they use their brilliance to help others grow.

Like Creators they will push themselves to the limit but rarely over it. They are driven by being admired by others.

Famous Collaborators: Masters who started out as Collaborators include Mahatma Gandhi, Oprah Winfrey, Martha Stewart, Barack Obama, Emmanuel Macron, and Justin Trudeau.

Tip: If you're trying to work out whether you're primarily a Collaborator or a Creator, here's how to distinguish between the two. Collaborators often create a program or project in order to have something of value to connect to others through. And vice-versa, Creators will try to connect their creations through others so they can see the light of day and generate value. If you had to give up creating or connecting and let someone else do it for you, which one would it be? All of us have each of these roles within us. The question is, which is your primary or driving role.

The Calculator

Their Art: Calculators focus on creating value. They create the *Money Flow System* that makes the Masterpiece sustainable. Their art generates true wealth by working out the right time to harvest the produce (or Masterpiece). They get their energy from developing a strategy, creating a Money Flow System and serving their clients in a way that sustains their Masterpiece. At their very best, they transcend the man-made system and create strategies that transform entire ecosystems for good. They're constantly observing trends to work out when the best time is to invest or grow their business, collection or empire.

Calculator Traits: Unlike Creators, they have their ear to the ground and like Choreographers they tend to be good finishers. They're brilliant at service and they'll sweat the deal until they have completed it. Like Choreographers, they tend to shy away from the big stage and tend to operate in the shadows, quietly accumulating wealth, their reputation or sometimes both.

They tend to see opportunities before others and will go after them with persistence. They can be very patient and are willing to wait for exactly the right moment to pounce—even to the extent of suffering personally if it's in service of a greater cause.

They have the potential to create Masterpieces that generate passive income and are brilliant at growing a tiny opportunity into something far greater.

Shadow-side: They'll often get frustrated that others, especially Creators and Collaborators who are not willing to wait for the right opportunity to come along, lack grounding and patience.

They can be accused of being soulless and, if they disconnect from their Purpose, lead lives that lack meaning. On the flip side, when they align what they create with their Purpose and do transcend the man-made system, they make brilliant leaders who create or transform entire ecosystems that elevate everyone within it.

Like Choreographers, they will rarely push themselves to the limit. They are driven by the opportunity to serve.

Famous Calculators: Masters who started out as Calculators include Nelson Mandela, Mother Teresa, George Soros, and Warren Buffett.

Unique Combinations

Everyone has a unique combination of these profiles. Over time, as you reclaim more aspects of yourself, you may find you strengthen your profile in areas where you are weaker. One way of looking at the different profiles is like this:

Creators and Calculators reflect the heart and head spectrum.

Collaborators and Choreographers reflect the inner and outer aspects of a team.

In other words, Creating emerges in the gut and heart; Calculation arises in the head; Collaborating is focused on the world outside, and Choreography on the world inside.

Another way is to think of an orchestra: **Creators** compose the music; **Collaborators** play the music which attracts the audience. **Choreographers** conduct the orchestra—they turn their back on the audience to ensure the ensemble creates more together than it can alone. And **Calculators** ensure the orchestra sustains itself by serving the ecosystem in which it exists concert after concert so everyone involved can realize their Purpose.

Mission (Outer Game)

A Mission describes the next chapter in an individual, team or company's life. It is your vision of the world you want to see in a given period of time, for instance the next three years, or the next decade. As my partner, Koenig points out this differentiates it from your Purpose, which is outside of space and time. Your Purpose is eternal whereas your Mission is temporal. It is what your world would look like when you have brought your Purpose to life.

Your Personal Mission will answer questions such as:

- What would your health be like (body, mind and spirit)?
- What would you love to do (Your Masterpiece)?
- Who would you love to be doing it with (Your personal partner, your family, your professional partners and your community)?
- Where would you love to live (which city, town or village, in which country or would you like to travel the world)?
- How will we generate a sustainable flow of money (streams of revenue)?
- And what will you do to help the next generation love what they do (your children and / or the world's children so you leave a legacy for good)?

Your Mission touches on all four aspects of The Cycle of Life we introduced in Chapters 1 and 2. It helps you focus your mind on an inspiring goal. When I work with individuals, I help them to focus on the most inspiring aspect of their Mission, to literally visualize it and then to imagine what it would feel like to bring this to reality. You may want to do the same.

Take a few minutes to draw your Mission—literally—draw every aspect of your life in three to five years' time. Avoid the temptation to see this as a test of your drawing capabilities. It isn't. Stick-figures will do. Simple outlines of houses or nature or whatever you want to depict is sufficient. What matters is you understand what you are drawing, not that you are able to exhibit it. Drawing is a simple way to access your unconscious mind. Once you have completed the sketch of your Mission, feel how it would feel if you brought that to life. I help participants of the #Masterpiece program to do this by taking them on a guided journey. I will explain more about how you can do this in Chapter 7. In Chapter 6, I will explain how you can create a Collective Mission within an organization. And in Chapter 9, I will guide you through the process in more detail—and provide a link to my website—so you can do this for yourself.

Value Proposition (Outer Game)

A Value Proposition is a sentence—sometimes a very long one—that explains how your Masterpiece adds value to the various stakeholders who benefit from it at any given moment of time. If your Purpose is the *fil rouge* of your life, your Value Proposition is the *fil rouge* of your Masterpiece. Everything you say in your communications—both online and offline—and do—whether they be products or services, flow out of this Value Proposition. If your Masterpiece is how you bring your Purpose to life, your communications and services are how you bring your Masterpiece to life. Articulate your Value Proposition and you understand how your Masterpiece serves others.

To give you an idea, as I mentioned earlier, my Purpose is to *free the world's creativity for good* whereas the Value Proposition of my #Masterpiece program and this book is to help you *love what you do all the time.* You are more likely to buy a book or purchase a program which helps you to love what you do all the time than one which helps to free your creativity. The Value Proposition brings the Purpose to life by describing how it adds value to those you serve.

Like your mission, a Value Proposition is temporal rather than eternal. Each Masterpiece you create has its own Value Proposition. Some authors, like Alexander Osterwalder (*Business Model Generation*), suggest each audience for each Masterpiece has its own Value Proposition. Instead, I prefer the simplicity of Tom Poland's approach, the author of *Leadsology: The Science of Being*. He encourages his audience to develop one-word Value Propositions. Focusing on one word can be very powerful. It helps you focus your Masterpiece on the value you create. Getting to that one word can be difficult though. It may take some time. Where I differ from Poland and Osterwalder is making the link to the Inner Game that I described earlier.

For me, a Value Proposition answers the following questions:

- **WHO** are you doing it for? Your ecosystem—who do you serve within the entire ecosystem?
- **WHERE** are they? Which city, town, country or region are they based in?
- **WHAT** value do you create for them? What does your Masterpiece provide that adds value and helps your audience grow both emotionally and functionally?
- **HOW** does this value benefit them? What are the specific benefits of your Masterpiece on a daily basis?
- **WHO** do you need to become in order to bring it to life? Why should someone believe you?

The key is what your stakeholders are crying out for you to do for them. This isn't what you would like to do for them. It isn't what you think they ought to do, nor is it what their ego wants, or they tell you what they want. It's what *their* Inner Game needs to grow and fulfill their true potential.

Think of one specific person you know that your Masterpiece will benefit. Then identify how it will add value to this person. Resist the temptation to communicate to everyone. If you try communicating to everyone, you will end up communicating to no one. As you learn more about your audience, you can always refine your Value Proposition.

Make the benefits as specific and grounded as possible too. Jeff Walker, creator of the Product Launch Formula uses the analogy of grounding a plane. Most of us define our Value Proposition and benefits at 30,000 feet—the height a plane flies at. Rather than say "I will help you live a dream life"—which sounds vague—I promise to "help you love your life all the time—you will wake up next to someone you love, look at your diary and only see events you love, live where you love and help others to love what they do too." This is very tangible and measurable. I have grounded my plane. You know exactly what you're going to get from joining one of my programs.

The best way to work out how your Masterpiece generates value for your audience is to ask them. Develop a draft Value Proposition, then find someone who would be your ideal client and share your draft with them. Ask them whether this would help them to grow and whether they would be interested in purchasing or investing in your Masterpiece. Avoid the temptation to read the Value Proposition aloud to them. Speak to them in their language. Remain open to their feedback. Then, incorporate their feedback and refine your Value Proposition.

Your Value Proposition creates more flow at any moment in time in one of two different ways. Think of a mountain stream. Nature increases the amount of water flowing past any one point either by increasing the *breadth* of the stream or the *depth* of the gradient. A stream broadens as it turns into a river and deepens as it goes over a waterfall. The same is true with your Value Proposition—you can either broaden the number of people who benefit or take one of those people on a deeper journey. Waterfalls tend to appear earlier in a stream's journey. This is why I recommend you do the same with your Masterpiece—take one individual all the way through your journey. Test out your Masterpiece before expanding it so more people can benefit.

Encourage money to flow

Koenig coined the term **Money Flow System** to describe how money flows between the various stakeholders within an ecosystem. As author, Douglas Rushkoff points out in his book, *Throwing Rocks at the Google Bus*[29], the vast majority of companies still use the "Sumerian business model" that extracts more capital for fewer people. The antidote to this extractive capitalist system is encouraging more money to flow through an ecosystem at any one time. In other words, we increase the velocity of transactions within an ecosystem so everyone, rather than just a few, benefits.

The problem is some of the time we take—we are more Outer Game—and some of the time we give—we are more Inner Game—and today, the relationship between these two behaviors is out of balance. Collectively we take more than we give, which explains why fewer and fewer of us are amassing greater and greater amounts of wealth. What would happen if we valued taking and giving equally—if we derived as much joy and happiness from both behaviors?

29 Rushkoff, Douglas. *Throwing Rocks At The Google Bus: How Growth Became The Enemy Of Prosperity*, Portfolio (2 May 2016)

Through the gift of presents, Christmas has institutionalised the concept of giving and receiving one day a year. Imagine if we valued giving and receiving equally every day of the year. This is exactly what nature does.

Different parts of an organic ecosystem play one of five different roles to increase giving and receiving within the ecosystem. Either, they **Seed, Grow, Pollinate, Harvest or Reseed**. Two of these roles increase the *breadth* of flow within the system and two of them increase the *depth* of flow within the system. We can map them against the Cycle of Life to illustrate how they relate to these two strategies and each other.

Seed—plants grow from seed, so does your Masterpiece. Use the **Choreographer** within you to ensure the ground is sufficiently fertile so the seed of your idea starts to grow. You may need to be patient, to wait for exactly the right moment to plant your seed—too soon and you are not ready—too late and your audience is no longer ready.

Grow—for seeds to reach the light so they can give back, they also need nutrients, minerals and water, especially in the early stages. Your Masterpiece needs the same. Use the **Creator** to develop breakthroughs that add significant value to those who benefit from your creations and grow your Masterpiece in leaps and bounds.

Pollinate—for a plant to contribute to the growth of the ecosystem, it must produce flowers and fruit that the ecosystem needs. As your Masterpiece grows, nurture the branches and leaves so it flourishes. Eventually it will produce buds. Use the **Collaborator** to nurture these buds so they blossom into flowers. As they do, help other parts of your ecosystem to pollinate and cross-pollinate these flowers so they turn into fruit. The flowers and fruit are a tangible part of your Masterpiece that benefit your ecosystem. The flowers are the Value Proposition that you share to see if your Masterpiece does benefit the ecosystem. The fruit is the Masterpiece itself.

Harvest—pollination turns flowers into fruit. Timing is critical to harvesting this fruit. Use the **Calculator** to harvest the fruit at exactly the correct moment to benefit the ecosystem. Too soon and the fruit will taste bitter. Too late and it will taste sour. Many **Calculators** generate money just by being in the right place at the right time to generate wealth.

Reseed—at the core of the fruit is the seed from which the next generation can grow. Once others within your ecosystem have consumed the "edible" part of your Masterpiece, use the **Choreographer** within you to invite them to spread the seed of the idea with their community so the next generation benefits from the value you have created between you. Remember **Choreographers** use processes and systems to scale Masterpieces effortlessly. Paraphrasing the founder of GeniusU, Roger James Hamilton, **Choreographers** *multiply* by using systems behind the scenes whereas **Collaborators** *magnify* by connecting people on the stage.

- **Choreographers and Collaborators** expand the breadth of the canopy so it can capture more sunlight.
- **Creators and Calculators** heighten the tree and deepen its roots so the canopy can reach the sunlight.

Your Masterpiece needs all four of these Artist Profiles operating in balance to maximize the potential value it generates for the ecosystem.

At the beginning of your journey, use the **Creator** and the **Collaborator** to refine your Value Proposition and generate value. Then, use the **Calculator** and **Choreographer** to scale it. We will explore this concept more deeply with the use of examples in the last chapter. For now, remember what you do is less important than *how* you do it. Follow this approach rigidly without connecting to your Inner Game and you will never create a Masterpiece that benefits the entire ecosystem. Connect to your Inner Game then use this approach and it will.

You may be wondering how this works in practice. At the end of each #Masterpiece program, everyone who contributed to the program (coaches, organizers, communicators team etc) gets together to play a variant of the *Findhorn Money Game*. We add up the revenue generated, remove the costs, then share what is left between us. We take turns to allocate the funds based on what we believe our contribution is worth and what we believe others' contribution is worth. As we do this, we explain why we are allocating the money in this way. We continue allocating and reallocating the funds until everyone is happy with what he or she has received *and* given to others. Of course, this process throws up some fascinating conversations about our perception of giving and receiving money. Indeed, the *conversation* about money always ends up being more important than the *allocation* of that money, because it reveals what stops us from creating a Masterpiece that reflects and generates value for the entire ecosystem. Sometimes, it leads to reclaiming aspects of ourselves we have suppressed. We will explore this idea more in the next chapter.

Communicate to encourage flow

Communications follow exactly the same principle—*how* you communicate is more important than *what* you communicate, and what you communicate follows the Cycle of Life. Lord Lever Hulme famously said, "half my advertising budget is wasted, I just don't know which half." In my experience, all communications which don't come from the Inner Game are wasted, and all communications which don't use the Outer Game to ensure they are relevant are wasted as well. In other words, communicate from the Inner Game and refine using the right words with the Outer Game.

Only start communicating when you have something of value to communicate. Resist the temptation to share an idea before it is ready. If you cut open a caterpillar's cocoon before the butterfly has formed, all you will find is a gooey mess.

Pollinate

Start communicating your idea once you have developed a draft Value Proposition. Before then, you will sabotage it. If you find yourself doing this repeatedly, you may discover there is something for you to reclaim (see Chapter 5 for more details on the **Reclamation Process**). Get feedback on the value (proposition) you create rather than the idea itself. Think of your Value Proposition as the bud of a flower. Communicate the potential of the bud to help those whom your Masterpiece benefits to grow. Then, when you're ready, develop your initial offering: the products or services that become your Masterpiece. Think of this as the flower. Allow the bud to blossom. Communicate what has blossomed to your audience and see if they pollinate your idea or not.

Harvest

When you're ready, invite those whom your Masterpiece benefits to join the first pilot of your Masterpiece—it may be a few chapters of your book, a mini-retreat, or if your Masterpiece is a relationship—the first date. Whatever it is, ensure you communicate your Masterpiece with the energy that inspired you to create it in the first place. Your audience will respond to your energy rather than the words you communicate. The words are just there to give you confidence while you communicate. Consider the pilot a test—you are testing the Masterpiece to see whether your audience is ready to part with money to pay for it.

When it comes to pricing your Masterpiece, Koenig makes the distinction between what *it* is worth and what *you* are worth. Often, we confuse the two. You are of infinite value and of no value at all! Your Masterpiece is not you. It has a life of its own. So, resist the temptation to use your Masterpiece to value yourself. Instead, consider what you believe it's worth and what your audience believes it's worth. The price you set is somewhere between the two. To start with, you may tell your audience it is worth what you believe it's worth but charge them what they believe it's worth and over time move the price up to what you believe it's worth. Often, we underestimate the value of our Masterpiece. And sometimes, we overvalue it. Do you tend to overvalue or undervalue yourself? Use your answer to help you find the right balance when it comes to your Masterpiece. Remember setting the price is an art in itself.

Reseed

Strengthen your communications after you have completed your pilot. Ask for feedback and where appropriate, testimonials. If the feedback is predominantly good, invite your audience to share their experience with their community. If the feedback is predominantly bad, use it to reinvent your Masterpiece. Then, consider how you can scale your Masterpiece. For instance, you may use social media such as LinkedIn or Facebook to find your audience, a system such as MailChimp or Keap to manage your emails and direct them to a simple website using WordPress or just a single (landing) page using LeadPages or ClickFunnels to communicate your message where they can sign-up and accept payment using Stripe or PayPal for credit cards, WooCommerce (for WordPress) or Shopify as the online checkout and QuickBooks or Xero to manage your accounts.

Grow

Consider how you can grow your Masterpiece. After the pilot, you may launch a second-generation product incorporating improvements you received through the feedback and or ideas you identified during the program. You may have ideas for additional products or services you can launch, some of which may appeal to different niche audiences or different geographic markets. You may find there is a premium product that appeals to an audience that wants an exclusive 1:1 relationship with you or a more basic product that appeals to an audience that cannot afford your standard product. The Creator in you will naturally generate dozens of ideas. This is wonderful. It is the purpose of the Creator. Balance the Creator with the Calculator—grow upwards and downwards at the same time. Ensure your roots are deep enough and sturdy enough to be able to harvest all the branches and flowers you nurture. It is far better to nurture one flower until it blossoms to its full potential before trying to cultivate another one.

Pollinate

When it comes to re-pollinating your Masterpiece the second time around, consider how your Value Proposition serves other people's communities. Growing your own community takes time. Other communities already exist. Identify the top two to three communities which would benefit from the value you create. Then, offer that value to that community for free. For instance, you may give a speech to that community, offer an interview or a podcast. Be willing to provide your very best content and ensure whatever you communicate comes from your Inner Game. They will respond to your energy rather than your message.

At the same time, be aware, there are many impressive gurus out there who have made their name by developing systems that are designed to help you launch your Masterpiece. I haven't come across any that are truly operating from the Collaborate paradigm and I have looked very hard. Follow these guidelines, pivot everything around your Purpose and you will develop a program that resonates at a higher level and therefore attracts those with whom you would love to work.

5 Changing Your mind

We have to learn to think in a new way.

Albert Einstein

To rebalance the world outside you, rebalance the world inside you. This is an infinite journey consisting of three different dimensions:

1. **The Inward Journey**
   Changing our relationship to the four key elements: Time, Power, Love and Money, that stop us from creating our Masterpiece.
2. **The Outward Journey**
   Mastering all four Artist Profiles: the Choreographer, Creator, Collaborator and Calculator.
3. **The Upward Journey**
   Growing from a seed into an entire ecosystem that influences its environment.

This chapter will focus on the first dimension—the Inward Journey to unlock the Inner Game—so the soil becomes fertile enough for the seed of your Masterpiece to grow. Deepening the roots encourages growth in the outward and upward journey. Or to put it another way, we will unlock the Inner Game (inward) to encourage growth in the Outer Game (outward) by bringing our Masterpiece to life (upward). We will explore the outer and upward journeys in the remaining chapters.

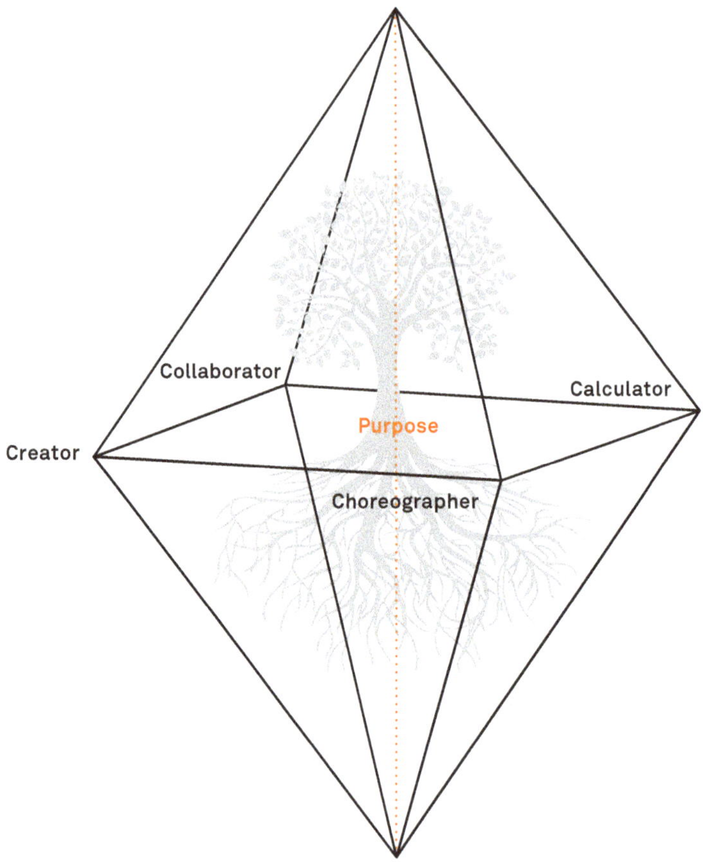
Collaborator
Calculator
Purpose
Creator
Choreographer

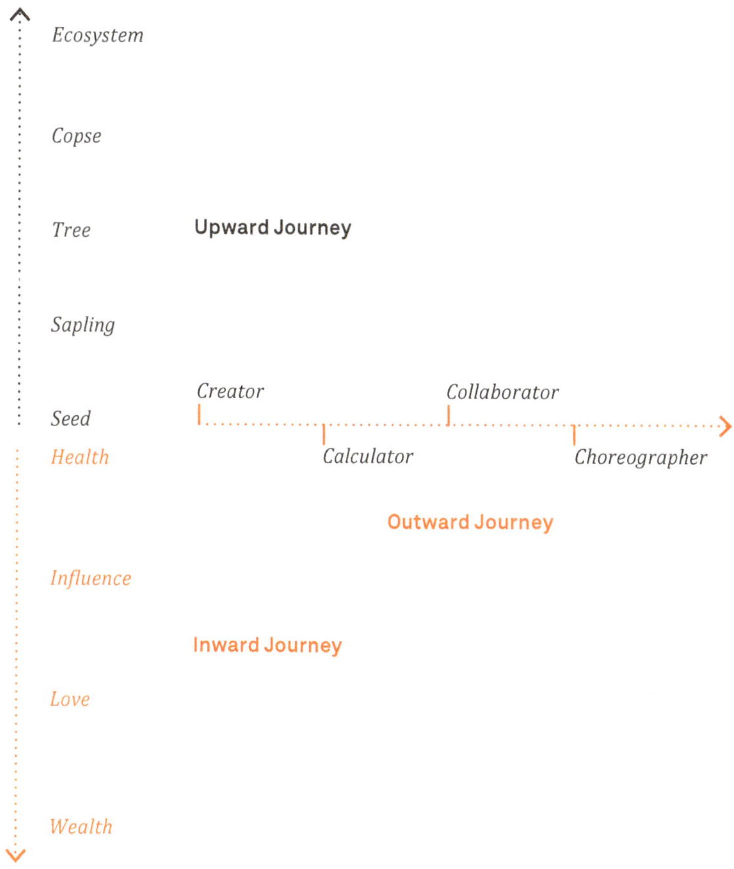

Turning the world inside-out

To move from a focus that starts with the outer to one that starts with the inner requires us to change our mindset by elevating our consciousness and to leverage our strengths (expand our Artist Profile). The psychologist, researcher, and author of *Mindset: the new psychology of success*[30] Professor Carol Dweck, differentiates between two types of mindset: fixed mindset and growth mindset. Fixed mindset is the belief that everything is defined by our genes

30 Dweck, Carol S. Mindset: the new psychology of success. 2006. New York: Random House.

and we can't change it, no matter what we do. We are either born intelligent, athletic, creative, musical, visionary, or not. Growth mindset says we can change everything, including our intelligence, our creativity, and our genes. We can learn to become more artistic, musical and intelligent.

Our mindset is more important than most of us realize and yet elite athletes demonstrate again and again its importance. They push back physical boundaries and make the impossible possible. A four-minute mile was impossible until Roger Bannister ran it. Now, the record is under three minutes and forty-five seconds. The same could be said of a two-hour marathon or running one hundred meters in under 9.6 seconds. Records are there to be beaten, but it is not what we do that enables us to do it—it is who we become in order to do it.

Everyone has had their own mind over matter experience—even if you're not an athlete. Colleagues called Steve Jobs' ability to do this his "reality distortion field" (taking their inspiration from the film *Star Trek*). Accessing it requires us to open our chakras. Sustaining it requires discipline (the Choreographer). This is a balance between the Inner and Outer Game, a state where the impossible happens, no matter what is going on around us.

According to research biologist Bruce Lipton, author of *The Biology of Belief*—if genes define our potential in any given moment, mindset defines how close we get to it. Our Masterpiece can change both. Put another way, how we interact with the world outside us can change the world inside us. Our Masterpiece helps us do this.

Mindset has become a popular buzzword today. The media and business tend to talk about it without realizing what it is. They know even less about how to change it. You cannot change a company's mindset; you can't even change an individual's mindset. All you can do is create the space within which the individual chooses to change. Any change in mindset comes from the Inner Game. The individual chooses to change. If enough people in an ecosystem choose to change, the ecosystem mindset, or the culture and myths that limit it will change.

> *Organizations do not transform—people do.*
>
> **Bob Anderson and Bill Adams**

Think different

What stops us from changing our mind and creating our Masterpiece is our fears. Many of these are so deeply embedded in our unconscious mind we aren't even aware they exist. We remain in the past rather than changing our relationship to it. When we change our relationship to the past, we create the possibility of a different future.

When we look at the world from the Outer Game, through the lens of the Control or Compete paradigms, we may doubt ourselves and believe others are better or more capable of doing it than we are. When we do the same through the lens of Create and Collaborate (the *WooWoo-we're-all-in-this-together-but-I'm-not-taking-responsibility-for-my-shit* mindset), we may depend on others to such an extent, we never take responsibility for ourselves and believe we can't do it without them. For instance, the most common excuses I hear from my clients for *not* creating a Masterpiece, are:

I don't have enough time
I'm not capable of doing it
I won't be accepted if I do it
I don't have enough money to do it.

Each of these excuses (or symptoms of inaction) correlates to one of the four elements: Time, Power, Love and Money, which in turn correlate to the first four chakras—we'll explore these more in chapter 7. When I dig a little deeper with my clients, I discover a fear always lies behind these symptoms. This fear is a variant of:

I didn't do it right
I'm not good enough
I'm unlovable
I'm worthless.

You may have your own flavor of these fears. Initially, as I mentioned when introducing Jung and Koenig's theories on reclamation, you may project this fear onto someone or something else. For instance, you may say something like:

My family is more important
My work is a higher priority right now
My partner or boss will never allow me to do it
I'm not creative enough
I'll do it when my children are older

When I have secured this promotion
When my relationship is more stable
When I have earned enough money

What stops us from creating our Masterpiece is not Time, Power, Love or Money. What stops us is our relationship to Time, Power, Love or Money.

We project our deepest fears onto these elements. Rather than face our fear, we suppress it deep underground. We suppress the voice deep inside us. The one that calls us to be who we truly are. We join the conspiracy; the conspiracy that creativity is only for a chosen few, that only the fittest will survive, that others know best, that worst of all, there is an élite—and you're not part of it.

It's safer here, playing small. We are surrounded by others who believe the same. We accept we can't do something. We accept the commonly accepted relationship to each of these elements. Until we don't. Until we stop. Until we wake up. Or until we think we wake up. We move from passive acceptance to active resistance. We write posts on social media. We go out on the streets. We tell our friends. We say racism or poverty, or inequality is unacceptable. We protest and in the process we legitimize it. Resistance creates resistance. It is the flipside of the same coin. It is the same thing.

Stop playing small. You were not born to play small. You were born to create your Masterpiece. Actively accepting your fears nullifies resistance. You can reclaim your relationship to each of these elements by understanding that your ancestors shaped your perception of time, power, love and money, and you inherited it. You can change this relationship, so you don't pass it on to the next generation.

To do this, you must face your deepest fears. Dig in the dark. Integrate the darkness. Accept the fear. Welcome it as a friend. Understand what it has taught you so far. Imagine what it can teach you in the future. Looking into the dark also exposes the light within you—even if that light has dimmed with age. Then, accept you are that light too. You are both the light and the dark—the Inner Game and the Outer Game.

For example, when I paint I am constantly moving between light and dark. The Inner Game is connected to the collective unconscious. It has no fear. Because it is both fear and fearless. It is power and powerless. It is love and loveless. It is worthy and worthless. When we use our Outer Game to bring that infinite power, love and value into the world, without resisting our fears for long enough, we create a Masterpiece. Accept you are both light and dark at the same time. And neither.

Whatever you resist is also in you.

Eckhart Tolle

Reclaim Your True Power

You were born whole, complete, connected to all that is. At birth, you had no ego; you were not aware of any separation between you and the entire universe. As I described in the Introduction, your little brain was producing primarily delta brainwaves. Your ego only started to form at the age of two when your brain started producing primarily theta brainwaves. By the age of twelve, the illusion of separation was complete. Each interaction separated you a little more—you separated from the universe by a thousand cuts. I will explore how this happens in more detail in Chapter 7.

There are thousands and thousands of different modalities that can help you reconnect. However, the vast majority end up being little more than temporary sticking plasters, because they don't treat the root cause or only partially treat it, which isn't treating it at all. You do yoga, learn to meditate, go on a retreat, and for a few blissful moments you feel connected again. The afterglow may last for a few moments, days, weeks or even months, but eventually your "old" reality re-emerges. You shift from the masculine vicious cycle to the feminine vicious cycle—from False Summit to WooWoo Mountain. To experience these moments of bliss, you try more modalities, a different coach, another retreat, but none of them appears to reconnect you for good. That's because this is a journey. It's not a destination.

More importantly, most modalities only focus on experiencing more "positive" emotions—more joy, love, happiness, peace, harmony etc. Yet, the universe is made up of both light and dark, yin and yang, positive and negative. So, you cannot reconnect to the entire universe unless you accept you are both joy and sadness, love and hate, peace and disharmony.

Koenig's **reclamation work** is different. It is designed to help you reclaim all aspects of yourself that you have suppressed so you reconnect to who you were born to be. You don't even need to know what "caused" the suppression in the past. All you need to know is what resistance you are experiencing in the present. The process is simple. The process is so simple that once you learn it, you can use it whenever you face resistance—even in the middle of a meeting!

It works on the basis of repeating a phrase and its opposite, even if it may initially appear like a lie—until your unconscious mind eventually accepts and embodies it. When you do this, you literally release the toxins in the cells, which are stopping you from reconnecting. You may find yourself laughing out loud or crying or sometimes both at the same time. This is just an outward reflection that the process is working.

Time

Over the last 10,000 years, we have changed our relationship to time: from eternal and expansive to temporal and linear, from being part of time to running out of time, from Inner Game to Outer Game. Your Inner Game is outside space and time. Your Outer Game believes it can manage time. It can't. You can't. It's an illusion, which is reinforced by your watch, smartphone, calendar, laptop, colleagues and partner.

Each subsequent transition has disconnected us further from time. Before the agricultural revolution, time flowed through us. It expanded and contracted based on our needs. We were part of time. And it was part of us. Today, we have lost our relationship to time.

To reclaim your relationship with time, rewire both your conscious and your unconscious mind. You can use a guided meditation (or Neuro-Hypnotic Repatterning - NHR) to rewire your unconscious mind. You can use a mantra or Neuro-Linguistic Programming (NLP) to rewire your conscious mind. I recommend you start with your conscious mind and then work on your unconscious mind before returning to your conscious mind. Which tool you use is less important though than accepting both your fear and the opposite of your fear, the Outer Game and Inner Game. For instance, you are both timeless and on time. If you accept only your fear—the root cause of being late—you climb False Summit. If you accept only the opposite of your fear—being at peace even if you are late—you climb WooWoo Mountain. When you accept both, you rebalance yourself and reclaim your relationship to time.

How to Reclaim Your Relationship to Time

Start by writing down the top five to seven things you associate with time—both "positive" and "negative." For instance, you may associate time with *freedom, peace, pressure, love and scarcity*.

Then, pick the one which has the most power for you. Let's say it's *freedom*. In this case, using Koenig's reclamation system, you would say "I am free" and you would add *with and without time*—i.e. "I am free with and without time" or "I am free with and without enough time." To start with, the sentence may feel like it's a lie. That's okay. Do it anyway. It's working its magic. At a certain moment, you may feel a little warm, tingles in your spine or hands, a charge of electricity run through your body, tears well up inside you or the need to laugh out loud. These are all indicators the process is working. .

Repeat the reclamation until it resonates and then look for the fear that underlies it. The fear is always the opposite of what you just reclaimed. It may not be the dictionary definition of what is opposite. It's what is opposite for you. Let's say you are always running out of time. When you dig a little, you realize you're a perfectionist, constantly repeating a task for example refining an email or chapter of your book even though you know you stopped adding value to it long before—you realize the fear beneath the freedom you are searching for is "I never do it right." In this case, you may say, "I never do it right and I'm okay with that." Or if you want to go deeper, you may say, "I'm a complete failure and I'm cool with that." Keep repeating it until you feel the phrase resonates in your body. Then, search for the opposite of this fear, for example "I'm always right" and add *with and without enough time*, i.e., "I'm always right with and without enough time." Again, repeat the phrase until you feel it resonates in your body. To start with, it may feel like a lie. That's fine. Keep going until you have a breakthrough.

Sometimes, the fear is so deeply buried, it takes time to dig it up. In this case, you may want to work with a friend or a coach. Keep asking yourself probing questions. In this case, *why are you late? What are you afraid of? What would happen if you are late?*

When we disconnect from time, we externalize it. We turn it into a "thing" outside us. It is no longer part of us. It is something alien—to be blamed. It becomes a repository for our frustration, and we end up saying things like:

- *I would have done it if I had enough time*
- *I just didn't have the time to do it*
- *I ran out of time*

Or we may project our frustration onto something else:

- *The bus was late*
- *My computer crashed*

At some level, all of these claims are a lie. The truth is you didn't make the time to do it, because it wasn't sufficiently important to you. Rather than blame time for not doing something, take responsibility for what you lack. Replace time with you—*I am not enough* or *I'm not good enough*. Ask yourself why was this task not important enough to you? Is it because it isn't aligned with your Purpose, Mission and Masterpiece? Or are you sabotaging your Purpose, Mission and Masterpiece?

Once you have reclaimed your relationship to time, the universe will then test you to see if you have. For instance, you may find yourself running out of time to complete a task before you take your partner out on a date or rushing an email to get to an important call. Try repeating both phrases until you feel they resonate in your body. Then, see what happens. You may find your partner or colleague sends you a message to say he or she is running late. Let go of the expectation that something will happen, because it will only happen if you have rewired both your conscious and "personal unconscious" mind[31] to manifest something different. If there is still resistance in either, nothing will change.

Reclaiming your relationship to time like this—particularly what may be perceived as the negative aspects of your relationship—may seem strange at first. However, to return to a state of connection with all that is, we need to reclaim everything—the good and the bad. How can you be connected to everything if you have suppressed parts of everything?

Whatever you suppress in your personal unconscious, emerges via your ego, and uses you. Imagine you have a hammer in your toolkit, but you're unaware of its existence. One day the hammer gets bored of being unused. So, it chooses to

31 I will describe the difference between the personal and collective unconscious in Chapter 7

use you instead. It starts hitting you on the head until you realize it's there and use it instead. The same is true of whatever we suppress. Whatever we don't use will abuse us until we do.

> *"The two most powerful warriors are patience and time."*
>
> **Leo Tolstoy**, War and Peace

Power

Over the last 10,000 years, we have changed our relationship to power—from something internal to something external, from something we are when we connect to the entire ecosystem through our Inner Game to something we do when we use our Outer Game to exert our ego over it. Your Inner Game is the doorway to true power. Your Outer Game is a fraud, claiming it is the doorway to power. It's a lie, created by your society and reinforced by the media, technology moguls and celebrities.

As we explored in Chapter 3, business has centralized power over the last 250 years since the Industrial Revolution. For instance, the wealthiest twenty-six people in the world (who between them have amassed fifty percent of the world's wealth) are all men, all made their fortune through business in the last fifty years, and all operate either from the Compete or Create paradigm. This modern perception of power was formalized in the 19th Century, although its origins date back to the creation of slavery and hierarchies in Sumer.

Today, the vast majority of us are totally unaware that we can inadvertently reinforce racism by protesting against it. We legitimize those who feed on this resistance to justify their existence. These so-called "leaders" play on deep fears within us—the fear of the unknown, the fear that foreigners will control us, or minority groups are criminals. These fears are so deeply embedded in us, we aren't even aware of them. They are in our genes, which we all inherited in one form of another—as another of my partners, Jean-Philippe Challandes puts it, we become either the oppressed or the oppressor—and sometimes both at different times.

Koenig differentiates between power *over* someone and power *with* someone. Challandes differentiates between power and potency—the untapped potential of something to influence. He adds when you exhibit potency, you become an authority—someone who authors or creates their own world—and you become an authority by unleashing other people's potential. If we combine these insights, we could say true power is becoming an authority that unleashes the untapped creative potential of others so that we share power *with* them. Or to put it another way, true power is reconnecting to our true nature so we elevate the entire ecosystem around us to become the world in which we would love to live in.

This is how we move from the Control to the Collaborate paradigm.

How to Reclaim Your Relationship to Power

To reclaim your relationship to power so you become an authority who unleashes other people's potential, you can use Koenig's reclamation approach I described above for time. Let's say you constantly get frustrated or angry when you can't influence a process—for instance, you can't go on holiday, because the government has introduced a new quarantine law for the country you were planning to visit or your computer crashes in the middle of an important conversation or you have to fill in dozens of complicated government forms. Keep asking yourself what lies beneath this symptom. You may need to dig through many layers until you get to the underlying fear. In this case, your frustration may stem from the fear of being controlled by others and therefore losing control of yourself, either mentally or physically. You worry others will reject you for being crazy. Using Koenig's reclamation approach, you might say, "I'm out of control and I'm ok with that" or "I'm a hopeless reject and I'm cool with that." Repeat this phrase until it resonates deeply with you. As you're doing this, you may want to ask yourself what the advantage of being out of control or a reject is.

For instance, rejection forces us to think differently. Many of the most innovative and creative people in the world were initially rejected for being crazy. The rest of humanity thought Copernicus was mad when he suggested the Earth was round. The same thing happened when Leonardo Da Vinci sketched the helicopter, The Impressionists exhibited their first exhibition, Nikola Tesla invented Alternating Current, and Albert Einstein developed The Special Theory of Relativity. To paraphrase Steve Jobs and Mahatma Gandhi, it is the crazy ones, the misfits, the rebels, the square pegs in round holes, the artists with crazy wild ideas who become the change they want to see in the world. Being rejected is a strength. It means you don't fit it. You think different. And that's what the planet needs now.

Being a reject has helped me to see things differently, to not buy into the mainstream view of the world, to marry the most amazing woman in the world, love where I live and love what I do. If I hadn't been rejected, I would still be living in London, tied to a job marketing other people's stuff—stuff that humanity doesn't need.

Once you have reclaimed the "negative," then focus on the positive. In this case, you may say "I am recognized with and without money." People may recognize your services by paying money for you to provide them. They may not pay you, but still recognize them anyway. Again, repeat the reclamation until it resonates with you.

Love

Over the last 10,000 years, we have changed our relationship to love—from something internal to something external, from it being part of us to depending on someone else for it, from Inner Game to Outer Game. Your Inner Game is love. Your Outer Game searches for it outside you. It isn't there. It's an illusion. Created by your fellow man and reinforced by advertising, stories, films, dating sites, colleagues and partners.

As we explored in Chapter 3, civilization externalized our relationship to love by introducing the institution of marriage. The translation of Grimm's Fairytales and their popularization by Disney on the big screen accelerated this separation to such an extent, we're hardly even aware of it. Getting married is not the end of the story, as fairy tales would have us believe, it's the beginning. You are love. No one can give you love and you can't give love either. You cannot go to a supermarket and buy some. It isn't on special offer on Black Friday or Valentine's Day. Love is the foundation of the Universe. It is all around us all the time. As Tony Robbins says, it is the air we breathe. There is as much of it inside you as outside you. It is infinite.

Giving someone love is like giving a fish water. Without it they die—and if they're dead, there's nothing you can do. They're dead. You can't save them. You can't bring them back to life. The reason we feel good when someone shows us love is because their expression of love triggers our own love. Searching for love outside you will never lead to a balanced relationship inside you. True love isn't dependent. It's interdependent.

Yet, we are constantly creating dependent relationships. Think of the classic boss to employee relationship, or the couple where one partner patronizes or mothers the other. Transactional Analysis (TA) is a psychological theory, developed by Eric Berne in the 1960s, which asserts there are three types of relationship: parent to child (Control, Compete and Create paradigm - oppressor and oppressed); child to child (Create paradigm where we are either fighting or playing); and adult to adult (Collaborate paradigm where relationships are interdependent).

Healthy relationships operate on the same level—either adult to adult or child to child. As an adult, it's fine to act like a child as long as the other person is doing the same. The only way to break the cycle is to learn to operate at the same level as the other person. My behavior before I met Anna reflects a particular aspect of TA, called "co-dependency" which can be explained through a model called Karpman's Triangle.

It suggests that individuals in co-dependent relationships play one of three different roles: the Rescuer, who constantly tries to save the victim; the Victim who wants attention but doesn't want to be saved; and the Persecutor who attacks the Rescuer. Each is "co-dependent" on the other. The Rescuer is drawn to save the Victim. The Victim accepts for a while, because they are willing to accept a few patronizing words in return for some attention. However, when the Victim has had enough of being patronized by the Rescuer, he or she becomes the Persecutor and shouts at the Rescuer. The Rescuer backs off and flips into the role of the Victim, saying something like, "I was just trying to help." An argument may ensue, depending on how well the players know each other and how often they have triggered each other in this way.

Couples, families, employees, and their bosses may move from one co-dependent relationship to the next, without consciously being aware of it. They just repeat the pattern. Most of us don't exhibit these extremes most of the time, but every so often we patronize or mother just a little. We get frustrated by our partner or a team member or even our boss and, rather than take the time to help them "get it" we tell them what to do and then, when they don't do it exactly as we envisaged, we get more frustrated and rather than invest more time, we take control, saying something like, "If I want it done properly, I'll have to do it myself."

Reclaiming our tendency to blame others for our own shortcomings implies accepting everything we resist in them is also in us. The world outside us is an energetic mirror, in which all of our shortcomings are exposed. Rather than accept we created the problem, we externalize it. We blame the other. Transformation starts with us, no matter how disruptive the other person may be. They are in your life for a reason. Take responsibility for everything that occurs in your world and give up control over it.

> *From abundance he took abundance and still abundance remains.*
>
> **The Upanishads**

How to Reclaim Your Relationship to Love

To reclaim your relationship with love, you can use the same approach described above for time. Let's say you are constantly arguing with your partner(s). When you dig a little, you realize you're selfish, constantly focusing on your own projects or looking after your own affairs rather than caring for your partner. You realize the fear behind this symptom is that you won't be accepted by others so unconsciously you push them away—to avoid dealing with it. Using Koenig's reclamation system, you may say, "I'm unacceptable and I'm okay with that." Or if you want to go deeper, you may say, "I'm a selfish, uncaring bastard and I'm cool with that.'" Keep repeating it until you feel the phrase resonates in your body. Then, search for the opposite of this fear, for example "I'm free'" and add the suffix '... *with and without attention from another person*', for instance *"I'm free with and without attention from another person."* Again, repeat the phrase until you feel it resonates in your body.

Alternatively, you can start by reclaiming the opposite of the fear. Start by writing down the three to five things you associate with love. Then, pick the one that resonates most with you and use the phrase *"I am xxx, with and without love."* Repeat it until it resonates deeply with you.

Our relationship to love is so deeply embedded within us, you may need to dig deeper into the unconscious using a guided meditation or Neuro-hypnotic repatterning before you can use Koenig's approach. I do this in the #Masterpiece program. This meditation is always transformational. You may also find this is the gateway to changing your relationship to the other elements too.

> *Your task is not to seek for love, but merely to seek and find all the barriers within yourself that you have built against it.*
>
> **Rumi**

Money

Over the last 10,000 years, we have changed our relationship to wealth—from something internal to something external, from it being part of us to depending on someone else for it, from Inner Game to Outer Game. Your Inner Game is true wealth. Your Outer Game searches for money outside you. It's an illusion created by society, and reinforced by advertising, banks, governments.

How to Reclaim Your Relationship to Money

To reclaim your relationship with money, you can use the same approach described above for time. Koenig maintains our relationship to money is the doorway to all the other relationships. I have no reason to doubt him. After all, money is linked to the base chakra (which we will explore in Chapter 7) where energy enters the body. If this is closed the energy will not flow up to the higher chakras for you to create your Masterpiece (and generate true wealth).

Valuing your Masterpiece or anything you create is one of the easiest ways to expose your relationship to money. Koenig starts his reclamation sessions by asking participants to write down what they associate with money. Let's say, you haven't created your Masterpiece yet, because you're terrified that it won't generate enough money. You realize the fear behind this symptom is insecurity—in other words, you associate money with security. Using the reclamation system, you may say, "I'm insecure and I'm okay with that." Or if you want to go deeper, you may say, "I'm desperately insecure and lonely and I'm cool with that." Keep repeating it until you feel the phrase resonates in your body. Then, search for the opposite of this fear, for example "I'm free" and add the suffix '*... with and without money*'—"I'm free with and without money." Again, repeat the phrase until you feel it resonates in your body.

As you reflect on your relationship to money, ask yourself two questions: what would you be left with if you had no money at all? Or what would you do if you had all the money in the world? Your answers may give you a better understanding of what true wealth is for you.

Koenig adds when it comes to valuing our Masterpiece, we often end up valuing ourselves—either undervaluing or overvaluing. We project value onto what we're creating. Instead, use your Value Proposition to consider the value you are creating for all of the stakeholders. Then look at it through the eyes of the person who is paying and consider what they are willing to pay for it. That may lead to two different numbers. The price you end up charging is somewhere between the two. If you're struggling to charge the higher amount, you may want to tell your client, this is what it's worth and this is what you will charge. As you gain more confidence, you may increase what you charge towards the higher amount. The key step is for you to acknowledge what it's truly worth.

If you're struggling to work out what the client believes it's worth, test the price with a partner and then with a client who you can trust. Ensure you describe all elements of your Value Proposition and the full scope of the product or service you offer. Observe how confident you are in describing your Masterpiece and listen carefully to your partner or client's response. This will give you clues as to what else you need to reclaim and what else you may need to add to your Masterpiece. The same approach works if you overvalue your Masterpiece—asking partners and clients for their perspective before you fix the price will help.

Mindset - the key to fulfilling your potential

The following example from the world of sport reinforces the importance of our mind over matter. The England rugby team may or may not have done reclamation work in exactly the way I have described above. Nonetheless, their revival since the Rugby World Cup in 2015 demonstrates the importance of changing our mindset to realize our full potential. England became the first hosts of a World Cup to be eliminated during the group stages and yet they have the biggest budget of all major rugby playing countries.

In rugby union there are fifteen players on each side who throw themselves at each other for eighty minutes. It's a little like American football without the helmets or protection. As the saying goes, football is a sport invented by gentlemen and played by hooligans, whereas rugby is a sport invented by hooligans and played by gentlemen.

Before the 2015 tournament, under previous coach, Stuart Lancaster, the team won twenty-eight of their forty-six games. Between that World Cup and the next one, under Lancaster's replacement, Eddie Jones, the team won forty-two of their fifty-four games including getting to the next World Cup Final and winning three out of five Six Nations Championships (compared to zero out of three campaigns for his predecessor). Their "win rate" increased from sixty-one percent to seventy-eight percent—the highest of any England coach ever. And at one point it was as high as ninety-six percent. It included defeating Australia three times in one series in Australia, which has never been done before by any team.

Of course, mindset is only one of many factors that influence whether a team wins or not. Players may get better. The opposition may get worse. And new players may emerge. But what's remarkable about England's transformation is Jones picked the same players as Lancaster. Nine of the fifteen players who started the game against Australia in October 2017, also started the game against Australia in October 2015. Given that one player was injured, another retired, a third almost retired, and an individual player's form may come and go, this is extraordinary. A coach can develop a better strategy or system, but it's the players who have to execute it on the pitch. He can't do it for them. He cannot make a player faster, more agile, or a better tackler. The only thing he can do is make them believe they are faster, more agile, and better tacklers. And that's what Jones and his team of coaches and sports psychologists appeared to do. Players who didn't perform under Lancaster found an extra yard of speed, an extra belief to squeeze through the gap, and an ability to ground out a win when they weren't playing well.

Jones demonstrates that sports, like art, can provoke us to think differently. His team illustrates what is possible when we put our minds to it. If success in élite sports can be measured in thousandths of a second or in fractions of a centimeter, then the most important part of our body is the top ten centimeters. At the elite level the difference between winning and losing is more mental than physical.

> *I've missed more than 9000 shots in my career. I've lost almost 300 games. Twenty-six times, I've been trusted to take the game-winning shot and missed. I've failed over and over and over again in my life. And that is why I succeed.*
>
> **Michael Jordan**

6 Changing Your Company

Believe you can change the world.

Dave Hewlett, Co-Founder of HP

Creating a Masterpiece for a company follows the same approach and principles as creating a Masterpiece for an individual: start with the Inner Game; articulate a Purpose; define the Mission; develop the Value Proposition; and bring it to life through communications and a Money Flow System.

In other words, start with Inner Game and pivot around it using the Outer Game to bring it to life. However, there are a few important differences both in terms of how to develop some of these components and how to ensure everyone in your company is aligned with them, and this is what we will explore in this chapter.

Creating a Masterpiece within a company has never been so important. At a conservative estimate, over eighty percent of companies operate primarily from the Control or Compete paradigm and those that operate primarily from the Create paradigm are largely oblivious to the unintended waves they are creating. Less than five percent of companies are operating primarily from the Collaborate paradigm. Companies claiming to operate from the Collaborate paradigm are a little bit like teenage sex—everyone claims they are doing it, not many are and those that are, aren't doing it very well.

The problem is the only tools most CEOs, Chief Human Resources Officers and Chief Transformation Officers are aware of were developed in previous paradigms. Rather than increase collaboration, they have the opposite effect and spread the disengagement pandemic. This in turn spreads the distrust crisis. Too many people don't love what they do and those that do aren't influential enough.

Creating a Masterpiece that contributes to society by resolving the biggest challenge the company faces is the antidote to this disengagement pandemic. When those involved start to love what they do, the energy of this Masterpiece spreads. It is more infectious than the disengagement pandemic. Everyone wants to contribute.

Consider John F Kennedy's famous declaration that America would put a man on the moon before the decade was out. That single minded-mission created a Masterpiece—the Apollo program, which transformed the lives not just of those involved with it, but of everyone in the United States and in the Western World. Americans and Europeans were inspired and transfixed by Neil Armstrong's infamous phrase—"that's one small step for man, one giant leap for mankind." Or consider the impact of Tesla on the car industry. Creating an entirely electric car was unthinkable in the latter part of the Twentieth Century—the knowledge, need, nor infrastructure existed to create electric cars. Now, it's the fastest growing car company ever and its market capital is two and a half times bigger than Toyota, the largest car company in the world by volume. Tesla's influence goes way beyond cars though—and this isn't just because it produces solar panels and storage devices. Its Mission is inspiring a whole generation to rethink how we use fossil fuels (or not), and how we generate and store electricity. In other words, its impact extends beyond the edge of its canvas. Yet, Tesla is far from perfect. Its leadership creates unintended ripples as we will explore in Chapter 8.

I believe we need to double the number of companies operating primarily from the Collaborate paradigm before 1 July 2026 to reverse climate change and create a virtuous cycle that leads humanity away from extinction. That means we are already late. Sadly, there are too few companies operating primarily from the Collaborate paradigm to act as role models for others. The vast majority of companies we look up to today operate from the Create paradigm—and that includes Tesla. Creating a Masterpiece that helps them reclaim what they have suppressed is the fastest way to help them move to the next level. Let's explore the problem by looking at the prevalent tools these Create companies use.

The problem with problem-solving

Even companies operating primarily from the Create paradigm use tools, such as design thinking and marketing, which were developed in the same paradigms (Control and Compete) that created the problem in the first place. Take design thinking: it is a process which anyone can follow to develop an innovative solution that addresses the needs of an audience or society. Like marketing it starts with the end in mind and all too often, that end is satisfying consumer desires.

The problem with design thinking is it starts with the problem, not the purpose. The first step in the design thinking process is to identify the person who faces the problem and to articulate the problem they face. Once their problem has been articulated, the second step is to think of solutions to resolve it. But if the articulation of the problem fuels ego (Outer Game) without growing essence (Inner Game), the solution will not solve the root cause. In other words, unless design thinking starts with the purpose of the individual you are trying to help and takes into account the entire ecosystem within which it operates, it will exacerbate rather than resolve the problem we are trying to solve, or it will create an entirely new problem.

The book industry illustrates how an industry can be devalued by focusing on a problem rather than a purpose. Amazon solved one problem and created another. In the 1990s, we were beginning to read less, because we didn't have time to go to a bookstore and books were expensive. So, Amazon eliminated the need to go to the bookstore and enabled consumers to purchase books online for less. They didn't stop there. Amazon then diversified into Kindle, enabling us to read books on a computer, tablet, or smartphone. Then, they bought Audible, which enables us to listen to books on the way to work. That sounds great. But, what has the real impact of this been?

Yes, we are reading and we are writing more than ever before, but the margins in the book industry have evaporated. As a result, only a tiny percentage of writers can make a living purely from writing. This elite group does very well. But, dig beneath the surface and we find the vast majority of writers are struggling—so are publishers. For instance, to balance their books, publishers often ask new authors to purchase a few thousand books as part of the "publishing deal." More at a lower price isn't always better. It fuels craving, competition and more effort for less return.

> *We don't need more stuff. We need more humanity.*
>
> **Seth Godin**

Amazon—innovation without purpose

Amazon operates from the Create paradigm and in the process exacerbates the imbalance. Jeff Bezos, Amazon's CEO, is on-course to disrupt more markets than Steve Jobs. He's already transformed books, retailing and cloud services. He could add logistics, grocery, and the smart home soon. That's six industries in less than twenty years—half the time it took Jobs to get to seven.

Bezos has done it by focusing on the widest selection, aggressive pricing and ease of use. Amazon has an inventory of 250 million items. That's sixty times bigger than Walmart—the largest retailer in the United States. The company prices aggressively to dominate the market. Thirty years ago, supermarkets made milkmen redundant by selling milk at a loss. Amazon does the same, running whole categories at a loss for years. And it simplifies buying with features like 1-click, Prime, which provides free shipping for an annual fee and drones, which are making deliveries even faster.

Amazon launches bold experiments that enable others to create. And it isn't scared to fail. The Fire Phone flopped. Amazon moved on. Unlike Apple, which channels its zen-like energy into a few products, Amazon takes a numbers approach. Bezos believes that we're all innovators and his inventions tap into this. He provides the building blocks for others to build on. This is a classic Create approach. For instance, Amazon Web Services enables start-ups to compete on a level-playing field.

However, this approach is accelerating the imbalance. Amazon's mission is to be "the most-customer centric business on earth." That explains what Amazon does, not *why* Amazon does it. Is it to create a more sustainable world? To end poverty? Or to level the playing field? It's been accused of tax avoidance in the US and the UK. And then there's the so-called Amazon Tax: Amazon owns sixty percent of US online retail, seventy percent of cloud services, and seventy percent of e-books, which makes it a monopoly. What if Amazon owns logistics, grocery, and the smart home too? We'll pay Amazon a tax just to live. And that's fine so long as it serves a higher purpose. But it doesn't. Amazon drives down prices and the more industries it monopolizes the more value it extracts from the system. You only have to look at Bezos' personal wealth to appreciate Amazon extracts wealth for a few rather than enabling it to flow through the hands of many. In 2020, Bezos became the first person to amass a fortune greater than $200 billion. This is unsustainable. The elements within a natural ecosystem don't hoard resources in this way, they share them so every element benefits.

> *Amazon is Walmart on speed.*
>
> **Douglas Rushkoff**

Alphabet—going backwards

Alphabet, the company that owns Google, is no better. Since Google disrupted online search with its zen-like brilliance in 1998, it became the second largest company by market cap (currently it's in the top 5), generating over 160 billion dollars in revenue in 2019, over thirty billion dollars in profit and employing almost 120,000 people. That's more than one-million dollars per employee in revenue.

Google encourages innovation, enables teamwork, and promotes leadership. When it went public, its founders encouraged its employees to spend twenty percent of their time working on their own innovations and this led to many breakthroughs. More recently, Google's Project Aristotle studied what makes the perfect team and the attributes of great management.

However, there was no greater purpose behind Google than "do no evil" and there was no Money Flow System to bring it to life. To make matters worse, the founders went on a spending spree, purchasing a series of disconnected start-ups. As a result, Google ended up with horizontal innovation, such as Self-Driving Cars which hasn't launched a product yet; Google Fiber which hasn't delivered on its promise; and Google Verily, a life sciences company. Google remains Alphabet's cash cow and includes search, ads, Android, Google apps, YouTube, and Google Maps. Whereas Google itself generated over $160 billion in revenue in 2019, these so-called "other bets" generated just $659 million. For many years, these other bets lost billions of dollars.

Their lacklustre performance led to the creation of Alphabet—a holding company designed to increase financial transparency for Wall Street and free each division up to focus on its own vision. On the face of it, this sounds sensible—they are combining the best of both worlds—West Coast innovation with East Coast banking. But without a greater mission, this strategy is hollow. What is the point? More control? Extracting more profit for a few? Is it addressing a greater purpose or an underlying problem?

Alphabet was created to pacify the markets rather than serve a greater purpose. It's an operating model, not a vision for the world. So, what could its vision be? To enable the world's greatest innovations? To inspire world class teams? To get the whole world to collaborate?

Moreover, the twenty percent it gave each employee to work on their own projects has effectively been squashed and innovation centralized. Employees need to ask their boss for permission, and leadership has told their bosses to give permission less often. Innovation has been reorganized into another division. Just as others are being inspired by Google's innovative operating model and working practices, it appears the company itself is taking a step backward, introducing a pyramid and silos through which control over strategy and results can be exerted to extract more capital.

Yes, Google, Apple, and Amazon have combined the best of both worlds—great innovation with great business, Creativity and Calculation, Collaboration and Choreography—but to what end? What is the purpose of these organizations? What is the real legacy of the dotcom revolution? Without putting purpose at the heart, it ends up being hollow and creating more imbalances than it resolves.

Unilever—marketing an illusion

On the face of it, Unilever is making a difference. However, when we dig deeper it appears something is missing. Paul Polman, its former CEO, appeared to be doing all the right things to move the company towards the Collaborate paradigm until the shareholders removed him for trying to move the headquarters to The Netherlands.

Polman, who like fellow Dutchman Van Gogh, trained to be a priest, did something equally radical as his countryman on his first day in the office. He stopped making quarterly market reports, claiming business shouldn't be so short-termist. On the surface, this change is relatively innocuous. However, he was making a statement about the unsustainability of the current financial operating system—and doing what he could, I suspect, to extract Unilever from it. Polman then proceeded to articulate the company's purpose: "To make sustainable living common place," and embody it in Unilever's Sustainable Living Plan which positions sustainability at the heart of Unilever's business model. This plan is based on three big goals, all of which are time-bound:

1. *Improve health and well-being for more than one billion people by 2020*

Unilever launched the "U in Unilever" campaign, which encouraged employees and each brand to develop their own purpose. Over 50,000 people have articulated their Personal Purpose and over 500 million people have been impacted by their brands. However, seventy percent of these come from just one brand, Lifebuoy, a soap, which promotes handwashing.

2. *Reduce its environmental impact by half by 2030*
Unilever's original goal was to do this by 2020. It's concerning for all of us that one of the most ardent supporters of the Paris Agreement on climate change hasn't made more progress here. What's impressive though is that Unilever takes responsibility across the entire value chain from "farm to fork," not just the two percent which comes from its manufacturing operations.

3. *Enhance livelihoods for millions by 2020*
Unilever champions the United Nations Sustainable Development Goals to increase equality, health, and education. Between 2006 and 2016, it enabled around 800,000 women to access initiatives aimed to develop their skills and has enabled over two million smallholders and entrepreneurs to improve their economic livelihood.

For Unilever, sustainability isn't a strategy, it's the strategy. It's a big bold bet on the future. In the first five years of the strategy, Unilever outperformed its biggest competitor P&G, growing its market value twice as fast, and demonstrating that sustainability is a business opportunity not a cost. In 2016, their sustainable brands grew fifty percent faster than the rest of the business and accounted for sixty percent of their growth. Employee loyalty skyrocketed too, indicating that a greater purpose really does encourage people to stay and others to join.

However, after the initial euphoria, the program started to run out of steam. Since Polman left, insiders say The Sustainable Living has become a tick-box exercise. In other words, like Google, Unilever has slipped back into the Compete mindset. I'll explain why shortly.

The Legacy of Silicon Valley
Silicon Valley has failed to live up to its promise to change the world for good and yet the world's biggest companies are based there and we look up to them as role models. When I first started working with the internet in 1999, I was inspired by the possibility of real change. Here was a vehicle through which business could transform itself. Over twenty years later, I believe the vehicle has broken down.

Yet, the original purpose of Silicon Valley was to do just this. Exactly sixty years before I joined the internet bandwagon, David Packard and William Hewlett established an electronics company in a Palo Alto garage and in the process founded Silicon Valley. The company became HP, the world's largest technology company in the 1990s, and the garage was dubbed "the Birthplace of Silicon Valley." For them profit wasn't the purpose of their newly founded company. It was to serve the community in which they operated. They saw themselves as an integral part of the ecosystem. Profit was a useful by-product. Since then, Silicon Valley has given birth to Apple, Google, Facebook, YouTube, Airbnb, LinkedIn, Twitter, Uber, Cisco, Intel, and Tesla. That's impressive, but has it been a force for good? Has it really delivered on the original purpose of its founders?

The culture in too many companies in Silicon Valley suggests not. Uber is the posterchild of this symptom. Uber's original purpose was to create "transport as freely available as running water." The intention was to create an ecosystem of sustainable cars available within minutes, the majority of which would be on autopilot. However, its actions rapidly began to diverge from this purpose. And this comes back to the actions and mindset of the founder or Source of the company, Travis Kalanick. He got distracted by the glamor and wealth. Drivers left because they couldn't earn what they were promised, and many cities and other taxi drivers sued them for operating illegally without insurance or permission. Kalanick resigned in June 2017 over harassment charges. Since then, Uber has taken steps to tackle the problem, but this doesn't mean they have addressed the root cause of the problem, nor does it mean Uber is now delivering on its purpose.

Too many organizations in Silicon Valley develop an inspiring vision to capture the imagination of investors, customers, and employees. But they don't ensure this purpose is aligned throughout the entire organization, because the Founder isn't aligned within him or herself. Outer Game actions aren't aligned with Inner Game spirit. The connection to a greater purpose only exists on paper. As a result, as the organization takes off, behaviors start to emerge that are not aligned with it and this creates resistance.

Take Steve Jobs. One day he could be so visionary he would operate from Collaborate and design a breakthrough like the iPhone. The following day, he could shout at the same team for not following his instructions. In other words, he would flip from self-mastery to Control, or from being Godlike to acting like God. Flipping between visionary behavior and bullying is unsustainable. And the casualty was his health and the culture of Apple. The culture reflects its leader. Instead of being open and innovative, Apple's culture is secretive and insular. Steve Job's arrogance is the flipside of Vincent van Gogh's lack of self-belief. Too much self-belief and you bully potential collaborators. Too little and collaborators stay away. Either way collaboration is limited.

> *The level of consciousness of an organization cannot exceed the level of consciousness of its leader.*
>
> **Frédéric Laloux**

What these companies illustrate is why we are where we are—the world's most successful companies, which many of us hold up as role-models are in fact accelerating the symptoms of imbalance. Rather than increase the flow of wealth between many, they extract it for a few. To create true wealth, we must extract ourselves from the 5,000-year-old, man-made system and reimagine an entirely new system. This takes incredible courage—and yet, as we shall see, there are extraordinary examples of individuals and companies doing just this.

Collective Mission

A Collective Mission describes the next phase in a team or organization's journey. It unites the members of that team or company for a specific period of time to achieve a specific outcome. As I mentioned earlier, the most compelling Missions are bound by time and space. JFK promised to put a man on the moon *by the end of the decade*—not just to put a man on the moon. By adding a date by which NASA would make this happen, he focused minds of everyone who worked there and forced them to think differently. As we explored in Chapter 3, creativity loves constraints. The more constraints we have (up to a certain level), the more creative we must be to work around them. Setting a time constraint focuses our mind and forces us to be more creative in order to achieve it. The converse is also true.

Creating a Collective Mission or Collective Purpose which is not bound by time increases disengagement and leads to Codependent Chasm. Purpose statements without a time-limit may be very well-intended but they end up competing with and diluting an employee's Personal Purpose. An employee doesn't know whether they should focus their mind and therefore their energy on the company Purpose or their own Purpose. Effectively, they have two bosses—their Inner Game and their CEO's Inner Game. Enigmatic CEOs, like Elon Musk and Steve Jobs appear to make this work. But they are imposing their will, which is still operating from within the man-made system on others. As I described in Chapter 3, they end up creating codependent companies.

I made the same mistake with my own company, as well as with some of my clients.

On the other hand, an individual can choose to contribute his or her Personal Purpose to a Collective Mission for a certain period of time, because a Mission with a time-limit is Outer Game whereas Personal Purpose is Inner Game. Rather than create a Collective Purpose that ends up diluting your own Personal Purpose, create a Collective Mission that allows everyone in your team or company to collaborate towards a specific goal. Your team or company will continue to contribute to that goal for as long as it helps them to bring their Personal Purpose to life in line with their own Mission.

If you remember what Koenig said about Source—in an organization primarily operating from the Collaborate paradigm, the Source's role is to create the space in which others can realize their Personal Purpose. It is not to tell the employee how to do it or what the values are. That's brainwashing.

When I run workshops to help my clients create them, I map out the entire ecosystem within which the company operates using an adapted version of the 5R methodology originally developed by USAID. I use this tool to help the Source of the company understand the unique role he or she can play within the entire ecosystem. For instance, a luxury fashion company may operate in the ecosystem of luxury or fashion, a pharmaceutical company may operate in the ecosystem of health or wellbeing and a technology company may operate in the ecosystem of technology or communications.

The first step (and the first R in the 5Rs) is to identify the **Roles**: who are the key players within the ecosystem? Seven to ten players is normally enough. For the health ecosystem, the Roles might be hospitals, the health ministry, pharmaceutical companies, insurance companies, doctors, nurses, specialists, researchers and patients. Leave your own company or organization out at this stage.

In the next step, identify the **Relationships**: who has power or influence over whom? I normally place post-it notes on a flip chart for the Roles and draw lines between them to illustrate the Relationships. The third step is to identify the **Results**: what outcomes does the ecosystem currently generate? Be generous. The more generous you are, the more likely you are to create a really compelling mission. In the health example, the results could be improved health, money, new treatments, research, employment. Then, look at the **Resources** required to generate these **Results**: what does the system need in order to operate? The health ecosystem needs capital, talent, research insights, technology etc. The final R stands for **Rules**: what are the implicit and explicit rules that regulate the ecosystem? Explicit rules are the laws—in this case, it would be both national health laws and any medical society laws. Implicit rules are the norms that the ecosystem follows: *this is the way things are done around here.* For instance, in the healthcare ecosystem, one of the implicit Rules is doctors and nurses always work extremely long hours.

Once you have mapped out the ecosystem using the 5R methodology, the next step is to identify the Results you want to generate in an ideal world. For instance, you may want to prevent disease, or prevent a specific disease or increase wellbeing, rather than simply improve health.

Now, you're ready to start articulating the **Collective Mission**. At this point, you may find it helpful to shift from Outer Game intellect to Inner Game intuition by changing your brainwaves—I'll explain more about how to do this in Chapter 7. Resist the temptation to think too hard about it. Allow the answer to pop into your mind. Take a coffee break, go for a walk or to the toilet. In the health example a Collective Mission may be something like: *End new AIDS infections by 1 January 2025* or *80% of us feel well by 1 July 2026.*

To help you develop your Collective Mission, look at your ecosystem map and identify what you would need to change in order to achieve the Results you want to generate in an ideal world. For instance, you may want to change the culture of hard-work and the failure of medical professionals to take care of themselves, which of course has a knock-on effect on the wellbeing of those they take care of. This may take your Mission in one direction—focusing on the wellbeing of healthcare professionals—or you may want to prevent disease, which would take it in another direction—focusing on the wellbeing of patients. Or you may see one as a prerequisite of the other—you cannot improve patient wellbeing until healthcare professionals improve their own wellbeing. Identifying what stops the ecosystem from flowing will also help you to develop the **Value Proposition** and the **Money Flow System**.

Collective Value Proposition

A collective Value Proposition serves the same purpose as a personal Value Proposition, it explains how the company adds value to its stakeholders via its products and services. It is the *fil rouge* or red thread that runs through the communications, products, services and Money Flow System for that Masterpiece. As we discussed in Chapter 4, the communications and Money Flow System for a Masterpiece pivot around the Source of that Masterpiece's Personal Purpose. Communications and the Money Flow System for a Collective Masterpiece work in exactly the same way as for a personal Masterpiece—they pivot around the Source of that Masterpiece's Personal Purpose. The Collective Value Proposition ensures these elements consistently add value to the Masterpiece's stakeholders.

Value Propositions for companies primarily operating from the Compete paradigm are different than those operating from the Collaborate paradigm. Competing for customers excludes the impact on society, whereas when we collaborate there is no competition—each company contributes something unique. From the perspective of the Compete paradigm, a Value Proposition helps the company to identify how it competes with others within its ecosystem. From the perspective of the Collaborate paradigm, a Value Proposition helps the company to understand how it contributes to transforming the ecosystem. Two or more organizations may share the same Collective Mission and have different Value Propositions. In other words, how they contribute to the Collective Mission differs. In our ecosystem, I am the Source of the main #Masterpiece program, one of the central trees in the ecosystem. Others run their own programs dealing with specific topics or specific audiences—additional trees within the ecosystem.

A Collective Value Proposition answers the same questions as a Personal Value Proposition. Again, the key is to identify what the benefits for that audience are and in Jeff Walker's words "ground the plane" by making those benefits tangible. The best way to do this is to speak to your customers and partners.

This is exactly what I did recently with a Swiss Medical Foundation I helped launch. We set up a workshop and invited all the partners who were interested in funding and supporting the foundation to attend. Partners who were moved by the Collective Mission attended. Those that didn't, didn't. This was key, because each of the potential partners either came from competing companies or from medical institutions, who tend to operate independently. The Collective Mission helped to unite them and focus on a bigger goal. Rather than develop a value proposition in a closed room and then attempt to sell it to the partners, we invited them to help us create it together. The beauty of this approach is each partner felt a sense of ownership. They became involved in the act of creation, the moment of its birth. And as I mentioned previously, there is no more powerful moment in the life of a business than the moment that you create it.

> *Your customers are the judge, jury, and executioner of your value proposition. They will be merciless if you don't find fit!*
>
> **Alexander Osterwalder**, author of Business Model Generation

Values

Values are how you bring your Masterpiece to life. They are the bridge between the Inner Game and Outer Game. If your Masterpiece is a painting and you're not entirely sure what the finished piece looks like, clear your mind, listen to your intuition and focus on placing each brushstroke in line with your Values.

Values are always personal. Many companies create Values top-down and then communicate them to their employees. If you are operating from either the Control or Compete paradigm, this makes sense. However, it won't increase employee engagement, nor will it help to change the culture of the company. Even if the board asks for their employees' input, they "approve" the final values and the Source has the final word. Using the top-down approach, a company's Values are the Source's Values. Asking employees to embody them is brainwashing.

If you operate from the Collaborate paradigm or aspire to operate from this level, creating Collective Values and communicating them throughout your organization is a waste of time. It dilutes an individual's personal values in the same way that a collective Purpose dilutes a Personal Purpose. Values are a lens through which you interpret the world outside you. No one else can interpret this world for you—not your employer, your boss or your partner—only you can do it.

We use a value map like the Barrett or Hall-Tonna framework to help assess everyone in a company's values. Each maps values against paradigms. Barrett calls these paradigms levels and identifies seven for both individuals and leaders:

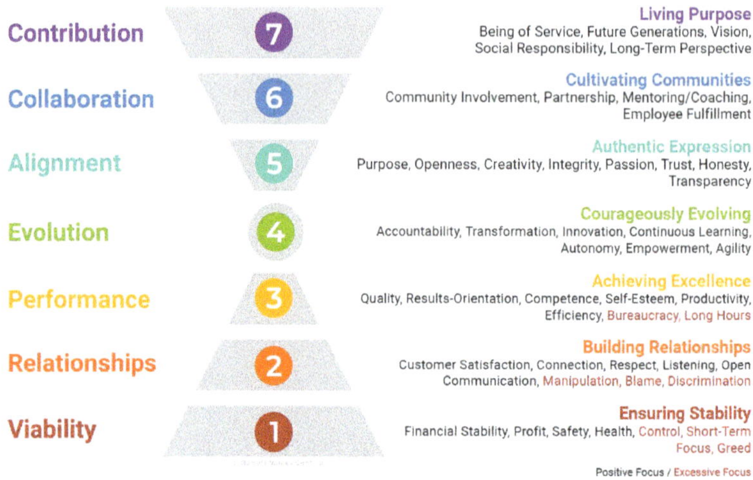

Reproduced with permission from Barrett Values Centre. © 2020 Copyright, Barrett Values Centre

These levels are based on Maslow's hierarchy of needs, rather than the five paradigms: Control, Compete, Create, Collaborate and Consciousness—I based on Wilber and Laloux's work. The models may have different origins, but the underlying principle remains the same: consciousness grows with each consecutive paradigm.

What I love about Barrett is the simplicity of the mapping against the paradigms and the emphasis on balance across these paradigms. Great leaders exhibit a balance of positive values across all paradigms. Barrett correctly points out values from the first three paradigms can be both positive and negative and he promotes the positive values.

What I don't love is calling these paradigms "levels" and the application of the tool to companies. It all ends up feeling a bit like Tesla and Google—an inspiring Mission with inconsistent application. The term "levels" is misleading because it implies a higher level is better than a lower level. I disagree. As mentioned in Chapter 3 each paradigm is a different tool—the more tools you have in your toolbox, the better prepared you are to deal with different situations. I can cope with this, but the application to companies is inconsistent with the intended outcome. Barrett works perfectly to identify individual values, but then assumes there is a collective set of (company) values against which individual employees can be measured. As I just explained, values are personal so comparing them to a collective encourages the individual to subjugate themselves to the collective. At best, this is promoting the Create paradigm. At worst, it reinforces Control and Compete. And, as we have seen, this accelerates the underlying root cause.

Instead, when I work with companies, I start with the Source of the company. I help him or her to articulate their Personal Values using a tool like Barrett or Hall-Tonna and assess how balanced they are. This may lead to one-one-one coaching to help the Source rebalance themselves—in the process, the Source's values may evolve. These become the **Core Values** of the organization. Then, I work with the executive to assess how balanced they are compared to these Core Values. This may lead to further coaching, either one-on-one or as a collective to help each individual rebalance themselves. Alternatively, it may also lead to identifying some people who do not fit within the culture. In this case, as Koenig puts it, rather than coach the individual inwards, *celebrate* the individual out of the organization by encouraging them to find a culture which is better suited to where they are in their own personal journey. From this point, I move out in waves or cohorts throughout the organization, repeating the same process—helping each individual to assess how balanced they are, explore how this relates to the core, and then coach in or celebrate out. We start these waves by inviting everyone to complete a values assessment, and then inviting those closest to the Core Values to join the first cohort.

Contrary to many large consultancies, I do not believe an organization needs everyone to rebalance itself; according to Wilber, ten to fifteen percent of any ecosystem is sufficient. According to Gregg Braden, it's even less. In a murmuration of thousands of starlings, if a few birds change direction, the rest of the flock will follow in waves. In Autumn, as the birds prepare to migrate, I'm lucky enough to observe them from my office window. The spectacle is absolutely mesmerizing—the whole murmaration can change direction in an instant. The same principle applies in organizations. Work with the Source, then move outwards in waves.

The Purpose of Business

What's missing in business today is purpose and balance in everything we do. Yes, we may have a vision statement for our business, but does it serve a greater Mission and even if it does, how often do we align our entire organization with it? Balance requires an organization to align everything it does with this Mission. You may think that's impossible. Well so are most vision statements and yet, we still sign up to them.

Aligning everything we do with a greater Mission isn't just the right thing to do, it's the most profitable thing to do too. According to Deloitte, seventy three percent of people who work at a purpose-centered company are engaged[32]—that's fifty percent more than at a non-Purpose centered company. According to Gallup, employee engagement increases earnings per share by 147 percent.[33] That's enormous. Unilever estimates the market for what it calls "sustainable living brands"—consumer goods brands whose sole purpose is to "do good"– is worth more than 2.5 trillion dollars.[34] This is just one sector, but represents four percent of annual goods and services and will grow exponentially, particularly as one of the most influential investors in the world has effectively mandated it. Just imagine if these businesses developed Money Flow Systems that increased the flow of this wealth throughout the entire ecosystem.

At Davos, in January 2018, Larry Fink, CEO of the largest asset management company in the world, BlackRock, announced the companies he invests in must focus on purpose or risk losing his support. According to *The New York Times,* this was a "watershed" moment after all BlackRock manages over seven trillion dollars, that's between five to seven percent of most big listed companies. Fink repeats his demand every January. He's correct. Business faces a stark choice—extraction or creation. It has the potential to accelerate human extinction or pull us back from the brink. Which path CEOs choose will define the future for all of us.

32 Deloitte. "Culture of Purpose—Building business confidence; driving growth 2014 core beliefs & culture survey." February 21 through February 28, 2014 https://www2.deloitte.com/content/dam/Deloitte/us/Documents/about-deloitte/us-leadership-2014-core-beliefs-culture-survey-040414.pdf.

33 Gallup, *State of the Global Workplace*, May 2019. https://www.gallup.com/workplace/257552/state-global-workplace-2017.aspx

34 Unilever. "Report shows a third of consumers prefer sustainable brands." 5th January 2017.: Source: Purpose: Fad or Future? Europanel, 2016. https://www.unilever.com/news/press-releases/2017/report-shows-a-third-of-consumers-prefer-sustainable-brands.html

A company cannot achieve long-term profits without embracing purpose and considering the needs of a broad range of stakeholders. A pharmaceutical company that hikes prices ruthlessly, a mining company that shortchanges safety, a bank that fails to respect its clients—these companies may maximize returns in the short term. But, as we have seen again and again, these actions that damage society will catch up with a company and destroy shareholder value. By contrast, a strong sense of purpose and a commitment to stakeholders helps a company connect more deeply to its customers and adjust to the changing demands of society. Ultimately, purpose is the engine of long-term profitability.[35]

Larry Fink, Chairman and Chief Executive Officer of BlackRock

35 Fink, Larry. BlackRock. "A fundamental reshaping of finance." Retrieved October 16 2020. https://www.blackrock.com/au/individual/larry-fink-ceo-letter?switchLocale=y&siteEntryPassthrough=true

7 Changing Your world

What you hold in your consciousness tends to manifest—the inner game runs the outer game.

Bob Anderson and Bill Adams

The fastest way to change the world outside you is to create a different world inside you. As I mentioned earlier, we have major symptoms of imbalance in the world outside us—too many of us don't love what we do but do it for the money or to support our family. This causes depression and *dis-ease* at the individual level, disengagement and distrust at the organizational level and inequality and climate change at the societal level.

We also explored how you can address these symptoms at the personal level by changing your relationship to Time, Power, Love and Money, and at the organizational level by helping the Source of your organization to rebalance him or herself by looking at their values and coaching them, before they then help others do the same.

In this chapter, we dig deep into the symptoms of imbalance at a societal level to literally change your world by accessing the **Zone of Creation**: a state where you reconnect to the infinite potential inside (and outside) you.

The vast majority of us use our Outer Game (Artist Profile) to address the symptoms of imbalance and in the process create more symptoms. For instance, we may try harder at work and create imbalance at home or try to reduce climate change but end up damaging the planet. Only using our Outer Game limits us. It is like trying to play rugby with both hands tied behind our backs. For most of us, our Outer Game is what we are left with after we have experienced life. It isn't necessarily what we're best at, nor what is needed, let alone who we are. It is just what worked for us in the past, so we focused on it; we may have become very good at it. For instance, at my lowest point on my journey, I was brilliant at analyzing a situation, but terrible at creating solutions to solve it. I was stuck in my head, rather than getting onto the pitch and playing the game. If we continue to use our Outer Game to tackle today's symptoms of imbalance, we reinforce the masculine vicious cycle we talked about in Chapter 1, constantly climbing False Summit and falling off.

On the other hand, when we access the inner world using our Inner Game, we access infinite worlds where our potential is limited only by our imagination. In the process, we elevate our energy, expand our Outer Game (Artist Profile) and get clarity around our Masterpiece. In the process, we end up changing our world.

Infinite Worlds Inside of Us

Different traditions have used different terms to describe the infinite worlds inside us. Carl Jung called it the collective unconscious, Albert Einstein called it the unified field, author Eckhart Tolle calls it consciousness, mediums call it the astral plane, and early Buddhists called it the records of Akasha (which have now become known as the Akashic records). I call it the **Zone of Creation**.

According to Jung's original definition, the collective unconscious is a portion of our deep unconscious that is shared between all of us. Following his theory, it is responsible for the collective myths we hold about spirituality, sexuality and life and death. Since Jung originated the term, the definition of the collective unconscious has broadened. When Eckhart Tolle uses the term consciousness, he refers to a state where we "awaken" to who we are really. According to this definition, we could say that our souls are unified with all other souls at the "Source" of what Albert Einstein called a unified field of energy.

We all have access to this unified field because it is both inside us and outside us. It describes everything in the universe that is not matter, and therefore what matters to us most. Each of these theories describes the same concept from a different perspective. So, before I describe the Zone of Creation and how you can access it, let me first explain when creativity appears and where it comes from.

Going out of your mind

We are most creative when we go out of our mind. I'm not talking about being mentally ill, I mean when we get out of our busy analytical brain and allow something beyond our brain to emerge.

The special theory of relativity came to Albert Einstein fully formed while taking a tram home. Gravity occurred to Isaac Newton while sitting under an apple tree. And the original Eureka moment came to Archimedes as he was about to take a bath. He was so excited that he jumped up and ran around the city naked!

When do your very best ideas come to you? I have asked this same question thousands of times to people all over the world of different ages, different upbringings, and different cultures and no matter where I go, I hear the same answers over and over again: last thing at night or first thing in the morning, when I'm cooking, cleaning, driving, or gardening. When I'm in the shower or the toilet. When I'm cycling, skiing, horse-riding, running, or at the gym. When I'm on the train or the plane. When I walk in nature, meditate or listen to music.

Maybe I didn't include your answer, however, I bet it is linked to these answers. So, what does link these answers? What is the common denominator?

Our most creative ideas occur when we are producing primarily theta brainwaves—what researchers call a *hypnogogic state*. We don't become aware of these ideas until we are producing primarily alpha brainwaves—that unique period between being awake and being asleep. The majority of the time we are awake, we are producing primarily beta brainwaves. As we fall asleep, we shift to producing alpha brainwaves and then theta brainwaves in light sleep and eventually delta brainwaves in deep sleep. We rotate between these three states: alpha, theta and delta, every ninety minutes while we sleep. We follow a similar rhythm during the day: beta, alpha and sometimes gamma (a heightened state of conscious awareness).

Combined these rhythms are called the circadian rhythm—the natural, internal process that regulates our cycle of being asleep and awake, which repeats roughly every twenty-four hours.

Producing theta brainwaves helps us to process and make sense of the information we receive.

Producing alpha brainwaves helps our conscious mind to "hear" or extract the insights from the information we have processed. That's why we often have our best ideas just as we are falling asleep or just after we wake up.

Producing delta brainwaves helps our bodies to heal. Psychologists might label them:

- **Delta and Theta** brainwaves = being in our unconscious mind.
- **Beta and Gamma** brainwaves = being primarily in our conscious mind.
- **Alpha** brainwaves = link between the two: the conduit between Alpha and Theta and Beta and Gamma.
- **Gamma and Delta** brainwaves = being connected to all the potential inside and outside us.

However, when we receive too much information the day before or the information is too complex for us to process, we don't produce delta brainwaves. Eventually, we wear our bodies down. If we do this chronically, our bodies may breakdown from nervous exhaustion, and at the very least, we limit our creativity.

> *I put my heart and soul into my work, and I have lost my mind in the process.*
>
> **Vincent van Gogh**

Getting out of your body

We are even more creative when we get out of our body. Now that may sound strange at first, you may wonder—*how can I get out of my body when I reside in my body?* But that's just it, you go beyond the constraints of your physical body. In that moment, your body becomes the vehicle through which you bring the unlimited potential inside and outside you to life.

We create breakthroughs when we connect to the **Zone of Creation** by opening our energy centers (or chakras) so the energy flows from the earth up through our body and out of our head in one infinite loop or torus.

The idea that creativity emerges from the right hemisphere of the brain is a misleading myth, fueled by the media, pop psychology books, and a misreading of science. According to this populist view, the right hemisphere is responsible for creativity, imagination, and being in the present moment, whereas the left hemisphere is responsible for language, logic, linear thinking, and locating us in space and time. This is only half true. Yes, the use of language and logic light up the left-hemisphere of the brain, but *both* hemispheres light up during the creative process. In fact, the more creative you are, the more likely you are to have both hemispheres in balance and vice versa, the less creative you are the more likely you are to have one hemisphere dominate the other.

Here's a second misleading myth—breakthroughs in creativity do not originate in the brain at all. Brain damage, disease and old age do not reduce creativity whereas all three of these conditions can reduce language. In some cases, brain damage may actually increase creativity. Auguste Renoir, Francis Bacon, Marcel Duchamp, Wassily Kandinsky, and, to some extent, Pablo Picasso showed no diminution of quality, innovation, or power throughout their lengthy careers. Claude Monet, Edgar Dégas, Auguste Renoir, and Henri Matisse suffered from bilateral cataract, retinal degeneration, and severe pain in their hands and joints respectively, and yet, despite these ailments continued to produce artwork. In some cases, such as Monet's *Waterlilies* and Renoir's later works, these were their greatest Masterpieces. The Dutch Expressionist artist, Willem de Kooning, was diagnosed with Alzheimer's at age sixty-six and lost interest in painting. However, after an eight-year hiatus, his wife coaxed him back, and he produced some of his finest Masterpieces.

The gut and heart are conduits for creativity

Modern neurologists expand the definition of the brain to include the stomach, the heart and the spinal cord (or "*stem brain*"). According to food scientists from Nestlé, there are around 500 million neurons in the mesh-like structure in the lining surrounding the gut and covering the entire gastrointestinal system.[36] This is two-thirds of the number of neurons that exist in the entire nervous system of a cat. There are around another 40,000 neurons surrounding the heart.[37]

Both Van Gogh and Jackson Pollock illustrated the importance of the heart and gut instinct through their art. Van Gogh and Pollock influenced and were influenced by the two godfathers of modern psychology and psychiatry—Sigmund Freud and Carl Jung. Freud and Jung agreed creativity increases when we get out of our conscious mind and into our unconscious mind. They also agreed there are two types of unconscious mind—the personal unconscious

36 Nestle Nutrition Institute. News Article, "Gut bacteria and the brain: Are we controlled by microbes?" Published online Apr 07, 2017. Retrieved November 2020.

37 HeartMath Institute. "The Mysteries of the heart." https://www.heartmath.org/resources/infographic/mysteries-of-the-heart/

and the collective unconscious—and that the creative force is an unstoppable impulse that must be expressed. However, they disagreed over the exact nature of the unconscious, the relationship between the conscious and unconscious, and therefore the exact source of creativity. This disagreement led to a deep division between them. Freud believed the conscious mind was in charge. Jung believed the unconscious was in charge. In Freud's world, art is a reflection of the unexpressed (sexual) emotions stored in the personal unconscious. In Jung's world, art is an expression of the collective unconscious or the Divine within us. Jung believed art was a Divine impulse. Freud believed art was a sexual impulse.

Recent neurological research appears to support both perspectives. fMRI scans of musicians indicate the act of creation occurs outside our conscious awareness. When freestyle rappers improvise, the executive control parts of the brain (primarily located in the left-hemisphere) reduce and conversely, the areas associated with creativity increase.[38] This might be expected. What is unexpected is that these moments of creativity occur well before the rapper is consciously aware they have. In other words, there appears to be some outside agent involved in the creative process. These findings appear to turn conventional thinking about creativity upside down.

> *From the living fountain of instinct flows everything that is creative; hence the unconscious is not merely conditioned by history, but is the very source of the creative impulse.*
>
> **Carl Jung**

Open the Chakras to Create your Masterpiece

Wisdom traditions would agree that creativity comes from outside our conscious awareness. These traditions take a broader, more holistic view than modern science. They fill the gaps in between the silos that science has not studied yet. According to Ayurveda, yoga, Tantra, Qigong, Reiki, Tao, and Buddhism there are seven main chakras in the body.

The first chakra is the doorway to creativity and is associated with money, grounding, decision-making and discernment. It's located at the perineum, right

38 Liu, S., Chow, H. M., Xu, Y., Erkkinen, M. G., Swett, K. E., Eagle, M. W., Rizik-Baer, D. A., & Braun, A. R. (2012). Neural correlates of lyrical improvisation: an FMRI study of freestyle rap. *Scientific reports*, 2, 834. https://doi.org/10.1038/srep00834

at the base of our spine. We connect this chakra to the ground when we sit and meditate. If our relationship to money is "blocked" or we aren't grounded, we are blocked too. It doesn't matter how much work we do on the higher chakras, around love or spiritual awareness. If this chakra is "closed" or obstructed, the energy won't flow. Pretty much every artist embodied the "starving artist" myth for a while—Rembrandt, William Blake, Johannes Vermeer, Van Gogh, Picasso, Jackson Pollock—however, some of them resolved their relationship to money such as Picasso, while others such as Rembrandt, Blake, Vermeer and Van Gogh didn't.

The second chakra or *lower dantian* is the center of creativity, spirituality, sexuality, balance, and wisdom. The same energy can be expressed in different ways through this chakra, which may explain the spiritual nature of artists like Claude Monet, Piet Mondrian, Wassily Kandinsky, Mark Rothko and Marina Abramovic, and the sexual promiscuity of artists like Paul Gauguin and Pablo Picasso. It also explains Jung and Freud's disagreement. I believe both of them were correct to some extent—artists have a choice whether to elevate this creative energy to higher chakras or expend it out of our body through sex.

We can block the flow of this energy to higher chakras by tensing our lower body. The second chakra is about three fingers widths below your navel and two finger widths back. I notice my paintings don't flow if I hold my breath and tense my stomach muscles while I paint. The energy starts to flow through me, but then my mind jumps to the end of the painting, imagining a magnificent Masterpiece and I hold my breath. I cling to the outcome. In that moment, I "suffocate" my creativity. I stop breathing and the energy stops flowing. Exactly the same thing happens when I do something I don't love, such as administrative work. I find myself holding my breath until I get to the end. It's only afterwards, I realize how much stress I am putting my body under.

Physical practices like yoga, Qigong and tantra help you relax, because they focus on the breath.

If the first two chakras are "open," the creative energy flows up the body to the third chakra in the solar plexus.

The third chakra of the solar plexus is the center of power. If this chakra is closed, we create an upper limit to our full potential. We may generate money and create many Masterpieces, but we are never fully recognized in our lifetime, because we are scared of being truly seen. For instance, Post-Impressionists Paul Cézanne and Paul Gauguin were only fully recognized after their death.

The fourth chakra in our heart is the center of love. This chakra "converts" creative energy into our Masterpiece in the world outside us. When it is blocked, our art is irrelevant or meaningless for others. When it is open, our art touches others. It moves them, without the need of words. I believe if your heart is blocked, you cannot create a Masterpiece.

The fifth chakra in our throat is the center of self-expression or *art-iculation*. Given its location, it is particularly associated with verbal expression—speaking and singing. We may still create Masterpieces if this chakra is blocked, but we may not be able to articulate what we are creating to others, so nobody sees it. Van Gogh is a prime example. He was a Dutchman living in France, who spoke with a strong accent and had only a small circle of friends. If you cannot find a way to articulate what you are creating to others, you may have to wait until after you die before your art is recognized by enough people for it to become a Masterpiece.

The sixth chakra at the top of our spinal cord (in our pineal gland), is the center of intuition and the doorway into the **Zone of Creation**.

The seventh chakra, on the crown of our head, connects us to a higher power.

If we apply the same tree analogy of the infinite loop discussed earlier, we see the first three chakras rooted underground, and the last three chakras are above ground with the heart at the center.

When we open the first three chakras—we create the fertile ground within which the seed of our Masterpiece can grow.

When we open the last three chakras—we create the means through which we can bring our Masterpiece to life and change our world.

When we are in flow, energy flows up from the earth through our feet, up our legs to the base of the spine, where we discern what to do with it. If we allow it to go all the way, it then continues via the first neural network in the stomach, up the spine through the second neural network in the heart to the third neural network in the brain via our pineal gland. If this opens too, the energy can flow

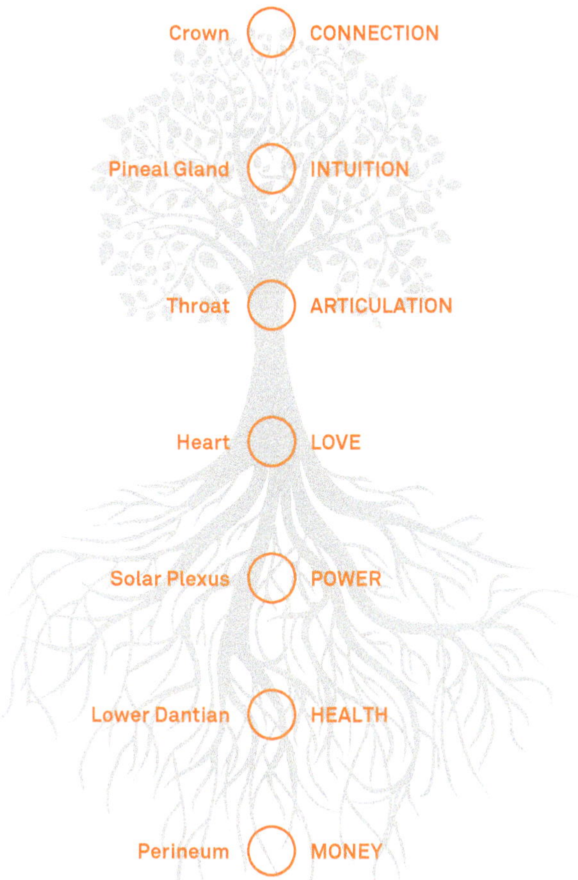

out of the seventh chakra at the crown of our head and back down to our feet, creating a bubble of electromagnetic energy flowing around us, called a torus. Each chakra produces its own mini torus, but the heart produces the most powerful electromagnetic field.[39] Alex Grey, the artist depicted the relationship between the chakras, energy field and torus in brilliant scientific detail in

39 HeartMath Institute. "Science of the Heart: Exploring the Role of the Heart in Human Performance," Vol. 2, 2015 https://www.heartmath.org/research/science-of-the-heart/energetic-communication/

Psychic Energy System (1980), Spiritual Energy (1981) and Universal Mind Lattice (1981).[40]

This is the Zone of Creation, a bubble of energy surrounding our body, emanating from each energy center of chakra. We can experience this state for a few seconds or a few hours depending on how empty our personal unconscious is and how open our chakras are, and how pure our body is.

When all chakras are open—you enter *the Zone of Creation!*

Opening your chakras helps you to access the Zone of Creation. You enter it via your intuition (or Inner Game) and use your intellect (or Outer Game) to activate various parts of your body to create your Masterpiece: via your hands to create art in the form of writing, painting or sculpture, through your heart in the form of love and compassion, through your voice in the form of talking or singing or up into your head so we have an "aha" insight or breakthrough. You can also transmute the energy out of our sexual organs to produce the greatest Masterpiece—new life.

In other words, you enter the Zone of Creation via your intuition and your intellect helps bring that art to life in physical form. Some people create new businesses, coaching programs or retreats, others sculpt, some create a family, while others write manifestos or theatre plays.

Your masterpiece is yours.

The Zone of Creation

The Zone of Creation is like the ocean. In the ocean, we can clearly distinguish one wave from another. However, it is much harder to tell where one wave starts and another one stops. Each wave travels at a certain speed. It has a certain height and length. This is its outward appearance or form. Underlying this physical appearance each wave has a resonance. The resonance defines the potential of the wave. Some waves can generate great power, others are more elegant or harmonious. Some waves are closer to other waves. They may

40 Psychic Energy System (1980), Spiritual Energy (1981) and Universal Mind Lattice (1981) can all be viewed on Alex Grey's website: https://www.alexgrey.com/art/paintings/sacred-mirrors/alex_grey_16_universal_

resonate more closely with them—perhaps they are in the same bay or the bay next door. These may be compared to people who are closest to us, and what some people call our *soul family*.

Other waves we resonate with less. They may be on the other side of the ocean. So, when I am accessing Van Gogh's energy, or the mountain's, or the person I am coaching, my resonance is similar to theirs. I have access to exactly what I need, when I need it. I don't paint with a clear outcome in mind. I go in with a clear state of mind, and let appear whatever needs to appear. It emerges naturally.

In the Zone of Creation, I am not aware of my body's most basic needs: I'm not hungry, I can paint for hours without eating; my fears dissolve. I'm afraid of heights, but when I paint, I can stand at the edge of an enormous cliff-face; my breath takes care of itself, sometimes it is the only thing I am aware of as my physical body becomes part of the ecosystem around me; and if I close my eyes, I may start to see visions, or at the very least gain insights about what I'm working on, from nowhere.

Everyone has access to the Zone of Creation.
The Zone of Creation is always available to everyone. This explains why some artists and inventors appear to come up with the same invention at almost exactly the same time. For example, Nikola Tesla was inventing airplanes at the same time as the Wright Brothers, radio at the same time as Guglielmo Marconi, and x-ray and electricity at the same time as Thomas Edison.

If our body is in pain or our mind is full, it is much harder to access the Zone of Creation. If we are overwhelmed by information from the world outside, our personal unconscious becomes full. You may like to think of your brain as a laptop, the personal unconscious as the laptop's hard-drive and the Zone of Creation as the internet, because it connects you to all other laptops in the world. If the hard-drive on your laptop is full, it doesn't matter how powerful your laptop is, your connection to the internet is slowed down by the overload of data. Your brain cannot process all of it. What's worse, there may be bugs in the data or it may be filed badly. Changing your relationship to money, power and love helps you to remove the bugs and refile the data so you can improve your connection. Changing your relationship to time helps you to stop trying to process too much data at the same time.

There's more to existence than meets the eye

Steve Jobs

The illusion of creation

At the quantum level, the Zone of Creation is both inside and outside—it is a formless substance from which we can create a different reality.

The world outside us isn't solid. That is a another misleading myth created by Newtonian science. Our first five senses tell us we can touch, taste, and see things, but when we get down to the sub-atomic level, we observe something different. We discover an atom isn't solid. It's more like a dust storm spinning very, very fast around a central axis. From a distance, it may appear the dust storm is solid. But when we get really close, like waves on a beach, we can't tell where the storm starts and stops.[41] The same is true of an atom. Just like the sandstorm and water, at the subatomic level, you can see right through an atom.

An atom consists of quarks and photons spinning at very high velocity around a central axis. If you could stand in the center of that atom, you would see these quarks and photons make up a tiny percentage of the entire volume. It's only the movement of these quarks and photons is so fast and they push quarks and photons in other materials away from them that they create the illusion that the atom is solid. It's not. It's made of nothing. To be precise, 99.999999% of it is not physical. To be more precise than that, this formless, non-physical thing is potential. If you look from inside the atom to the outside, you would see that same potential is outside too. So, to be more precise, 99.999999% of everything is potential. This is the unified field Einstein speaks of.

Now, the prevalent myth about Quantum science, perpetuated primarily by advocates of Newtonian science (who probably haven't consciously experienced the Zone of Creation for themselves) is that Quantum science only operates at the subatomic level. However, the quantum world infuses everything. Everything is potential. It infuses everything you see. It is in everything you don't see. It is inside us and outside us.

41 Lipton, Bruce. *The Biology of Belief 10th Anniversary Edition: Unleashing the Power of Consciousness, Matter & Miracles*. Hay House; 10th Anniversary ed. edition (11 October 2016).

We are not outside our ecosystem; we are part of it.
The implications of the preceding insights are significant: we cannot separate ourselves from the world outside us because the world outside us is us: there is no edge to our body—it is constantly ebbing and flowing, like waves in the ocean; and there is no inside our body, because the majority of what is inside, at the subatomic level, is the same as what is outside—unlimited energy or potential. There is no Inner and Outer. It is an illusion created by our first five senses and interpreted by our brain.

The world outside us only exists when we rely purely on these five senses to separate ourselves from it. Reality does not exist outside me, because what is outside me is me. Separation can only exist inside me, virtually, in my brain. When I change my brainwaves, from beta to delta or gamma, I become aware of my connection to the whole and this sense of separation disappears.

> *In this world, only an act of observation can confer shape and form to reality—to a dandelion in a meadow, or a seed pod, or the sun, or wind, or rain.*
>
> **Robert Lanza**

Space and time are illusions too. They are tools, like a Virtual Reality (VR) headset, that enable us to make sense of our reality. They are parameters on the canvas of life. Observation changes what we perceive on this canvas, because we are part of it. What we call it—the outer world, our environment, ecosystem, the Universe, the ocean—doesn't matter. All we can do is be aware of our connection to it—and that depends on the work we do in our inner world—to process what is in our personal unconscious by reclaiming what we have repressed.

There is a constant dance going on between the Inner Game and Outer Game. Our senses and Newtonian science lead us to believe that the world outside us impacts the world inside us and for us to reverse the direction of this arrow we need to do something physical. We need to take action. We need to launch a product and market it. On the other hand, our essence and Einsteinian science indicates that we can reverse this arrow and use our thoughts to impact the world outside us by thinking something metaphysical.

My experiments painting in extreme locations all over the world have shown me how the relationship between myself and my environment works in practice. When I am painting, the mountains or trees talk to me. They tell me of their pain, of their wisdom, of their knowledge, of what they have gone through to get to where they are, and all of that flows through me onto the canvas. I see the mountain in a different way. It comes alive, in three dimensions; it is moving, talking, sharing, allowing me in. It is as though I can see through the mountain, what shapes the mountain, right into its heart to what makes it who it is—underneath the glacier and the trees, underneath the snow and the outward appearances. I gain an insight into the depths of what it is to be a mountain, and that's what appears on the canvas.

On another level, I am dancing with the mountain and the mountain is dancing with me. A few summers ago, media expert Tony Johnston and I decided to paint and film Mont Blanc—the tallest mountain in Western Europe from Lac Blanc—a small glacial lake on the other side of the valley where it is possible to see a perfect reflection of the entire Mont Blanc range in the lake.

So, one morning we set off, despite a poor weather forecast. EMB Weather Services, located in Chamonix, provides the most detailed and accurate weather forecast I have ever come across. On this particular day, it was predicting that the clouds would remain low over the mountains all day, hovering at around 2,800 meters. That's over 1,000 meters short of the peaks and would lead to a different painting than the one I intended to paint.

We arrived in the valley and could see the forecast was correct. Nonetheless, we set off. We took the first gondola up and then the chairlift. Part way up, Tony started to film me and asked me a series of questions including this one: "Are the clouds going to lift?"

I responded, "The intention is that it's going to lift. It's pretty low at the moment. It's covering Mont Blanc, but miracles do happen."

The walk to the lake from the top of the chairlift took us around an hour and a half. Our back was to Mont Blanc for most of the walk. At a certain point, we stopped for a drink and a bite and Tony told me to turn around. The clouds had lifted. We could see Mont Blanc. I was so excited. We continued with our spirits lifted. However, by the time we arrived at Lac Blanc, the clouds had descended once more.

Tony interviewed me again. "That cloud has been in and out, a bit of cloud, a bit of sunshine, clouding over again, and now a couple of drops of rain."

I responded, “I'm confident though that we're going to get a good shot of Mont Blanc.”

I continued setting up and that's exactly what happened. The clouds lifted along the entire range. Not all at the same time. Bit by bit, one part would reveal itself so I could paint it. Then another part would reveal itself. I took advantage of these glimpses of the mountain range and painted each peak.

This experience and many others led me to conclude there is a correlation between my state of mind and my environment. When I access the Zone of Creation, I see how my thoughts create my reality. When I'm too egotistical, I let the energy go to my head and the clouds come down. When I reconnect with a positive feeling, they lift up.

The first time it happened, I was in South Africa on the same metaphysical retreat I mentioned in Chapter 1, just before I met my wife. During the week, I faced my greatest fears head-on and reclaimed them. Every morning of the retreat, I got up early and walked up toward a peak above the lodge where we were staying. One morning, feeling particularly energized, I decided to walk to the top. I reached it and despite my fear of heights, walked out onto the ledge that overlooked the valley. A sense of incredible power and extraordinary calmness filled me. I felt in harmony with myself and connected to nature. At one point, and I can't remember exactly why, a thought crossed my mind about a torrential downpour. Within minutes I felt a couple of spots of rain. A few minutes after that the downpour was so heavy, I was soaked through to the skin. Thunder and lightning cracked overhead. So, I headed back down the mountain quickly. The path had turned into a mountain stream and even my shoes were filling with water. But I felt alive, energized, at one with everything.

Something similar happened in the blizzard Tony and I got caught in, in a tropical storm in the Caribbean and in front of Mount Fuji. Clouds have miraculously disappeared while I have meditated in front of mountains. And the sun has appeared, contrary to the weather forecast, many times when I'm painting.

It is not possible to explain these phenomena by using logic or Newtonian science. It is only possible by using intuition or Einsteinian science. Our thoughts influence our environment. This isn't happening some of the time. It's happening all the time. The problem is most of the time our thoughts are polluted by what we have not yet reclaimed. Consequently, we are creating unintended waves. If we process what is in our personal unconscious and then access the Zone of Creation, we can create a different reality.

> *Intuition is really a sudden immersion of the soul into the universal current of life.*
>
> **Paulo Coelho, The Alchemist**

Accessing the Zone of Creation

There are four steps to access the Zone of Creation and create your Masterpiece.

Step 1. Remove Resistance
Step 2. Shift Your Brainwaves
Step 3. Become a Transceiver
Step 4. Bring the Formless Into Form

Each step generates a different outcome which we can map onto the Cycle of Life. In the first step, we cultivate the fertile soil. Then, in step two, we change our brainwaves so we shift from doing to being, from Outer to Inner. This prepares us to connect with the entire ecosystem in step three. In the final step, we bring the impulses we receive to life by grounding them without polluting them.

Or to paraphrase Dr Joe Dispenza, who described the science of accessing the Zone of Creation brilliantly in his book, *Becoming Supernatural*; we move from the world of *sometime* to the world of *no time* to the world of *anytime* in which time flows through us. We move from a world where we do *something* to the world where we do *no-thing* to the world, where we can do *anything* so we rediscover what we love doing. We move from a world where we are *someone* to a world, to where we are *no one*, to a world where we connect to *everyone* in which we can create an ecosystem of love. We move from a world where we are of *some worth* to a world, where we are *worthless* to a world of *infinite worth* in which we can create our own worth.

I am proposing you access the Zone of Creation to bring the Masterpiece you were born to create to life. According to the Akashic records your Purpose, Masterpiece, Mission and Legacy are already defined. Think of the Akashic records like an infinite library. In that library there are billions of books. One of them has your name on it. You can access the Zone of Creation to find your book, open it and discover what you were born to create.

We access the Zone of Creation when we allow the energy to take us out of our mind. Practices like guided meditation allow you to access the Zone of Creation. I enable you to create your future from a world of infinite possibilities rather than the ones your conscious mind has limited you to thus far in your life. You literally step into a different reality. Doing the reclamation work can help before the guided journey to ensure your ego doesn't kick in while you are exploring these infinite worlds and afterwards to ensure it doesn't stop you from bringing what you saw to life.

Step #1: Remove Resistance

The first step is to remove all resistance to the world outside you. You can do this by reclaiming your relationship to the four elements I have described throughout this book: Time, Power, Love and Money.

Outcome: By removing resistance and reclaiming suppressed elements of yourself, you process the information in your personal unconscious and open your chakras so you can access the Zone of Creation.

Step #2: Change your brainwaves

The second step is to shift your consciousness from the Newtonian world, where you are producing beta brainwaves, to the Einsteinian world, where you are producing theta or delta brainwaves. As I described in the introduction, between the ages of zero and two we produce primarily delta brainwaves; between two and six we produce primarily theta brainwaves; between the ages of six and twelve we produce primarily alpha brainwaves; above the age of twelve we produce primarily beta brainwaves; and sometimes, when we're hyper-focused, we may produce gamma brainwaves. As adults, we can only access delta and theta brainwaves through meditation, hypnosis, a state of flow—when we access the Zone of Creation—and sleep.

The following story illustrates how accessing theta brainwaves can change our reality instantly. During lockdown Sasha, my daughter, learned to cycle a bike. She had practiced a few times the year before, but hadn't mastered the art of starting and stopping, so she fell off. This time, she jumped on the bike with lots of enthusiasm and pedaled away frantically weaving this way and that until eventually she fell off. She tried a few more times with the same result before she gave up, pushing the bike back in tears, saying, "I don't want to ride anymore, Mommy."

My wife, Anna didn't give up on her though. She grabbed the bike, jumped on and started pedaling away furiously. It was hilarious. Here was a grown woman cycling on a child's bike. Her knees were coming up to her elbows and she was weaving this way and that even more precariously than Sasha. But she was laughing out loud as she did so. Daniel, my son, started laughing. So did I. Eventually, Sasha started laughing too. At this point, Sasha stopped Anna, grabbed the bike, jumped on and cycled off into the distance as though she'd be doing it her entire life. Ever since, she's loved cycling. She may have fallen off a few times, but she's never given up—and I don't expect her to.

Falling off the bike the first time triggered fear in Sasha. She reinforced this fear with each consecutive fall until she got to the point where the fear was greater than the joy she experienced cycling the bike—and she gave up. More importantly, her brain was creating a neural network, or a series of connections between neurons in her brain, which makes up a thought—and associating this thought with this fear. If she had continued to fall off, eventually she would have created a vicious cycle which would have embedded itself in her gene expression. In other words, her genes would have stopped her from cycling completely!

Take another example. Think of the first time you drove a car. How did it make you feel? Worried, uncertain, scared, out of control? How do you feel driving a car now? Confident, relaxed, calm? What happened in between these two moments? You repeated the behavior so many times, your brain developed a neural network that associated driving with a second emotion, which overrode the first emotion.

Now, let's say you have a car accident and you feel scared, shocked, or embarrassed as a result. These emotions can override the second neural network and create a new thought—driving may be scary—which leads to a different behavior. If you run the experience through your brain repeatedly, constantly remembering the accident, your mind will narrow the world of infinite possibilities into one form—driving *is* scary. In the process, you will go from being a confident driver to a nervous driver. If you continue to do that for long enough, it will influence your gene expression and you will suppress the gene for being a confident driver.

According to epigenetics, our gene expression is not static, it's dynamic. This may be different from what you learned at school—epigenetics only gained in popularity in the last thirty years. Think of our genes like a menu in a restaurant. You rarely, if ever, order everything on the menu when you go to eat. The same is true with your genes. We only express around five percent of our genes at any one time.[42] However, there are genes for being a confident driver, for bringing a Masterpiece to life, for being in love, for being healthy, wealthy, and living a meaningful life. You have everything you need inside you—the inner artist and art director, the Choreographer, the Creator, the Collaborator and the Calculator. In most of us, these genes are "switched off," or more specifically, they are not expressed. On the flip side, there are also genes for feeling unloved, undervalued, unseen, and being disorganized. Which genes would you like to order from the menu? The choice is down to you… or more specifically, it's down to your relationship with Time, Power, Love and Money.

The problem is that most of the genes we want to order, for instance, being a creative genius or an abundant entrepreneur, or having unstoppable energy, or unconditional love with an amazing family appears to be off the menu. We order, but our dish never comes. We keep on ordering, but it doesn't appear. This is because what we haven't reclaimed is stopping us. Paraphrasing the author Ben Angel, we can see the Masterpiece we want to create—let's say you can see the partner of your dreams 100 meters away from you. You keep on running towards this person, but as soon as you get ten meters away an invisible elastic band pulls you back to the place where you started. You end up sitting on your backside. So, you try again and again and again, but each time you get pulled back to the starting point. Something doesn't quite work. The relationship breaks down. You give up and go back to your current reality. Programs from your past create your current reality. We live in the past, until we wake ourselves up, reclaim what is stopping us and select an alternate future from the infinite options available.

In Sasha's case, if she continued repeating her vicious cycle, she would have switched off the gene for cycling a bike. However, my wife's actions broke this cycle before it was fully formed. By making Sasha laugh while she was cycling on Sasha's bike, Anna helped Sasha re-associate cycling with joy and happiness. Because joy is a higher-level emotion than fear, joy replaced fear in Sasha's mind. All this happened in the blink of an eye. Yet, this is what encouraged Sasha to try again so quickly and because she is only six and is primarily producing theta

42 Dispenza, Joe. *Becoming Supernatural: How Common People are Doing the Uncommon*. Hay House, Inc, Oct 31, 2017.

brainwaves, she rewired her brain with this new information immediately. She accessed the Zone of Creation and chose a different reality. Her brain rewired itself and she jumped on her bike and rode off. You can do the same, even if you don't have Sasha's advantage of naturally producing theta brainwaves nor a parent who is modeling the behavior for you (by jumping on a bike) and making you laugh first. As an adult, we need to change our brainwaves *and* create an alternative reality for ourselves.

Outcome: By changing your brain waves, you move from doing to being and can access an entirely new possibility that can enter your life.

Step #3: Transmit your Masterpiece using your Pineal Gland

The doorway to the Zone of Creation is our Pineal Gland or sixth chakra. According to Dispenza, when we activate it, it acts like a transceiver. The third step in this process is to crush the crystals inside your pineal gland so it becomes a transceiver through which you can receive a different signal from the formless world of the Zone of Creation, and transmit a different signal into your world to create a different form.

A television transceiver does exactly the same thing—it takes a signal that we can't see, a television wave, and converts it from the invisible spectrum into a visible image which we can see on a television screen.

The pineal gland is a small gland about the size of a single grain of rice, just at the top of our spinal cord where it meets the brain. It regulates melatonin, the chemical that regulates our sleep patterns: our circadian rhythm. We produce more melatonin at night and less during the day. When we build up enough pressure—energy, in the form of spinal fluid—on the outside of this gland, it bursts open, secreting a tiny amount of milky white fluid. According to Dispenza, this fluid "upgrades" the melatonin. It converts it into dimethyltryptamine, the same active ingredient found in ayahuasca—the hallucinogenic plant drink that shamans use to induce out-of-body experiences. Both can trigger transcendental experiences where you appear to step out of your body and step into the Zone of Creation. The difference is ayahuasca is toxic and the body reacts violently to its ingestion. Whereas upgrading melatonin is entirely natural. It shuts down the fears we have embedded in our genes long enough for us to immerse ourselves in the formless unified field, select a new reality we want to live out, and bring it back into the world of form.

The moment this gland bursts open can feel like you are having an orgasm in the brain. This is exactly how Tantra describes it. Rather than ejaculate milky white fluid out of your sexual organs to create a Masterpiece in the form of new life, ejaculate milky white fluid out of your pineal gland so you create your Masterpiece in the form of bringing a new reality into being.

When the pineal gland shuts down the world of cause and effect by secreting this fluid, it also triggers the pituitary gland to secrete its own fluid. The pituitary gland is also found at the top of the spine. The active ingredient in this fluid is oxytocin—known as the love drug—which encourages bonding between couples and mother and child at birth. MDMA, the recreational drug commonly known as Ecstasy, does exactly the same thing. The sensation it creates is more sensual than sexual—a feeling of unconditional love for everyone and everything, rather than a desire to make love. As if this isn't enough, the pituitary gland also produces a form of valium, which calms us down. In other words, opening our sixth sense to access the Zone of Creation creates a chain reaction which unleashes a cocktail of drugs inside us—the possession of which would get you arrested in most countries.

The relationship between the pituitary and pineal glands changes over time. Under the age of seven, when the brain is producing primarily theta brain waves, the pineal gland takes the lead, allowing children to connect more easily to the Zone of Creation. Beyond the age of seven, as the brain produces primarily alpha brainwaves, the pituitary gland takes the lead, suppressing the activity of the pineal gland in the process.

Opening the pineal gland

Opening the pineal gland takes some practice. If we combine what we have learnt from neurology, physiology, psychology and wisdom cultures, our breath is the conduit. We draw energy into our feet from the world around us, up our legs, through our base chakra, into our lower *dantian*, up our spine through each of the other chakras until it reaches our pineal gland. When we channel this energy with the breath, the pineal gland opens naturally. If there is any resistance in any of the chakras—particularly the lower chakras, associated with time, power, love and money, insufficient energy will reach the pineal gland. Dispenza compares the process to sucking on a straw—although it doesn't have to be quite as energetic as he suggests—it can be quite subtle. Either way, we pull the *kundalini* or *prana* energy up the spine until the gland secretes its liquid. Once the gland opens, the energy then circulates around the body in waves or cycles—out of the top of the head, around the body and in through the feet. In my experience of painting, it is possible to stay in this state for hours.

Outcome: by opening your pineal gland and crushing the crystals inside it, you can receive information from the Zone of Creation—the formless world—and transmit it to the physical world—the world of form.

Step #4: Bring the formless into form

The final step is to bring the formless impulses we receive from the Zone of Creation into form without allowing our conscious mind to pollute them.

To create a Masterpiece, we bring the formless from the Zone of Creation into form without polluting it with what we have not yet reclaimed. The Zone of Creation is infinite. When you connect to it, you access infinite worlds, infinite possibilities. These infinite worlds exist as potentiality, waiting for you to bring them into reality. Or to put it another way, the Inner Game is formless—it doesn't exist until you bring it into form using your Outer Game.

When a new idea starts to take form in your mind from the Zone of Creation, it is formless. At its inception, it is not even the seed of an idea—it is just an impulse, a hunch, pure energy. And that pure energy can take multiple different forms in your mind. If you feed it, by giving the impulse attention, the idea begins to take form in your mind. Let's say the impulse is to write this paragraph in this book. If I try to grasp the idea too soon, because, for instance, I need to meet my family for lunch, the form the idea takes may be "polluted" by my unresolved relationship to time. My ego kicks in. I rush the birth of the impulse into an idea, and I immediately fix the idea in time and space by writing it down. Now, I have narrowed the infinite possibilities this impulse could have taken into one single form—a paragraph in a book, the form of which is influenced by my unreclaimed relationship to time. For instance, a fear of not being accepted by my family if I am late. In other words, my relationship to time pollutes the purity of the impulse. The paragraph takes a form, which is out of alignment with my Inner Game—and its power is diluted. The result is I compromise my Masterpiece—one paragraph in my book—which has a knock-on effect on the entire book and the purity of the energy behind it is compromised. The whole thing resonates at a different level.

I first noticed this phenomenon while painting. I noticed whenever I lost connection with the painting for a split second—for instance, I allowed myself to step back and admire the painting, I got a big head. The same thing happened when I admired the clouds lifting over Mont Blanc. I literally allowed the energy to go to my head, rather than allowing it to take me out of my head and access the Zone of Creation. In that moment, I would place a brushstroke with my intellect rather than my intuition. A single brushstroke could unbalance an entire painting and take me a couple of hours to resolve it. The painting was never quite the same again. The purity of the energy was compromised, because I had overworked it.

The same is true with any impulse you receive from the Zone of Creation. If your ego influences the impulse as it transitions from Inner Game to Outer Game—from impulse to thought and from thought to the expression of that thought through what you say or do—then you will have limited the potential form the impulse takes. It fixes you in the past, rather than frees you to create a new future. As a result, you create unintended waves that reinforce your current existence.

If on the other hand (as I did with the impulse which has now turned into the last four paragraphs), I allow the impulse to rest as an impulse without attempting to bring it into form too soon, my Inner Game can reflect on which of the infinite forms the impulse could take is the most appropriate one for it to contribute to my book. This is exactly what I did by going to lunch, not because I was worried about being late, but because I consciously chose to allow my unconscious mind to identify which form would be most appropriate. In other words, you don't actually have to do anything, other than be consciously aware of what you are doing. Allow the collective unconscious to speak through you. Your Inner Game will do the rest. Hold the tension of the opposing forces without trying to collapse them too soon, and allow the breakthrough to emerge. This is true creation and you'll know it's a breakthrough, because you have never had the thought previously or been able to express it with such clarity.

Outcome: bringing the formless into form without letting your conscious mind pollute the impulse inevitably leads to the creation of your Masterpiece.

Getting out of your head

There are multiple different ways to access the Zone of Creation. All of them follow the same approach: put feeling before thinking by reclaiming what you have suppressed; change your brainwaves; open the pineal gland; and bring the formless into form.

The first time I was consciously aware of accessing this world was when I was painting in Italy a few years after I had restarted. The creative director of my agency at the time, Edwin, encouraged me to get drunk before I painted. I said, "Get drunk? Why?"

He said just try it and see what happens. So, the next time, I went to Italy, I drank a bottle of wine and started painting at ten o'clock in the evening. I painted through to three o'clock in the morning—and then, I fell asleep. That night, I had vivid dreams. It was as though fireworks were exploding in my head all night long—and the colors were so vivid—colors I had never seen before. These colors infused themselves into the painting.

I repeated the same process the following night. When I went to sleep, I had dreams with vivid fireworks again. The same thing happened the third night. At the time, I didn't know I was accessing the Zone of Creation. It is only looking back I can see what happened. Every morning, I woke up, looked at the painting and was amazed—it was as though someone else had created it. It was the best painting I had ever created, and this was the first painting I ever sold. Accessing the Zone of Creation (by accident), I changed my world and contrary to my father's prediction when I was sixteen, started making money as a professional artist!

Without knowing it, I had followed exactly the approach I have just outlined: I was filled with joy; I changed my brainwaves by getting drunk; I opened the pineal gland as I painted; and I brought the formless world of vibrant colors I saw in my dreams into form through painting.

Then, I realized I had a problem. The next two paintings I created I sold as well. But both times I got drunk to shift my brainwaves. I knew this wasn't sustainable—I was in danger of depending on a toxin to access the Zone of Creation. Many artists, such as Mark Twain, William Blake, John Milton, Jackson Pollock, the Beatles and too many other musicians to mention have done just this. I knew this wasn't my journey. So, I went on a voyage to explore how I could access this world naturally. Little did I know, I was going on a journey to discover I released these kinds of drugs naturally when I accessed the Zone of Creation.

All Art is a Self-Portrait: Changing Your Portrait

Accessing the Zone of Creation changes your world. It is literally a different world. But you can't explain the change using logic alone. You elevate your level of consciousness and step into a different reality. The world you resonate with is different.

When I paint, the most obvious indicator that I am accessing the Zone of Creation is the environment—it changes. I see how my thoughts extend beyond the edge of the canvas. It stops snowing, the lake calms down, the clouds disappear, it doesn't rain. The first time it happened I had no idea what was happening. Quite the opposite, I thought I was going crazy. It's only now, thanks to the developments in epigenetics, neurology, physiology and quantum physics and scientists like Dispenza and Robert Lanza that I can explain what is happening without sounding like I have gone out of my mind—even if that's exactly what I have just done!

Changing the world is not a conscious act though. You cannot change *the* world—that is your Outer Game, your ego wanting your Masterpiece to create an effect—you can however change *your* world. There is a world of difference between the two.

Changing *your* world relieves the burden. You don't have to change everyone or everything else in order to change your world. You are not responsible for their world. You are only responsible for your world—and you can change *your* world by causing an effect as I just have just outlined. This may sound incredibly selfish and even more egotistical than using the Outer Game. It isn't. Actually, you're influencing your world all the time. It's just that you're unaware that you're doing it—and you're unaware you're doing it, because nothing appears to be changing—and nothing appears to be changing, because you're not changing yourself. If you're not changing yourself, by reclaiming whatever you have suppressed, your world will stay the same. It is only when you reclaim aspects of yourself and access the Zone of Creation you bring another reality into existence and your world starts to change.

As I mentioned previously, all art is a self-portrait. It reflects the artist's mindset at the moment of creation. It doesn't matter what form that art takes; it could be a painting, a sculpture, a book, a business or a relationship—it will always mirror the energy of the artist who creates it in that moment.

What differentiates a Masterpiece from other pieces of art is that in that moment of creation, he or she plunges into the Zone of Creation. They become the ecosystem. There is no separation between them and it. Thus, the art they create is a self-portrait of the entire ecosystem.

The Masterpiece resonates with others, because they dream (unconsciously) of reconnecting to the entire ecosystem again as well. The Masterpiece provides a doorway to help them access it. They see themselves in it. If the form (or medium) the artist uses to create the Masterpiece is sufficiently relevant, it will attract a greater audience. But what attracts them is not the form, it is the energy that created that form. You are still reading this book, because you are drawn to the energy with which I created it rather than the words I am using. I could use any words. The words don't matter. The energy does.

> *If you can dream it, you can do it.*
>
> **Walt Disney**

What Stops Us From Accessing the Zone of Creation?

Two things can stop us from accessing the Zone of Creation: our mind and our body. I have described how our mind can distract us throughout this book: in Chapter 1, I described my own struggles with my mind; in Chapter 2, I described Van Gogh's struggles with his mind; in Chapter 3, I described where these struggles come from, the dawn of civilization; in Chapters 4, 5 and 6, I described how you can reclaim what you have suppressed by changing your mindset in yourself and in companies. In this chapter, I have described how you can return to a state of grace where you are connected to the Zone of Creation—in this space, you are *mind-less*—your mind switches off and your fears disappear. What I haven't yet described though is how your body can distract you too.

If your body is in pain, even if it is quite subtle—a blocked nose or a painful hip will do it—it is much harder to still your mind and shift your brainwaves from beta to theta. You cannot become no-body if your body is in pain. Yet, you cannot bring the formless into form without a body. Your body, like your mind, is a bridge between the Inner Game and the Outer Game. If the bridge is wobbly, it is much harder to cross into the Zone of Creation.

Others are far more qualified than me to speak about how you can care for your body. More importantly, your body is unique so the nature of any imbalance and the solution to rebalance it will be unique too. If I started to make recommendations, I would end up writing another book. What I can do is share my story, which illustrates both the relation between mind and body and how healing your body follows the same principles as healing your mind. Your body is whole; whatever you resist within it persists and grows; if you resist it long enough, it will influence both your gene expression and ultimately your health. In other words, mental resistance to what is outside you and physical resistance to what is inside you create imbalances.

Diseases are symptoms that your body is off-balance. They are warning signals to slow down. Actually, we get the warning signals before the disease develops. If we ignore them, the symptoms get worse until we stop. According to Ayurveda, there are six levels of health—from chronic disease at the bottom to vibrant health at the top. Western medicine only deals with the bottom two to three levels. Without a symptom, your doctor cannot diagnose the problem, and without a diagnosis, she can't prescribe you a drug to treat it. If it gets this far, she will invariably treat the symptom, rather than the underlying cause.

You may remember I disconnected from my Inner Game after I took my father's advice and stopped painting, then drank myself into hospital twice to compensate. In the process, I pushed my body so far out of balance, it took twenty-five years to recover. My doctor treated the symptoms, not the depression let alone the disconnection from my Inner Game that caused it.

Without realizing it, my drinking antics led to a candida (fungal) overgrowth in my gut. I didn't notice at first. It was like boiling a frog in water by gradually increasing the temperature. The frog only notices it's boiling when it's too late. I only noticed my body was so off balance when I repeatedly had an allergic reaction to a benign fragrance at home. My allergies got worse and worse without me noticing: I got hay fever every summer, my skin was itching, and I was sneezing a lot. In addition, my whole body had started to ache, I was tired, I got headaches after one glass of wine, and felt like I was about to breakdown. It got so bad, I was constantly sneezing, aching and exhausted. I would wake up every morning and blow my nose. I carried tissues with me everywhere.

I had had enough. This wasn't how I wanted to live my life. So, I changed my diet—for six weeks, I followed the radical candida diet, which eliminates all sugar, carbohydrates, refined foods and dairy products—it was brutal. I lost six kilograms, which I couldn't afford to lose, but it worked. In parallel, I took a food allergy test, started taking anti-fungal pills, nutrient supplements, probiotics and eating superfoods such as almonds, avocado, chia seeds, acai berries, blueberries, spinach, guarana, maca at least once per day in a coconut milk smoothie. I stopped sneezing. I started breathing better. I went an entire hay fever season without taking a single pill or spray. Everyone around me was suffering, except me. I have had hay fever since I was seven. Forty years and one radical diet later and it is gone.

I limit other potential addictions. I hardly drink anymore—not bad given that I ended up in hospital twice as a young man from drinking too much. In addition, I have severely reduced my use of social media and am reducing my dependence on work. Most of us work too hard. And then, we relax by scrolling through social media. To break these addictions, I re-evaluated what I truly value and then reclaimed my relationship to my own self-worth and worthlessness.

At night, I aim to get a minimum of seven hours sleep. Anything less and I am running my body down—I am not producing enough delta brainwaves to heal my body. Every so often, I will sleep for ten or eleven hours just to reset my body. Not getting enough sleep also severely messes up the balance within our microbiome. Most of us are suffering from long-term exhaustion, because we're not looking after our bodies enough. This is not about being macho, it's about being healthy.

I also started taking nootropics, such as matcha green tea or coconut oil to help me get into creative flow. I removed all added sugars and now eat couscous and quinoa instead of rice and pasta.

And finally, exercise is also important. It can reduce stress, relax the stomach, and stimulate the lymphatic system and liver to detoxify the body. In winter, I ski. And in summer, I have just bought a road bike. Anna and I often go for evening walks as well to review the day. It helps we live in a beautiful place. You can do the same, wherever you live.

My conclusion is the relationship between our body and mind is critical. If we pollute our mind, it will eventually manifest in our body. If it manifests in our body, it stops us from accessing the Zone of Creation. If we can't access the Zone of Creation, it is much harder to create a Masterpiece. In my case, candida in my gut blocked creativity from flowing. Consequently, it was harder to draw the energy above the second chakra and access the Zone of Creation. The irony was, the Zone of Creation can also help you heal. So, I was trapped in a vicious cycle—I couldn't heal my body in the Zone of Creation because I couldn't get there. I had to take care of my physical body first.

You need to take care of your body too: treat the body with care by feeding it what it needs in terms of nutrition, supplements and sleep; reclaim what stops you from accessing the Zone of Creation. In this lifetime, you only have one body. Medical science already offers the possibility of replacing or upgrading parts, and consumer marketing offers quick fixes to produce theta brainwaves, but that misses the point.

In recent years, there has been an explosion of online gurus, meditation apps, meditation music, nutritional supplements, online and offline programs and wearable devices, all marketed to help you produce theta or even delta brainwaves. Between them, they promise to transform your life—reduce your stress levels, increase your productivity, accelerate your creativity. All of them promote the idea you can manifest whatever you want—the home, the car, the job, the partner—without aligning it to a greater purpose or mission. But what's the point? There is a reason it takes monks and yoga-practitioners so long to learn the art of stilling their mind. They need to accept and reclaim whatever they have resisted outside them, so they use this greater power for greater good. As my mentor, Ashoke used to say, "power without connection is dangerous." He told me the secret to mastering my art was to meditate every morning *and* pray. Meditation increases power. Prayer increases connection. Producing theta brainwaves at the flick of a switch may shorten the journey to find moments of inner peace, but what we do with that inner peace will determine our ability to rebalance the planet.

To create your Masterpiece requires a balance of body, mind and spirit. As soon as I started taking better care of my body, #Masterpiece, the program, emerged. So, if you are struggling with aches and pains, allergies, indigestion or congestion in your sinuses, take it as a gentle warning there is something for you to reclaim. If you ignore it, it will persist and grow, eventually taking the form of a disease. The more dense the physical form, the harder it is to transform. But it is still possible. So, if you are suffering from any physical symptoms, no matter how minor they may appear to be on the surface, you may want to consider what you need to change to stop it from going any further.

Until you make the unconscious conscious, it will direct your life and you will call it fate

Carl Jung

Balance creates breakthroughs

Lewis Hamilton, the British racing driver, demonstrates how a balanced mind, body and spirit creates breakthroughs, whereas an unbalanced mind, body or spirit creates breakdowns. It doesn't matter how talented you are. If you are out of balance, you will never fulfill your potential. When Hamilton started in the sport's première event, Formula 1 (F1), he had the raw talent (Outer Game), but not the balance to make the most of it. In one incident early in his career, after failing to win a crucial race in Japan, Hamilton was so depressed, he stayed in his hotel bedroom for three days.

Motor racing is one of the most physically demanding sports in the world and F1 is its pinnacle. Drivers experience forces as high as 6G (six times the force of gravity) on the body. That's double what an astronaut experiences when a rocket takes off—and is easily sufficient to put enough pressure on the pineal gland for it to work its magic. Most of us would become unconscious beyond 5G. Yet, Hamilton doesn't just remain conscious, he appears to access the Zone of Creation while he's driving.

"The driver is balancing on the edge of adhesion at all times during cornering, in an exercise that could perhaps be likened to walking a tightrope at 100mph down a steep hill around a corner in high wind."

Andrew Benson, BBC, Chief F1 Writer

The most demanding part of F1 is qualifying. Drivers compete over one "flying lap" to work out the order in which they will start the race. Starting first (in pole position) provides a driver with a significant advantage over his rivals, particularly at tight street circuits like Monaco where overtaking opportunities are limited. During qualifying, drivers are right on the edge physically and mentally, pushing the car and themselves to the absolute limit. Thousandths of a second matter.

Hamilton holds the record for the most number of pole positions and is widely acknowledged as the fastest driver in his era. What makes Hamilton special is his ability to pull out a qualifying lap from almost nowhere. He may have had bad practice sessions and even be off the pace at the beginning of the session itself, but then miraculously he appears to turn it on when it's needed. Clearly, Hamilton loves it. He rises to the challenge and thrives in the moment.

All the indications are that Hamilton accesses the Zone of Creation during qualifying. At times, Hamilton can be up to a second-and-a-half quicker than his rivals. That's unheard of. Here's how Hamilton's great idol, Ayrton Senna, who was the fastest man in his generation described qualifying for the Monaco Grand Prix in 1988:

> *'When I am competing against the watch and against other competitors, the feeling of... being the best, gives me a kind of power that... actually detaches me completely from anything else as I am doing it...corner after corner, lap after lap... I was already on pole and I was going faster and faster. One lap after the other, quicker, and quicker, and quicker. I was at one stage just on pole, then by half a second, and then one second...and I kept going. Suddenly, I was nearly two seconds faster than anybody else, including my team mate with the same car. And I suddenly realized that I was no longer driving the car consciously. I was kind of driving it by instinct, only I was in a different dimension. It was like I was in a tunnel, not only the tunnel under the hotel, but the whole circuit for me was a tunnel. I was just going, going - more, and more, and more, and more. I was way over the limit but still able to find even more... It frightened me because I realized I was well beyond my conscious understanding.'* [43]

Hamilton appears to do the same, not just in qualifying, but also when it's raining. At times in wet conditions, Hamilton may be lapping two seconds quicker than the rest of the field, including his team-mate who is driving the same car. On one occasion, during the 2008 British Grand Prix, Hamilton was lapping five seconds faster than any other car. He won the race by a minute and eight seconds. That's unheard of in a sport defined by thousandths of a second. Hamilton appears to use the rain to his advantage as though he and the car are at one with it. There is no resistance. It is sublime—an art. The car is on the edge—and the track turns into a skating rink. Hamilton relishes it. I suspect he may even induce these conditions to help him. Whenever he is in a tight spot in the World Championship, it rains and Hamilton wins. Is this a coincidence? I think not.

43 Donaldson, Gerald. Blog article, "Senna's Magic Monaco Lap." Published online May 23rd 2019. Retrieved November 5, 2020. http://www.f1speedwriter.com/2018/05/sennas-magic-monaco-lap.html

I suspect Hamilton doesn't talk about it though, because he doesn't know how to describe it without sounding like he's crazy. After a dominant victory at the Spanish Grand Prix in 2020, Hamilton described being in a "perfect zone of clarity". Writers immediately drew comparisons to Senna's qualifying experience in Monaco in 1988, but Hamilton wouldn't be drawn further. Senna attracted considerable criticism from his rivals for his comments in the 1980s and perhaps Hamilton doesn't want to attract the same unwelcome attention today.

It wasn't always this way though. Hamilton has always had the raw talent. But he hasn't always turned it into results. Instead of blaming the situation, he learned from it. He reclaimed whatever stopped him from performing at the highest level. For instance, in his first season in F1, Hamilton missed out on winning the World Championship by one point. The following year he went one better. He won the World Championship by one point. That year, he was in the same team as the fastest driver on the grid, double-world champion, Fernando Alonso. They didn't get on well: in his desire to win, Hamilton disobeyed team orders and slowed Alonso down, then accused Alonso of holding him back twice during qualifications, once in Monaco and once in Hungary. How they responded to these events defined their future. Alonso gave his bosses an ultimatum—essentially to choose between Hamilton and him. Even though Alonso subsequently withdrew the threat, McLaren asked him to leave at the end of that season. He has not won a World Championship since and left the sport in 2018—returning again for the 2021 season. On the other hand, Hamilton has gone from strength to strength, particularly after joining Mercedes in 2013. He looked for areas where he could improve physically, mentally and spiritually. At the time of writing (November 2020), he has just won the Formula One World Championship for a seventh time, equaling Michael Schumacher's record. What the confrontation with Alonso exposed was that raw talent alone wasn't sufficient. Hamilton needed to reduce the resistance in his life and focus on winning.

Eight years later, Hamilton had another confrontation with a teammate, and again learned from the resistance to make himself better. This time it was Nico Rosberg. In 2016, Hamilton narrowly lost the Championship to him. Like Alonso, Rosberg exposed what Hamilton needed to work on—consistency. Hamilton didn't have a system (the Choreographer) to perform at the same level every weekend. Rosberg did. He may not have had Hamilton's raw speed, but he out-thought him—both tactically and psychologically—by developing a system that enabled him to out-perform Hamilton across the entire season. Hamilton made too many mistakes and Rosberg exploited them.

Rosberg retired at the end of the 2016 season exhausted by the effort of out-thinking Hamilton, knowing that Hamilton would learn from the experience and develop his own system. He did. In addition, he let go of his mind-coach, telling himself it was his mind and he had to find a way to get the best out of himself. He also let go of his physical trainer, telling himself it was his body and he had to find a way to get the most out of it. More recently, he has tried yoga and started mediating.

Of course, critics would say it is all down to the car—Hamilton has the fastest car and that's why he wins. I would say Hamilton has the fastest car, because he influences its creation. He works more closely with his engineers to get the most out of his team (using his Outer Game). But his team-mates have access to the same car and Rosberg is the only team-mate to have beaten Hamilton across an entire season—that's once in thirteen years and counting. Moreover, when Ferrari had the fastest car in 2018, Hamilton still found a way to win. That's because, Hamilton has also learned how to use his Inner Game to access the Zone of Creation and create a different reality. When Hamilton joined Mercedes in 2013, they didn't have the best car. Now, they do. In comparison, Alonso left F1 in 2017, complaining he couldn't get a seat in a decent car. The car wasn't the problem.

Every time Alonso moved to a new team, that team or his car had problems: for instance, at McLaren, the Honda engine wasn't performing, but as soon as he left, the car got better; and Honda moved to partner Red Bull where they also performed better. Something similar happened when Alonso left Ferrari. The car got better the year he left. In other words, Hamilton's Inner Game appears to have a positive influence on team performance, whereas Alonso appears to do the opposite.

Hamilton demonstrates both power and connection. Increasingly, he is aligning everything he does with a greater Purpose. His rivals don't. Hamilton is now using the platform he has created to speak out about the issues that matter to him. For instance, when he became vegan in 2017, he did it for two reasons, one personal—the desire for more consistent and sustainable energy throughout a race—and the other societal—he believes it serves a greater purpose, to help tackle climate change. More recently he has become outspoken on racism. He is the only black driver in F1 and has suffered from racism throughout his career. At the beginning of his career, racism upset Hamilton, as he grew older he ignored it, now he stands up to it. He has already agreed to lead a commission in the UK to increase equality in F1 and he is doing something similar with the FIA, F1's sports' governing body. He believes racism is endemic to the system in which he operates. He maintains the authorities and other drivers, particularly the older generation don't understand the problem fully. He's correct. Most of us are oblivious to it. Toto Wolff, his team boss at Mercedes-Benz, recounted the following interaction with Hamilton, which illustrates this well: "[Hamilton] asked me once, 'Have you ever had the active thought that you are white?' And I replied, 'I have never thought about it.' He said, 'I think about it [the fact I'm black] every day.'"[44]

Each of Hamilton's pole positions, race wins and World Championships is a Masterpiece in its own right. But Hamilton's greatest Masterpiece could be the stand he takes on racism. This will be his true legacy. It already transcends his sport. His team, Mercedes-Benz, are fully supporting him.

In the 2020 season, postponed because of COVID-19, they repainted their cars black as a symbol of their support for Hamilton's beliefs. This shift, from ego to essence, from acting as an individual to elevating an entire team to influence an ecosystem is the mark of a true artist. If he continues to apply what he has learned from other racers and the weather, he will change his world for good.

> *Equally Michael Schumacher's record puts a spotlight on me that I know won't be here forever. So, while you're here, paying attention, I want to ask everyone to do their part in helping to create a more equal world... I was told by many that my dream was impossible, yet here I am. I want you to know that you can do it too... let's keep rising to the occasion.*
>
> **Lewis Hamilton**

Taking care of your body, mind and spirit are prerequisites to creating your Masterpiece. Your spirit enables you to access the Zone of Creation, your body enables you to bring what you experience there to life and your mind can either facilitate or restrict this connection.

44 Benson, Andrew—"Challenger, champion, changemaker—the real story of Lewis Hamilton." November 2020, published online: https://www.bbc.co.uk/sport/extra/c1nx5lutpg/The-real-Lewis-Hamilton-story

8 Growing Your Masterpiece

When love and skill work together, expect a Masterpiece.

John Ruskin

Too few of us love what we do. This is a source of the imbalance in the world today. Imagine living in a world in which you love what you do and are inspired by what everyone else is doing. Imagine waking up every morning, looking at your agenda and loving what you see—the meetings, events, calls; and loving the uncertainty of not knowing quite what magic is going to occur, but knowing it will occur all the same. Imagine loving yourself so much you spend more time with your family, love where you live and enable your children or the world's children to pursue what they love too. This is the world we are creating. In this world, inequality in all its forms and climate change dissolve as a global problem. No, this isn't a dream. This is a Mission: a world where **81% of us love what we do by 1 July 2026**. Why this percentage and date?

As mentioned in Chapter 3, according to Gallup, only 15% of people globally are engaged in their work. In other words, more than 80% of us are *not* engaged. Koenig and I believe if we reverse this figure, so more than 80% of us love what we do, the world's biggest challenges—inequality and climate change—will dissolve. We need to make this change within five years; before these changes become irreversible.

Let me say this once more: You are an artist. You are born with the ability to create. Your Masterpiece reflects your Personal Purpose and it is the fastest way to bring it to life.

Artists create art because they must. Artists create to grow personally. They respond to their calling—the voice inside them. They focus on the journey rather than the destination. They know creativity loves constraints—which is why they set a start-date and an end-date to focus their mind. You too, must tie down the artist inside you and focus "her" on a deadline so you can get the best out of *you*.

The world needs you to bring your Masterpiece to life, because humankind benefits from its creation as much as you do. In this final chapter, I will reveal how the Artist Profiles come together to create the four components that constitute a Masterpiece.

Remember that:

1. Choreographers create the Culture in which Masterpieces grow.
2. Creators create and refine the Idea behind the Masterpiece.
3. Collaborators create the Community that it serves.
4. Calculators create the Business Model that makes it sustainable.

You need all four in balance to create a great Masterpiece.

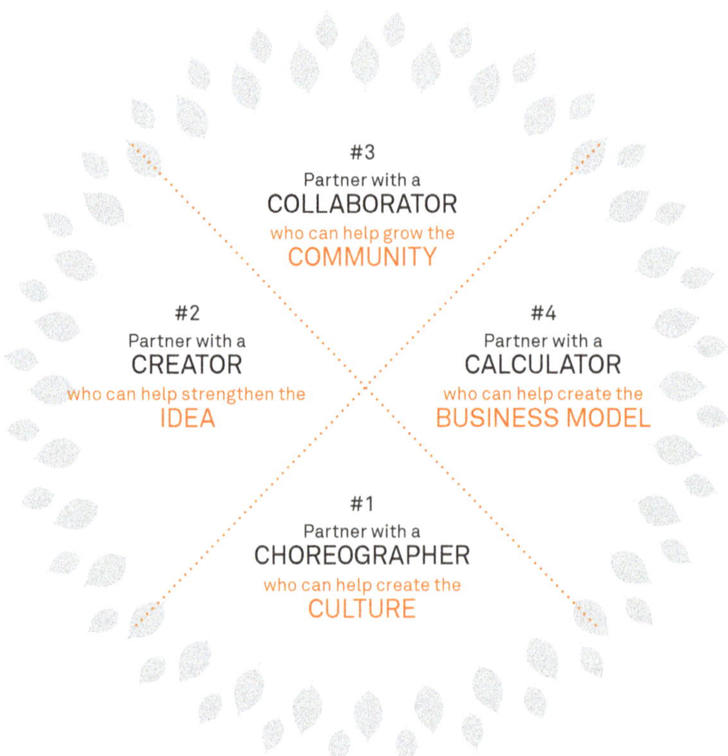

The Gestation Period

Masterpieces are rarely recognized immediately. In fact, they only become a Masterpiece when others recognize them as such. Van Gogh and Tesla both died before their greatest Masterpieces were recognized. This is partly because Masterpieces are one step ahead of their time. However, it is mainly because Creators doubt themselves and too often attempt to do it alone.

There is always a gestation period between the moment of creation and the moment of recognition. With new life, we know this human gestation period is around nine-and-a-half months. With a Masterpiece, it can be immediate or extended by years.

For instance, Picasso's *Guernica* was recognized immediately. It touched a raw nerve. He painted it in 1937, at the height of his powers, in response to the aerial bombing of a small town in Northern Spain. His intention was to fuel anti-fascist sentiment and prevent war. It was displayed at the World Fair later that year in Paris and immediately afterwards went on a two-year world tour. On the other hand, Van Gogh's Masterpieces were recognized ten years after he died.

Collaboration with other Artist Profiles is the key to reducing the gestation period from creation to recognition. Your art helps others grow. It serves them. And by serving them it serves you.

Collaboration inside and out

Collaboration is more important than ever. In 1905, Albert Einstein published his paper on the special theory of relativity, challenging the Newtonian assumption that time and space were fixed entities. To do so, he worked alone, even if he built his work from other people's ideas. To create a breakthrough of a similar proportion in physics today takes hundreds, if not thousands of people. For instance, over 3,000 scientists from around the world worked on the Atlas Experiment at CERN to find the Higgs-Boson particle in 2012.

You can either collaborate with others outside you, or collaborate with different aspects of *you*, by changing your relationship to the things that stop you. I do both. When you accept and reintegrate the various aspects of yourself you have repressed, you become whole again. You remove your (co)dependence on anything outside you.

How do you know if it's your Masterpiece?

- Your Masterpiece elevates you
- It helps you rebalance your health
- You experience love
- It generates true wealth

If it doesn't, it is unlikely to be a Masterpiece yet.

This is an infinite journey to constantly resolve what stops you from becoming you. Inner balance leads to outer balance and vice versa. It is an infinite loop between the Artist and the Art Director. In pursuing this journey, you radically reduce the gestation period between an idea's creation and its recognition by the world. You remove the doubt that all too often brings a Masterpiece to a grinding halt. In the process, you open the door to true collaboration with the world outside you.

A Masterpiece contains and balances all four elements of the Artist Profile. It must. And yet, all too often, we forget to recognize or involve those who can help us bring our Masterpiece to life. We become so absorbed with our own creation we neglect its realization. This path is unsustainable. It leads to exhaustion and burnout as Van Gogh and Nikola Tesla discovered to their cost. Rather than partner, we attempt to do it alone, and the gestation period extends often indefinitely.

The Cycle of Life

A Masterpiece follows the same cycle as life itself. The linear perception we have of time is an illusion. Everything in nature moves in cycles: a day is one rotation of our planet; a month is one rotation of the moon around our planet, and a year is one rotation of our planet around the Sun. We are not separate from this system. We are part of it. When our bodies are in harmony, they mirror the cycles around us. Each day we follow a cycle of sleep, creation, expansion, contraction and back to sleep. Each month and each year, our bodies follow a similar cycle. This is the cycle of life. New life is born, grows, creates value for its ecosystem and regenerates or dies. It goes on and on. It is one endless infinite cycle of life. Your life is just one infinitesimally small part of this cycle.

Yet, in our headlong rush to get ahead, we have forgotten the cycle of life. Instead of respecting it, we suppress it. The cycle of life is currently out of balance. More life is dying than any other point in the history of our planet. Species are becoming extinct at one hundred to one thousand times the average rate and are expected to increase to 10,000 times.

We ignore the natural cycles outside us, because we ignore the natural cycles inside us. We keep on pushing and pushing and pushing in one vicious cycle: from idea to growth—from creation to expansion—from Spring to Summer—and back again—without slowing down enough to wait for the harvest, let alone stop to regenerate ourselves in winter. Since the invention of the lightbulb, we have pushed ourselves so far beyond our limits that we are more out of tune with our natural cycles than ever.

Is it a surprise then, that our seasons are increasingly following the same pattern? I think not. In those parts of the world where four seasons exist, we seem to be moving from Spring to Summer and back again. In the Alps where I live, Winter is shorter and there is less and less snow year on year. We are not separate from this climate; we are part of it. We create it. If we want to change our climate, we need to change ourselves. When we slow down enough to regenerate ourselves, we regenerate our planet too. Your Masterpiece is your fruit. It is your chance to rebalance this cycle and make a worthwhile contribution.

Creating your Masterpiece also follows a cycle. From when the idea is waiting to emerge, through to when it starts to grow, to its first blossoms, to the harvest before cycling back around and regenerating again. The Masterpiece grows to the next level. We can map this journey against the relationships we need to change within us and the Artist Profiles we need to partner with outside us.

Growing Your Masterpiece

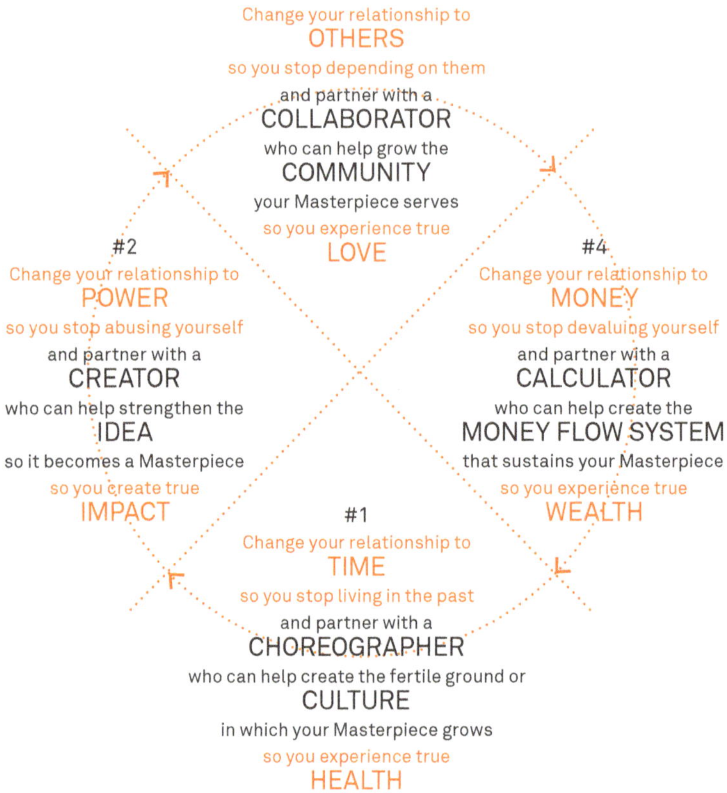

From a seed to an ecosystem

For a seed to grow into a forest it must go through hundreds, if not thousands of cycles. The oldest tree in the world is over 9,000 years old. Trees take their time. They start to grow when the conditions are right for them. Eventually, they grow into trees and then forests. Forests maximize the potential of all trees within them to live longer and produce more fruit.

Growing the ecosystem

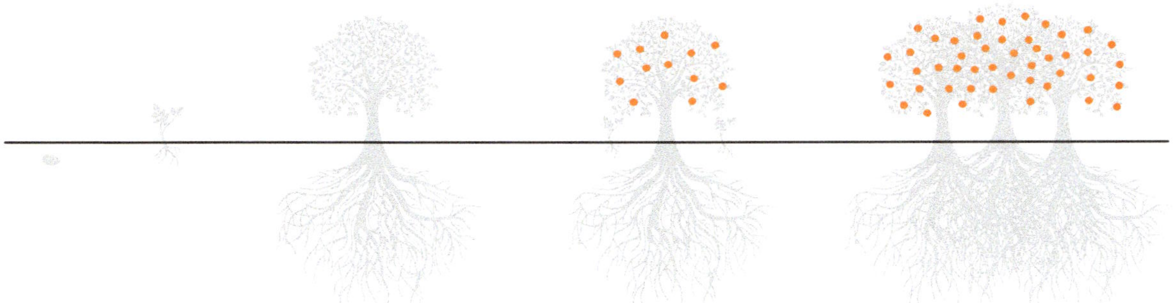

	Seed	*Sapling*	*Tree*	*Copse*	*Forest*
Status	Inactive - potential hidden	Growing - blown in all directions	Superficial success Susceptible to storms	Producing fruit Doing too much / overshadowing	Producing lots of fruit Lacks true meaning
Solution	**Identify Imbalance**	**Articulate Purpose**	**Create Masterpiece**	**Cultivate Ecosystem**	**Change environment**

Seed

A seed may lie inactive, underground for decades, even if its purpose is to grow into a forest. It waits and it waits, and it waits. It must find fertile ground, a culture that nurtures it and provides it with the right support. To begin with, it is inert. Nothing happens. All of its potential is hidden underground. But inside, new life is getting ready to emerge.

For us to shift from inactivity to growth, we must acknowledge and accept the fears that stop us from becoming who we are. We must nurture and cultivate our own fertile ground within us.

When the conditions are right, the seed germinates. It bursts through its encapsulating shell and starts to grow. And its first action is to grow downwards, to create its roots, not upwards. Only once it has a solid base on which to grow does it start to grow up. The first few days or weeks are spent underground. There is no light. The seed doesn't know for certain if it is heading in the right direction. It simply trusts the process of unfoldment. Then, at a certain point, it bursts through into the sunlight. However, just because it has emerged does not mean it will survive. This is the start of a whole other journey.

The seedling's interaction with its immediate environment and broader ecosystem determines its chances of survival. It needs a combination of fertile soil, water, nutrients, sunlight, and connection with its own species and others to grow to its full potential: a balance of the world above ground and the world below ground.

Sapling

As the seedling grows into a sapling, it is at the mercy of the elements and other species. It can easily be blown around by its environment or attacked by other species. This is where the support of other more mature trees is so important. Other trees can provide support and direction, because they have already been there. For us to make the shift from being blown around to growing strong enough, we need to articulate our Purpose—the life force that flows from the ground beneath us, through our roots, into our trunk, up our body, and out into the world. We must do this before starting to create our Masterpiece.

Then, we need to identify and accept the fears that block the growth of our roots underground. These fears are the rocks and stony ground that prevent our roots from growing deeper and therefore our canopy from growing higher. If we don't remove them or, at the very least, become aware of them, we prevent ourselves from reaching our full potential. And more importantly we are not playing our part in creating the canopy that supports all of us. As a result, other trees have to fill the gap in the canopy left by our absence—by our selfishness. What stops us from doing this is fear—the fear that we will not be promoted, seen, accepted or valued by others. But when we surface our fears—we literally bring them above ground—they magically evaporate, like water exposed to heat. Darkness disappears when we shine a light on it.

Trees

Trees that reach their full potential collaborate with other trees. Some species of tree emit fragrances above ground to warn their neighbors of the imminent danger of predators. For instance, in Africa the acacia tree can produce toxins to stop giraffes from eating it. When it is being attacked, it emits a smell which allows other trees in its close vicinity to do the same. Other species communicate underground via their roots, often using fungi as an intermediary.

In a forest, trees are interdependent. For instance, all trees that connect to each other photosynthesize at exactly the same speed, even if some trees are more mature and have more leaves than others. In other words, they share the sugars and nutrients between them to ensure everyone in their ecosystem gets what they need when they need it. They do this, because trees are stronger together: they can store more water together than they can alone; and they can also regulate their climate. Those that support each other are most likely to grow to their full potential and live longer.

And yet, even in a forest, there are some loners, trees that don't appear to share their gifts with their neighbors. These trees appear to have superficial success above ground. They may grow quite high, but their fruit is limited. They don't produce their "Masterpiece," and they often struggle to sustain themselves. These trees receive the least support from others within their ecosystem. All of us know "trees" like this. On the surface, everything looks like it is growing in harmony, but underground, there is a problem. The roots are superficial. The tree is isolated. And when a storm hits, it is often the first to be blown over.

Trees that grow alone on mountain tops where they are most visible, live shorter lives and are less likely to reach their full potential than trees that grow in lush forests and are part of an ecosystem that supports itself.

For us to make the shift from isolation to connection, we learn to appreciate that our Masterpiece is not how we are seen and appreciated, but how we serve others within our ecosystem.

Copse

Healthy trees interact with other species. To produce fruit, they invite pollinators above ground to flit around and cross-pollinate their initial offerings and below ground they encourage unseen species to nurture the culture and retain its fertility. The right combination of these forces inside and out helps the tree grow to its full potential and maximize its produce.

However, as we start to produce our own fruit, we often overshadow our neighbors inadvertently. Rather than nurturing young saplings, who can strengthen our ecosystem and attract more species to pollinate all of us, we try to grow as fast as we can. We overshadow others. Our intention is to show how amazing we are. But in so doing, we stop others from showing how amazing they are. If we limit our neighbors, we limit ourselves.

A shared canopy benefits every tree in the ecosystem. It creates a microclimate beneath the canopy that reduces water evaporation, retains more minerals, sugars and nutrients and attracts more species. For us to make the shift from overshadowing others to elevating others to their full potential, we learn to appreciate that nurturing our ecosystem, even if we can't see any immediate gain is more important than a quick gain. We play the long game. We stop trying to demonstrate how amazing we are and instead help others to become as amazing as they are. We do this by focusing ruthlessly on what we love, across all trees in the forest and enabling others to do the same. This way, together, we produce more fruit.

Forest

Trees don't grow constantly throughout a cycle. They grow in Spring and Summer to produce fruit and then in Autumn, encourage other species to harvest their fruit so they expand the ecosystem that sustains them organically. At the end of each cycle, trees stop growing. After the harvest, they stop pushing upwards and outwards. They rest, refocusing their lifeforce within. They allow the leaves which helped them to create their produce to fall. To the uninitiated, it appears they are dying in one brilliant, beautiful, blaze of color. But we know, from experience, most trees do this at the end of every cycle. They regenerate themselves and get ready for the next cycle. They appear to die but are really being reborn.

Throughout these endless cycles, it may appear that the tree depends on its environment and these other species for its survival. But the tree isn't consciously aware that it is separate from its environment. It is the ecosystem in which it exists. To a tree within a forest, there is no separation between it and other trees; there is no separation between it and other species; there is no separation between it and its climate. It is only the human brain that creates the illusion of separation. We label one thing a tree, another the ground, another sunlight and another the various species that support it. We separate ourselves from our true nature rather than accepting who we are—an integral part of an ecosystem. The fate of everything in an ecosystem is inextricably intertwined. As it grows and expands, the ecosystem benefits more and more from the investment it made in a single seed's growth. It works in harmony to maximize value for all. And the secret to its success lies underground. Above ground the leaves may intermingle, but below ground the roots intertwine, sharing information, nutrients and sugars so every part of the ecosystem benefits.

This is how a forest shapes its environment. Think of a rainforest. It induces rain to nurture and sustain the entire ecosystem. If we cut down or remove too much of our ecosystem, the whole ecosystem collapses and we have to start again.

Creating an entire ecosystem like this takes time. A mature forest may take centuries or millennia to grow to its full potential. This is the gestation period. We don't have centuries. We don't even have decades. We only have a few cycles.

> *The best time to plant a tree was twenty years ago, the second-best time is now.*
>
> **Chinese proverb**

Choreographers help create Cultures that nurture Masterpieces

For an idea to grow into a Masterpiece it must find fertile ground, a nurturing culture which provides the support the idea needs for it to break through the encapsulating shell of other people's expectations. If you are not a Choreographer, partner with someone who is. I did—and the result was a breakthrough.

One of my partners, Tamami Ushiki, is a Choreographer. Her art is creating the business model and culture that bring ideas to life. She has created the largest series of education programs for entrepreneurs and spiritual seekers in Japan very successfully. She brought my Legacy Retreat (the forerunner to the #Masterpiece program) to Japan to help participants create their Masterpiece.

"Above ground" in the Outer Game, her greatest contribution was to realize the program would grow fastest if we trained a series of Purpose Facilitators, who would take the work into companies and other communities when I wasn't there. She created the system to scale my idea.

"Below ground" in the space between the Inner Game and the Outer Game, she believed in me. Her belief in me grew my belief in myself. She integrated my Masterpiece into her Masterpiece and I integrated her Masterpiece into mine. This grew both my Masterpiece and hers. We helped each other to balance both our Inner and Outer Games.

But she didn't just help me. She also brought energy healer Master Choa; the wealth creation program Money & You; and Roger James Hamilton—the founder of the largest community of entrepreneurs in the world, to Japan. She didn't create these ideas. Her art is choreographing events behind the scenes to nurture these ideas. People are drawn to her. Everyone wants to work with her including some of the most famous coaches in the world.

If you can't find a Choreographer to partner with outside you, and ones with the right mindset are very rare, partner with the Choreographer inside you. To do this, change your relationship to time. Stop pushing constantly. Stop reacting to events in the world outside you and connect to the world inside you. Hibernate, if that's what it takes. Every year, Bill Gates takes himself away for a week to a cabin on a lake in the middle of nowhere. No internet, no phone, nothing. He uses this time to read, reflect and regenerate.

When we take time to truly reflect, we become present. We stop living in the past, reacting to present events based on our past experiences. We see how much time we waste, running around in tight circles, reacting to this post, that email, or that phone call without stopping to examine why. When we do, we realize the only impact we have is on us—on our health. And it is negative. As one of my clients, Dr Garth Brink, puts it in *Time* his upcoming book: "To be well requires my time to be spent well."

When we change our relationship to time, we stop resisting time and start embracing it. We partner with our inner Choreographer, break out of our own encapsulating shell and create a culture that can nurture our health and our Masterpiece.

Creators create ideas that become Masterpieces

For an idea to grow into a Masterpiece it must emerge and become strong enough to serve its ecosystem. If you are not a Creator, partner with someone one who is to help you clarify and strengthen your idea. I am a Creator. So is Peter Koenig, who I have mentioned throughout this book.

Koenig creates idea after idea. His first Masterpiece, *Moneywork*, emerged during his work with corporations in the 1980s. He realized what stopped leaders from doing what they were called to do was their relationship to money. This led him to study our relationship to money in depth, develop a tool that would help to free us from our money constraints and write a book that encapsulated his thinking: *30 Lies about Money.*[45]

He built on this work with his second Masterpiece which explores what founders do to create and manifest their Masterpieces. He calls it "Sourcework." If we think of a Founder like the conductor of an orchestra, then the players are his products, the audience is his community, the music is the culture he creates, and the connections between all these components is the business model. The music ties everything together. Sourcework points out there can only ever be one conductor of an orchestra. Peter calls this the "Source." When the founder is still actively involved in the business, it's relatively easy to work out who the Source is. When he leaves, it becomes harder.

What makes Peter's work brilliant is how he encourages others to integrate his Masterpieces into their Masterpieces. He infuses his magic into their magic. In the process, both become more magical. This creates a legacy that will live long after Peter stops. He has created his own tools (individual players) which combine into one system (the orchestra) based on an underlying culture (the music) that unites everyone harmoniously. Peter estimates there are as many as two hundred individuals all over the world, who are integrating his Masterpieces into their Masterpieces. Some of them integrate the tools. Others integrate the entire system. Some just take the philosophy itself. Everything Peter does is a direct reflection of his Personal Purpose: *enable everyone to spring back on track so we love what we do.*

45 Koenig, Peter. *30 Lies About Money: liberating your life, liberating your money*. iUniverse Inc, 4 November 2003.

If you are a Creator, your biggest challenge is focusing your inner artist long enough for your work to become a Masterpiece. Michelangelo spent four years working on the statue of David, his first Masterpiece. He then spent another four years working on the Sistine Chapel, his second Masterpiece. Four years! We can't even focus for four hours on a single project. This is why the first step to creating your Masterpiece is creating the Culture within which the idea can grow, not the idea itself.

The challenge with focusing your time on any one project is knowing which project to focus on. Imagine a cylinder made of glass. Next to it is a jug of water, a few rocks, a heap of sand, and a pile of smaller stones. Everything in front of you will fit in the cylinder, but only in the right order. What do you put in first? The sand, the water, the stones, or the rocks? Ponder this for a moment.

The solution is to start with the rocks and to fit the stones around them at the same time, then the sand, and finally the water. Remember water flows around rocks. The same is true in life. But how often do we focus on the water and the sand rather than the rocks and the stones? How often are you easily distracted by something when your Masterpiece is waiting for you?

Overcome the distractions and stop wasting time. The secret to doing this is simple. Focus on one or two big rocks (both professional and personal), fit the stones around the rocks as you do this, then let the sand and the water flow around them effortlessly. Focus on the big things and everything else flows around it.

Creating a Masterpiece doesn't need to be hard work or take long hours. We have transcended the protestant need for perspiration. The work we need to do today is emotional. To paraphrase Thomas Edison: today, creating your Masterpiece is one percent intuition and ninety-nine percent emotion. The less effort you put in, the more intuitive you can be. It is a virtuous circle. And it starts by you listening to you.

> *Creativity takes courage.*
>
> **Henri Matisse**

If you can't find a Creator to collaborate with—and there are plenty—change your relationship to Power. Stop abusing yourself and saying you're not doing it right. You are an artist too. The world needs to hear your voice. Start meditating, join a singing class or write a journal. When you reclaim your true power, your inner Art Director focuses your inner Artist on creating and strengthening the Masterpiece that will have the most impact on your Purpose.

Collaborators create the Community the Masterpiece serves

For an idea to be recognized as a Masterpiece, it must transform the ecosystem in which it operates by serving its Community's true needs. Collaborators will help you create and nurture that community. If you aren't a Collaborator, partner with one or two. I do.

Remember Kari I mentioned at the beginning of the book? Kari is a Collaborator. Her Masterpiece is called United Cities. United Cities is on a mission to transform businesses so they contribute to the communities in which they operate (cities) and in doing so achieve The United Nations Sustainable Development Goals. After twenty years working in the United Nations, Kari realized something wasn't right. She wasn't creating the impact she intended, so she left to lead a community of 400 CEOs, all of whom were interested in contributing to the UN's goals. However she struggled to generate funding, so pushed herself harder to breakthrough. She played to her strengths: charming Foreign Ministers and CEOs, and delivering talks all over the world to thousands of people. Everyone fell in love with her—but she still struggled to generate money. She created tools, but didn't have products for her community to invest in. Everyone loved the idea, but there was no business model to generate the revenue.

The problem was, while Kari exuded love on the surface, she didn't love herself enough to stop and take care of herself and regenerate. She was running on empty. Her inner world was incongruent with the outer world she wanted to create. Above ground, the tree was growing branch after branch, but below ground the soil was becoming exhausted—drained of the minerals and nutrients it needed to keep growing. The tree was in danger of falling over, let alone producing fruit. There was nothing to harvest. Kari was running the feminine vicious cycle, codependent on others. By ignoring her inner voice she remained disconnected from her true self and wasn't able to fulfill her Purpose.

Kari broke through when she rebalanced the world inside her. She returned to her roots and refocused on her Purpose: *to inspire love so we all accept who we truly are.*

The first turning point was a speech to hundreds of participants she gave in her home city of Älesund in Norway on the Sustainable Development Goals. Everyone was in awe. I was there. We could feel it. It wasn't only what Kari said, it was how she said it that mattered. She brought her philosophy to life. She embodied her Purpose. Then, she and her team attended one of our retreats in the mountains above Chamonix in France and she stopped trying to do everything to chase the money. She created the space for a team member to grow the community in Norway. The third and final turning point was when she started to take care of herself. Rather than constantly pushing herself to complete more and more meetings in an endless vicious cycle that created a culture of dependency, she stopped for a moment. In that moment, she rediscovered her own brilliance: the ability to manifest an entirely different reality. When Kari stopped and refocused her energy, she attracted Calculators and Creators to create the business model and products. Banks started to offer her millions of dollars in funding. So did governments and philanthropists. CEOs clamored to support her program. When Kari stopped pushing, the Universe started pulling for her. A whole team formed around her and started bringing her Masterpiece to life.

Your Masterpiece emerges in the darkness, deep within. It is a calling that you cannot refuse. You may ignore it, again and again. But if you refuse it repeatedly, you create resistance that impacts your health, your wealth and your relationship to others.

If you can't find a Collaborator to partner with—and there are plenty of amazing Collaborators—change your relationship to others. As we discussed in the last chapter, stop (co)depending on others to be accepted. Accept yourself. You are good enough. Observe yourself in those closest to you. Identify what you resist most in them, and change it in yourself. Learn everything you can about yourself, through them. When you change your relationship to others, and partner with the Collaborator inside, your love attracts the community which needs your Masterpiece most and you experience true love.

Calculators make the Masterpiece sustainable

For an idea to become a Masterpiece it must be sustainable. It must generate value for its ecosystem and itself. Calculators help you create the business model that ensures your Masterpiece sustains itself. If you don't know a Calculator, collaborate with one. I do. He's my accountant.

Another of my partners is speaker, author and intrapreneur, Gib Bulloch, who is predominately a Calculator and a Choreographer. Like Tamami, he doesn't actually coach. He creates the business model and culture to enable others to bring his vision to life. His Masterpiece is Scotland's first business decelerator, Craigberoch. The purpose of the decelerator is to help business leaders to slow down, reconnect to themselves and create innovation that will tackle the world's biggest challenges. The bonus is it also helps to regenerate these businesses and businesses on The Isle of Bute, where he was born and founded the initiative.

Gib created a business model that brings together a unique cast of Creators and Collaborators—artists, improv practitioners, neuroscientists and coaches, to help the participants slow down and think differently. Like my other partners, Gib had to go on his own journey for Craigberoch to emerge through him. His first Masterpiece was Accenture Development Partnerships (ADP), the not-for-profit arm of the largest consultancy company in the world, Accenture. He grew this into a quarter billion-dollar business with a smart business model that shared the risk and reward between his clients, Accenture, and those who volunteered to work for ADP. However, after a decade, Gib came to a crossroads. He knew something needed to change—which turned out to be him.

For a breakthrough to emerge, we often need to breakdown first. Gib did, literally. He documented his journey in his first book, *Intrapreneur: Confessions of a corporate insurgent.*[46] After trying Sufi spinning during a retreat in India, he awakened the artist inside him and started to have insight after insight. He returned home with a dangerously high fever which lasted a few days. But after it subsided, the insights continued to come. He couldn't find the "off" switch. Within days, his body burned out and he ended up in a mental asylum for a week. Following this experience, Accenture made him redundant. After attending Peter Koenig's course and my Legacy Retreat, his Masterpiece—The Craigberoch Business Decelerator—started to emerge. Craigberoch is a direct reflection of Gib's Purpose: *to unleash the power of purpose to create a sustainable business revolution.*

If you can't find a Calculator to collaborate with, change your relationship to money. As we discussed in the last chapter, stop depending on money to feel free or secure. Start feeling free and secure independent of money. You are worth it.

46 Bulloch, Gib. *The Intrapreneur: Confessions of a corporate insurgent*. Unbound, London, 5 April 2018.

Identify what you associate with money and free yourself from this association. When you change your relationship to money, you partner with your inner Calculator and start to generate true wealth.

Corporates: Start with the Culture

Attempting to create a Masterpiece without continually doing the inner work to nurture yourself will compromise your Masterpiece. The taller a tree grows, the deeper its roots need to be and the more it needs trees of a similar stature around it to weather the strongest storm. If you don't deepen your roots or surround yourself with similar trees, at the very least, you will create a culture that is codependent on you. And at most, your Masterpiece will be blown away by the storm or even worse you will create unintended ripples that continue to unbalance the planet.

Both Steve Jobs at Apple and Elon Musk at Tesla did the inner work to create multiple Masterpieces, but not enough work to create cultures that freed others to do the same. They stopped short of helping others to articulate their Purpose and bring it to life. They imposed their way and created a culture dependent on them.

The easiest way to create a sustainable culture is to start from scratch. However, there is an alternative if that culture has become as exhausted as Kari. Simply, return to the roots. Look at the founder's original philosophy and create a Mission and Values that embody those beliefs. Then, align the culture with it.

Culture is the collective mindset. You can't change a culture. You can't change someone's mindset either. But you can give them the keys and show them the map. It's remarkable what happens when you give someone a choice.

> *You are the culture you are trying to change.*
>
> **Bob Adams and Bill Andersen**

Apple

Companies like Apple and Tesla create innovative products which transform industries. In the process they generate significant profits for their company. Above ground, these companies create phenomenal products, communities of raving fans and business models that generate eye-watering growth, but underground the culture is insufficient to sustain them. The components above ground are enough to create Masterpieces, but when their Founder dies or moves on to the next creation, the innovation which was their lifeblood—dies. The product is just the most visible fruit on the tree. But the entire tree is needed in order to continually bear fruit. The iPhone, its successor the iPad, and its predecessor, the iPod, transformed seven industries: communications, computing, music, photography, filmmaking, television, and banking. Today, up to 80% of Apple's revenue comes from the iPhone and the iPad. Combined they helped Apple become the first company valued at more than one-trillion dollars. However, the company remains over dependent on these innovations which were the brainchild of one man, Steve Jobs. He was the Founder, and therefore the "Source" of Apple.

Since Jobs' death, Apple has not produced an innovation that has had a similar seismic impact to the iPhone or iPad. Some commentators would point to the Apple Watch, which has become the most popular watch in the world. However, Apple sold 2.2 billion iPhones and over 350 million iPads in the first ten years, compared to 100 million Apples watches in the first five years after launch. However, if Jobs hadn't created a community of raving fans and an innovative business model, based on flagship, zen-like stores, online sales, iconic advertising and world-class instore customer support, how many watches would Apple have sold?

Jobs' final Masterpiece was the doughnut-shaped global Headquarters that he helped design in Cupertino, California. He intended it to shape a culture where people would mix and innovation would emerge, just like he had done at Pixar, the animation company he also led. However, he created Apple from scratch with a culture that depended on him, whereas he became CEO of Pixar, which had a culture which was independent of him. Above ground, it appears that Apple is doing at least as well as Pixar after Jobs died. But underground, the culture tells a different story. Apple isn't producing more fruit, because its roots died with Jobs.

Tesla

Like the iPhone, Tesla's Model 3 is transforming industries. Tesla started by launching the Tesla Roadster, the world's fastest accelerating car to catch public attention. It then launched the Tesla Model S, the world's best car according to the reviews, to attract the luxury market. And then, it launched the Model 3 – the world's most valuable car if you compare features and price. All three Masterpieces supported Tesla's original Mission: to accelerate the transition to sustainable transport. To do this, Tesla recreated the concept of a car from scratch, building it around a battery and a computer rather than around a combustion engine and adding a computer as an afterthought. This makes a Tesla the world's most advanced and sustainable car. Like Apple, its philosophy or culture goes way beyond simply producing a product.

Tesla extended this philosophy to its business model. It turned conventional business thinking upside down: creating flagship stores that don't sell, employing salespeople that don't sell anything either and spending $0 on advertising. You can't buy a Tesla offline. You can only order it online, and the people in the stores are only there to organize a test drive and answer your questions. Instead of expensive advertising, Tesla relies entirely on the media, their non-sales salesforce and word-of-mouth to get their message out. As a result, Tesla became the fastest growing car company in history.

But Elon Musk, its CEO, didn't stop there. This was just phase one. He understood the fundamental problem is how electricity is produced, not how electricity is used. So, in 2017, he pivoted the company to focus on a new mission: accelerate the transition to sustainable energy. He launched two more Masterpieces—generating electricity via solar tiles and storing the electricity in an enormous rechargeable battery that could be housed at home. Musk did this by merging Solar City, another company he led with Tesla. He continues to create more Masterpieces at Tesla in the form of cars and trucks that target different markets.

However, like Apple, Tesla is overly dependent on one man. If Elon Musk died, innovation would dry up at Tesla just like at Apple. Like Apple and Google before it, Tesla would probably revert from the Create model to the Compete model. In other words, it would shift from dependence on one individual to dependence on an organizational structure.

We need a new type of artist in the corporate world, one who creates cultures that produce Masterpieces independently of them. We need to grow entire woods and sustainable ecosystems rather than lone trees on isolated hilltops. One will sustain entire communities indefinitely, the other will collapse when the tree dies. This requires the leader to dig deeper and deeper roots, by reclaiming suppressed aspects that stop partnership internally or externally. According to their biographers, neither Jobs nor Musk found peace. Instead, both flipped back and forth between moments of God-like brilliance (pure creation) and moments when they appear to think they are God (bullying).

HP Inc.

The good news is, I have had the privilege of working with a number of inspirational leaders within corporations who are helping to create sustainable ecosystems that produce Masterpieces. They are quite literally taking these companies back to their roots. Nate Hurst, HP Inc's former Chief Sustainability Officer is one of these leaders. Dave Hewlett and Bill Packard created Hewlett Packard, the printer and computer giant that founded Silicon Valley, in 1939, on the principle of serving the communities in which it operated.

> *Why are we here? I think many people assume, wrongly, that a company exists solely to make money. Money is an important part of a company's existence, if the company is any good. But a result is not a cause. We have to go deeper and find the real reason for our being.*
>
> **Dave Packard**

However, soon after Hewlett and Packard stepped down from the board in the 1990s, the company lost its way. The principles on which the founders had grown the company to be the largest technology company in the world were suppressed. Meg Whitman, who had taken over the helm, was forced by the market to divide the company in two: HP Enterprise, a business-to-business company, and HP Inc. a consumer electronics company.

I met Hurst in 2017, just after the dust had settled from the separation. He already had an idea what he wanted to do but didn't know how to align his team or get them to step up so he could step up. We ended up running two workshops in Silicon Valley. In the first, we helped his boss and her team to articulate their Personal Purpose. Six months later, we did the same with Hurst's team. We also helped them to create a Collective Mission, the Masterpiece, Value Proposition and three-year roadmap to bring it to life. Around the time we ran the workshop, HP Inc. produced its first sustainable Masterpiece—a printer cartridge made entirely from recycled plastic. The plastic came from bottles in Haiti. Recycling them provided work for many who had lost loved ones or their jobs during the earthquake.

Hurst built on this opening. He commissioned a film to tell Renatte's story. Renatte lost her husband during the earthquake and was left alone to bring up their five children. Recycling bottles helped her get back on her feet. She was able to buy a house and look after her children. Hurst used the film to persuade HP's executive and strategic boards to integrate Key Performance Indicators into their day-to-day management. Next, they produced the world's most sustainable laptop—the HP Elite Dragonfly. Admittedly, only part of its speaker was made of recycled plastic. But Hurst and his bosses had a bigger vision. They see sustainability as a journey. They have plans to produce the first entirely recycled laptop by 2025.

HP isn't stopping there. They are focusing their energy on 3D printing, because it has the potential to reverse the most worrying byproducts of the Industrial Revolution. The Industrial Revolution centralized production in the hands of the few who owned factories. It raped the planet of raw materials, led to complex and unsustainable supply chains, which crisscrossed the planet and suppressed creativity by turning farmers into factory workers. 3D printing enables everyone to produce what they need, where they need it, when they need. It unleashes creativity, reduces distribution costs and has the potential to be far more sustainable.

Hurst helped HP Inc. reimagine itself by rediscovering and reinterpreting its roots and culture in a way that was relevant to addressing today's challenges. HP Inc. is reinventing itself to serve the communities in which it operates once again. Thanks to Hurst, the founder of Silicon Valley was back, leading the HP way again.

With his job done, Hurst moved on to take up a new role at Wells Fargo, the world's fourth largest bank. Imagine if he could do something similar in the financial world!

Patagonia

> *Doing the right thing ended up making us more money... you've got to reinvent capitalism altogether. It leads to a whole bunch of poor people and a few extremely rich people. Ultimately, capitalism is going to lose its customers. There won't be* anybody to buy the product because everybody is going to be so poor.[47]
>
> **Yvon Chouinard**

47 Beer, Jeff. Fast Company, "Exclusive: Patagonia founder Yvon Chouinard talks about the sustainability myth, the problem with Amazon—and why it's not too late to save the planet." Published online 16th October 2019. Retrieved online: November 4, 2020.

Patagonia's culture grew out of Chouinard's love for the mountains, experiences, and philosophy: do what you love, design the most elegant, effective and environmentally friendly products, then hire your friends and family to help. He saw there was an absence of good climbing clothing and embarked on solving that; a mission that would become his Purpose.

For Chouinard, his experiences in nature taught him to eat lower down the food chain, play hard, but never exceed his limits and be true to himself. Climbing, surfing, kayaking and fly fishing were all pathways for him on his inwards journey to discover his true self—and create a culture with deep roots. Instead of adding more, Chouinard decided to be more. He believes if we produce and own good quality, well designed and repairable products, they can last a lifetime. Which is why sustaining our planet has been at the heart of everything Chouinard does. In fact, when he realized the metal spikes or pitons his first company manufactured to stop climbers from falling were damaging the rock faces, he changed what he produced and started a campaign for "clean"' climbing. Clean climbers don't leave a mark on the way up so others find the climb in the same pristine state.

When he launched Patagonia, he started it based on the same culture. Patagonia combines the best of both worlds. Its bottom line is its impact on the environment, not its profit. In fact, Patagonia has removed itself from the constraints of the financial operating system. It remains a privately-owned family company. Every time Patagonia makes a decision for environmental reasons, from removing polystyrene cups, or recycling cardboard at its head office, to sourcing only organic cotton for its t-shirts or and ensuring its second level suppliers such as mills adhere to the highest standards of employment, Patagonia's profits increases. For Chouinard, profit is a by-product of doing good business. And the company invests ten percent of that profit or one percent of its revenue into environmental causes, whichever is the higher.

When Patagonia hit a crisis in 1989, Chouinard reinforced this culture. It led him to articulate Patagonia's mission publicly. Up until that point, the company had been growing consistently and rapidly and was well on its way to becoming a billion-dollar company. But as soon as its growth stuttered, it became painfully obvious that Patagonia, like just about every other company, had become addicted to growth. It had overextended itself. But more importantly, like HP Inc. it had lost sight of the values on which the founder had created it. The crisis led Chouinard and his leadership team to some awkward navel gazing. What did they want from Patagonia? Why were they in business? What did they believe in? What emerged was Patagonia's mission and the impetus to develop an inspirational, sustainable model based on its culture that would ultimately inspire other businesses to follow: "Make the best product, cause no unnecessary harm, and use business to inspire and implement solutions to the environmental crisis," said Chouinard. More recently, he updated and simplified Patagonia's purpose to: *We're in business to save our home planet.*

Articulating the mission helped to reinforce the culture. Before the crisis, Patagonia's leadership team were constantly trying to organize teams into boxes. Afterwards they implemented a more organic structure that enabled people to collaborate more effectively between teams and allowed individuals to take ownership of what they do in small self-organizing teams, akin to the Collaborate model described in Chapter 4. Chouinard understood talented people will not do something because they are told to do it. They avoid it until they own it.

Like Tesla, Patagonia does not rely on marketing, it involves its community. Perhaps, most importantly, the culture creates resilience. Rather become a lone tree on a hilltop, Chouinard has created an ecosystem that can weather the strongest storms. During the Great Recession of 2007-2012, when other clothing manufacturers were struggling, Patagonia increased its revenue by twenty-five percent. The majority of its Masterpieces don't come from him, they come from within the company. That is true sustainability. That's Chouinard's art.

> *We want people who, once they buy into a decision and believe in what they are doing, will work like demons to produce something of the highest possible quality... Since we can't order our employees around, either they have to be convinced that they are doing is right, or they have to see for themselves it's right.*[48]
>
> **Yvon Chouinard**

48 Chouinard, Yvon. *Let My People Go Surfing: The Education of a Reluctant Businessman—Including 10 More Years of Business Unusual*. Penguin Books; Updated 2nd edition (6 September 2016). P 177.

Creating the wood to support you

It's time to stop growing isolated trees on mountain tops. The view may be spectacular, but the effort to remain standing when the storms come isn't worth it. And the storms will increase over the next few years. It's time to create entire ecosystems that nurture all of us.

To cultivate a "wood" that supports you, enable others to create Masterpieces at least as high as your Masterpiece and ensure the culture is conducive to their growth. The higher the trees surrounding you, the more likely all the trees in the wood, including your own, will weather the storm.

Trees that grow together sway in harmony when the wind increases—their leaves mingle in one movement. If you look at a wood from above in a breeze, it's hard to tell one tree's leaves from another tree's leaves. Trees don't resist the wind. They move in harmony with it. To the trees, there is no separation between them and the wind. Both are part of the same ecosystem.

As a wood grows, it influences its own ecosystem. Each tree reinforces the others. The leaves are only the most visible part of their collaboration. The real collaboration is occurring underground. Roots intertwine, strengthening each tree's foundation. Trees don't worry whether there will be enough water or minerals to share between them. They create their own ecosystem around them. Mature trees support younger trees and attract other species to join them in a self-reinforcing loop. When trees come together like this, they literally change the weather, creating micro-climates that are conducive to their own growth. Think of rainforests. Their presence precipitates the rainfall needed for the ecosystem to thrive.

This is exactly what we are creating with WorldClass Academy. A few of us have come together to create an ecosystem that will nurture our Masterpieces and yours. It started with Tamami and I partnering to deliver The Legacy Retreat. I couldn't travel to Japan thanks to the COVID-19 travel restrictions. So, I delivered part of the program from my office in Switzerland via video conference. Tamami and her team delivered part of it in person in Tokyo. The outcome was way more powerful as a result of our collaboration. That got me thinking. Then Peter, Kari, Jean-Philippe Challandes (who specializes in changing our relationship to power) collaborated to deliver an online program, called 6 Days to Pivot. That led me to invite Gabriel Uribe (who specializes in turning the creation of Masterpieces into a daily practice) to join us.

What is emerging between us is an ecosystem designed to help you bring your Masterpiece to life. Each of us has our own Masterpiece. So we help each other strengthen our Masterpieces. And we run programs based on our Masterpieces that help you bring your Masterpiece to life. The more we partner, the stronger our roots become and the more our leaves intertwine. Our collaboration is already touching millions of lives. However, this isn't enough. Our intention is to change our ecosystem. Between us, we have a diverse range of experience and skills. What unites this diversity is the common mission I mentioned earlier—for **81% of us to love what we do by 1 July 2026**. If everyone loved what they did, our environment would change for good. This is why we are inviting the misfits, the crazy ones, the artists with wild ideas—anyone who has ever been rejected—and resonates with this mission to apply to join us. Because we think differently. We're the ones who change our world. And we need this more than ever.

Creating your Legacy

> *Only on the fringes of an ecosystem, those outer rings, do evolution and adaptation occur at a furious pace; the inner center of the system is where the entrenched, non-adapting species die off, doomed to failure by maintaining the status quo… only those businesses operating with a sense of urgency, dancing on the fringe, constantly evolving, open to diversity and new ways of doing things, are going to be here one hundred years from now.*[49]
>
> **Yvon Chouinard**

What were you born to create? What would you like to be known for after you leave? What impact would you like to have on the world? Your Legacy is how you will be remembered. It combines everything you think, say, and do. Yes, everything! We tend to be remembered both for our greatest Masterpiece and greatest flaws.

Everyone creates a legacy whether they like it or not. Martin Luther King is remembered for transforming racial segregation in the US and his extra-marital relations. Tiger Woods, the golfing great, is also remembered for having affairs. Vincent van Gogh's legacy is his sunflower paintings and cutting off his ear.

49 Chouinard, Yvon. *Let My People Go Surfing: The Education of a Reluctant Businessman—Including 10 More Years of Business Unusual*. Penguin Books; Updated 2nd edition (6 September 2016).

Sigmund Freud's is the unconscious and sexual repression. Nelson Mandela's is being father to a nation, but not to his children. Steve Jobs' is the iPhone and bullying employees. Even Adolf Hitler left a legacy, it just wasn't the one he intended.

You can choose to consciously create your legacy or let it drift. Your legacy can be a pile of ashes or your vision for the world. That's the choice we all face. The most powerful legacy you can leave is your Personal Purpose expressed in the world around you. It is a perfect alignment between the Outer Game and the Inner Game. Legacies that are remembered start with a Masterpiece. The secret is to remove the barriers which stop its creation. The purer your connection to your Personal Purpose and the more balanced your Inner and Outer Games are, the more likely you are to create a Masterpiece.

But a Masterpiece on its own doesn't guarantee leaving a legacy. Many end up creating a legacy that is out of alignment with who they are. It doesn't reach its full potential, because the Outer Game serves the ego rather than the essence. We serve ourselves rather than humanity. We manipulate rather than serve. This creates resistance in the world outside us. Conflict within us creates ripples outside us. If left untouched these ripples lead to divorce, disease, distrust, debt, addiction or depression—and even the global challenges we see around us: devaluation of entire industries or ecosystems, and the devastation and destruction of natural habitats. Those who have left the greatest legacies discovered how to rebalance and allow their Inner Game to drive their Outer Game.

> *Whatever we resist persists and grows.*
>
> **Carl Jung**

This message was brought home to me when I was painting in Provence a few years ago. It was late July. In front of me stood rows of lavender fields in full bloom and an old gnarled tree. Behind me stood the imposing figure of Mont Ventoux and all around me the Mistral wind gusted up to seventy kilometers an hour. The wind became so strong that I used three easels with rocks on them to hold the canvas. And even then, the canvas moved, acting like a sail, banging into my brush. After three very frustrating hours, I gave up and went back to the Bed & Breakfast where I was staying.

When I came back the following day, the wind continued, but as I started to paint something shifted in me. I centered myself and listened carefully. The tree started talking to me. It was swaying in the wind, just letting the wind move through its leaves, and it began to advise sagely that I should do the same. I looked at the lavender—it allowed the wind to flow through it too, just like waves in the ocean. So, why was I the only one fighting the wind?

I let go and suddenly the painting started to come alive. I used a different technique I'd never used before, and worked with the wind. I let the wind just flow through me onto the canvas. And the painting transformed beyond recognition. In ten minutes, it became the best piece I had created until then.

How could you incorporate the wind or the environment into your Masterpiece? How could you enable others to contribute? What would happen if you worked with their energy rather than against it?

Everything is connected. You are not a drop in the ocean, you are the entire ocean in a drop. We often fight others or the environment, even if it is there to help us. We slam an open door instead of walking through it. To change your world, you need to change yourself. You are part of the global choir. And the world needs to hear your voice. Speak up. Start singing. You have a unique window of opportunity right now to do so. Humanity has never been in more need. And it has never been easier to do it.

It's easy to read a book from the stands. It's much harder to stand up, walk onto the pitch and start playing. But if you don't play, you won't get the result you intend. What you decide will change your world for good. Will you let others decide the outcome of the match? Or will you step into the arena, face up and live the life you were born to create?

Life is a game. What role do you want to play in it?

I look forward to seeing you in action.

9 Doing this in Practice

So, now it's time to consciously manifest your Masterpiece—the next chapter of your life.

Use these six steps to tap into your sixth sense and begin to manifest your Mission and Masterpiece. Alternatively, if you would like me to guide you through the journey, just visit https://theartistinside.me. It will redirect you to a series of videos and apps, including:

- The Inner | Outer Game
- The Legacy NOW Test
- A guided journey to manifest your Masterpiece

1: Step three years ahead into the future and hand-draw every element of your Mission:
Relax. This isn't a test of your artistic ability. It's an invitation to tap into your imagination. No one is going to ask you to exhibit your drawing. Stick-figures will do. Simple outlines of houses or nature or whatever you want to depict is sufficient. What matters is you understand what you are drawing. It is a simple way to access your unconscious mind. Use your drawing to answer the following questions:

How is your physical, emotional and spiritual health?

- What would you love to do? What Masterpiece have you brought to life?
- Who would you love to do it with? Who are you in a relationship with?
- Where would you love to live? When do you spend time with your family?
- How do you generate a sustainable flow of money for yourself and others?
- How do you enable others to love what they do too?

2: Reflect and experience it like it's already true
What would bringing your Mission to life feel like? How would it feel to love what you do, love who you do it with, love where you live, and take care of your health, as much as those who love you take care of you? What would it feel like to create your Masterpiece? See this experience in acute detail in your mind's eye. What would you see and hear?

Then, feel in your body and mind what it would feel like to experience that moment. Would you feel more joy, peace, happiness, love? Allow these emotions to permeate every cell of your body.

3: Face your fears
Next, write down any fears you associate with bringing your Mission and Masterpiece to life. For example, the fear of not being good enough, not worth it, too old, too young, not experienced enough, not being accepted for doing it, lacking the right skillset.

Write down any and all the fears that emerge.

4: Reclaim the fear
Reclaim these fears, using Koenig's reclamation tool:

Focus on both the "positive" and "negative" polarities.

For the negative polarity, you may say, "I'm not *good enough* and I'm okay with that." Then, ask yourself what is the advantage of not being good enough? In this case, you may realize that not being good enough was the greatest thing that ever happened to you, because it encouraged you to grow and that led you to meet people and have experiences that helped you on your journey.

For the positive polarity, you may ask yourself what is the opposite of not being good enough? Let's say it's trust. In this case, you might say, "I am *trusted* with and without recognition (or money or power or whatever it is)." **In the above two examples (negative and positive polarity), replace the words in *italics* with whatever fears you wrote down in Step 3**.

Keep going until you feel no resistance to the Mission you described in Step 1, and all you feel is the emotion you wrote down in Step 2. Now, check you're not overly attached to your Mission. If you hold it too tightly, you restrict the magic. Ensure you feel a sense of "space" around it. This allows others to contribute to your Mission too. If you hold it too tightly, you will crowd them out.

5: Change your mind

Once you have done the reclamation work and you feel no resistance to the fears about bringing your Masterpiece to life—meditate, listen to meditation music or a guided journey. Do whatever you need to do to start producing theta brainwaves.

Then, using your breath, draw the energy up from the ground through your feet, up your legs, into your root chakra, up your spine, through all the other chakras to the top of your spine. Imagine the pineal gland opening naturally. Relax. Take your time. Repeat this process a few times until you feel yourself entering a deeper state. This may take some practice. This helps you access the Zone of Creation.

6: Bring your dream to life

Relax. Remain balanced. Allow whatever needs to emerge to emerge through you. See whatever you need to see, whatever you need to hear and feel whatever you need to feel. Stay in this altered state for as long as you need to. You are now beyond space and time, in a state of pure consciousness. Words don't do justice to the experience, so just enjoy it. When you return, write down whatever you need to.

***

Note: If you do this six-step process, remember, you will be tested. In the metaphysical world of no time and no space, you will have a choice, a doorway to step through. If you have done enough reclamation work before you enter this world, you will step through the doorway. If not, do more reclamation work until you're ready. Once you return to the physical world of time and space, you will be tested on what you reclaimed again. If things haven't manifested yet, or your fear manifested instead, then repeat one or two of the most relevant reclamations silently in your head, until you reconnect to your Inner Game and see a different choice emerging. Initially, it will emerge as just an impulse—the energy behind the idea. Allow it to emerge in its own time. Let it grow into a thought naturally. Then, bring it to life by saying something different or doing something different. When you do this, your world changes forever. You step into Consciousness. In this state, you are connected to everything. There is no separation between you and *it*... whatever you call it doesn't matter when you are there. All that matters is that you are.

Ask Alexander

Here are some of the most popular questions that I have received from clients—and my answers. If you have a question that isn't included below, send it to me and I will answer it: **ask@alexander-inchbald.com**

Q—*I have been using your six-step approach for a month now and I'm not showing any results.... what should I do? Or am I doing something wrong?*

A—What stops us most of the time is resistance to someone or something we're not consciously aware of. For instance, you may be following this approach so rigorously, you're actually "controlling" it and therefore preventing the magic from happening. Or you may have a secret addiction or aversion to money that you have kept hidden from everyone, including yourself. In the first example, the reclamation work would be around Power—"I'm a controlling, manipulative b******, and I'm okay with this." In the second example, it's around money—"I'm a hoarding addict and I'm okay with this." Or something like this.

Remember to reclaim the opposite as well—for example, "I'm free with and without power" or "I'm free with and without money." However, becoming aware of your resistance, let alone working out what the reclamation is, on your own isn't easy. It may take months of practice. And that's why we created the #Masterpiece programs—removing resistance to whatever you experience in the world outside you is at the heart of them. Have a look at the additional materials section to find out more.

Q—*I am a successful CEO with a team of 200+ employees. I am currently trying to help our team shift their mindset and embrace a new frontier of work-life balance. How can I be an effective leader and still competitive in my industry?*

A—Let's distinguish between your Collective Mission, your Collective Masterpiece and your Purpose. The Collective Mission defines the next chapter in your company's life, your Collective Masterpiece is the fastest way to get there and your Purpose animates both. Of course, you may use these terms differently—this is just how I use them. You may share a similar Collective Mission with other companies in your industry and outside your industry. For instance, your Mission may "enhance wellbeing"—and many other companies may share this mission. Does this mean these companies are your competitors—or your partners? It all depends on your perspective. If you consider others as competitors, they will compete with you. If you consider them as partners, they will partner with you—perhaps not immediately, but over time, even the most resolute enemies can find reconciliation. What would happen if you stopped thinking of others as operating within your industry and you started considering that all of you exist within the same ecosystem?

To visualize this, you may want to return to Chapter 6 and map out the ecosystem using the 5R framework. Now, consider what contribution you, and only you, can make to the ecosystem's Mission? In a permaculture, humans have different capabilities than plants—we have hands, which enable us to move things. What capabilities do you have that others in your ecosystem don't have? This will provide an insight into your Collective Masterpiece. While your Mission is the same as others within your ecosystem, your Masterpiece is your unique contribution to it—and that contribution isn't about maximizing the height of your tree at all cost. That approach leads to selfish hoarding of minerals and water, which would benefit others within the ecosystem. Your responsibility is to develop a Masterpiece that nurtures the soil, and generates resources that benefit the entire ecosystem. This is an entirely different long-term way of thinking. Indeed, if there is no ecosystem, there will be nothing to compete over anyway.

Q—*I would consider myself a creative person with good business sense, however I have repeatedly collaborated in partnerships that started out really well but over time didn't work out for different reasons. Where am I going wrong? I often end up frustrated and disappointed.*

A—The same principles apply as the previous question—it focused on businesses—this one focuses on individuals. So, continuing the analogy from the previous question, are you trying to grow your tree at all costs or the entire forest? Are you trying to do it all yourself, or do you create the space for others to contribute to the growth of your fruit and you to contribute to theirs? If you're trying to do it all yourself, are you allowing your perfectionism to dominate? If so, you may end up inadvertently "crowding" out potential partners—stamping all over their seedlings rather than helping them to grow or growing your canopy so wide, you block out the sunlight. What would you need to reclaim so you stop being such a selfish, dominating, manipulative perfectionist? At an even more subtle level, do you find yourself going into every meeting with an agenda? You know what you *want* from the other person. You may be happy to listen to the other person for a while, but you're really just using that as a ploy to extract what you need. If so, the other person will feel it at a very subtle level and is more likely to walk away. You are inadvertently pushing them away.

Kari, who I talked about in the introduction and Chapter 8, taught me this lesson. She used to do something similar with CEOs or Foreign Ministers—until she didn't. She stopped. Instead she started to play a game—what would happen if she had no agenda? What would happen if she was clear on her mission, embodied her Purpose (Kari's purpose is around Love) and then just left the space open for others to surprise her? So, she started to experiment. What she discovered surprised even her. If she just listened and held the "space," two things happened: first, these CEOs or ministers would start sharing so openly that their openness surprised themselves; secondly, about twenty minutes into the conversation, something "miraculous" happened—these CEO and ministers would offer something that supported Kari's Mission, but wasn't on her radar. In other words, when Kari just focused on who she is and held the space for others to be who they are, they created something that supported both of them—just not in the way she imagined. You may want to consider doing something similar.

If you think this is just about "active listening," or it's so obvious that you can't believe I included this story, read this passage again. It isn't. I made that mistake too. There is something very subtle and very deep going on here. The first time this happens, we may discard the idea that comes up as being so far away from what we envisaged going into the meeting that we stamp all over it. Just be aware of that thought. Then, see what comes up next. You may start to see how you could (personally) benefit from it. Just be aware of that thought too. See what comes up a second time. If you can avoid the temptation to either push it away or grab it, if you give it sufficient space to grow, you may just find a "miracle" occurs. It all comes down to focusing exclusively on what you love. That creates the space in which others can contribute what they love. To return to the analogy above, maybe you could share your resources so each other's trees grow flowers, your connections to pollinate these flowers, or the processes to convert this energy into fruit that can be harvested and eventually seeds that can be replanted?

Q—*Why do so many talented artistic people have money issues, or lack of money?*

A—To master the Creator profile (in the Artist Profile), we have to reject the 5,000 year old man-made system that I described in Chapter 3. Money is a central part of this system. Rejecting this system enables us to think differently outside it. We become a rebel, a misfit, a reject, an artist with wild ideas. We unleash the artist inside us—and then, we become addicted to the act of creation. We fall in love with it—and that's understandable, because being in the Zone of Creation is very seductive. In the act of creation, we are in flow—we are at peace, in harmony. In the Inner Game, we don't have to deal with the outside world—with invoices or banks or mortgages. So, we stay there. Some of us get seduced to such an extent, we push the financial world outside us away. We reject it subtly, as something "evil" or bad—and we use all sorts of excuses to justify our actions. We invoke the drama queen within us to protect our creative space. "She" may stamp her feet and come up with manner of excuses to stay in the Zone of Creation. Some of them may be valid. But unless, we are consciously aware we are doing this, we become the victim of the drama queen. To live from what we create—our Masterpiece—we need to re-embrace the system we rejected in order to create it. We need to reclaim the Art Director within us, so we balance our time between Inner and Outer, between creation and realization, between the Zone of Creation and the realization of what is created in that zone. To do this, we must reclaim all resistance to the man-made system. If we resist it in any way, we are still pushing it and money away from us. So, we must reclaim our relationship to money.

Q—*Can 7.8 billion people all love what they do every day? Who would clean the toilets or empty the rubbish bins? Shouldn't we all learn to do things we don't enjoy too, e.g., live in the "real world"?*

A - There is an apocryphal story that President Kennedy once visited NASA, the space agency, where he met a cleaner. JFK asked the man what he did, and the man replied, "I help to put a man on the moon." Whether the story is true or not misses the point. What we do is less important than how we feel about it. And how *you* feel about it is more important than how *others* feel about it. Your responsibility is not to *take* responsibility for everyone else loving what they do. It is to take responsibility for loving what *you* do. You have no idea what other people love or don't love. That's their responsibility.

According to this story, the cleaner found meaning and love in cleaning. The same principal applies in an ashram. If you visit one, you may be asked to clean the toilets. The purpose is not just to keep the place clean, nor is it to humble you, although it may. The purpose is to help you understand *how* you do something is more important than *what* you do. You can clean toilets with love. The physical act isn't important. The feeling you allow the physical act to engender in your body is. Your senses may create a feeling of discomfort—that this task is somehow beneath you—that the smell is somehow abhorrent. When my mentor, Ashoke, taught me to meditate, he told me to put sugar on my tongue until I could taste salt or smell a rose until I smelled lavender. You are not your senses. You are way more than that. Can you transcend your senses and find love in every action? If so, stop judging others for what they choose to do. You cannot change *their* world. You can only change *your* world—and the best way to do that is to love what you do—not just some of the time, all of the time. When you do that, and you ruthlessly focus only on what you love, you elevate your energy to such an extent the world around you magically changes.

Q—*My partner doesn't love what I do. She thinks that I spend too much time working on my innovations and inventions and neglect the family and household chores. She doesn't see the genius in me at all. How can I ever create my ultimate Masterpiece with this type of resistance or lack of support?*

A - About the time I got married Ashoke explained to me his sole responsibility was to his soul. It was not to heal other people even though his clients valued his healing highly. His "soul contract" was all that mattered to him. I would say my sole responsibility is to bring my Purpose and Mission to life by loving what I do, not just some of the time, but all of the time. I love spending time with my family, but I won't be able to ski regularly with my grandchildren (my Mission) if that's all I do—I will remain unfulfilled and my life will lack meaning. So, I commit to spending a certain amount of time with my family—and I keep that commitment. Then, I focus the rest of my time on my Mission. I do certain household chores with love (or as much love as I can muster). For the rest, Anna and I ask others who find more love in these tasks to help us. These are two conscious choices I have made about how I live my life. In order to make them freely and consciously, I reclaimed what Anna accused me of being—selfish and negligent: "I am selfish and I'm okay with that." The distinction is I am intentionally and consciously being selfish when I focus on my Mission, because I want to ski with my grandchildren when I'm 74. My wife may dislike it, but her resistance to me dissolves, because I stop resisting her. Personally, I found it reassuring that Nelson Mandela acknowledged he had been a terrible father to his children after he became President and father to his nation. He then consciously chose to spend more time with his grandchildren.

Q—*I am investing a lot of time doing what I love, but I am missing time with my family: what tells me that I am in balance between work and private life?*

A—Work-life balance is a myth. Trying to balance two Outer Game actions against each other won't lead to fulfillment or meaning—nor will it help you to bring your Purpose to life. On the contrary, you may will end up making compromises and sacrifices—trying to pay one thing off against the other thing and invariably failing. Instead, I would encourage you to balance your Inner Game with your Outer Game by *only* doing what you love. Do you love spending time with your family? If so, what do you *love* doing with them? Hiking, skiing, playing games, watching films, eating together...? Then, carve out time in your diary on a daily, weekly or monthly basis, and commit to that. Remember it's not the quantity of time you spend with your family that creates wonderful memories. It's the quality of that time. So, when you're with them—be with them. Avoid checking your phone every few minutes. Just be there. Consider planning your next six months with your partner and children (if they are old enough). You may want to set aside weekends or entire weeks to be with them. Then, keep that commitment, even if something "comes up" at work. Do the same at work. Write two lists: what do you *love* doing at work? It's normally what you're really good at. Then, write down what do you hate doing at work? It's normally what you're not really good at—it saps your time and energy—and more importantly puts you in a bad mood. Now, find someone who loves doing what you hate. You may say that's impossible or you can't pay that person. I get it—really, I do. However, there are many different ways to value someone's contribution. Consider how value flows between you organically, rather than a traditional transactional relationship.

Q—*What advice would you give to a young person entering the world of work who needs a job—hopefully a rewarding one—but struggles to reconcile their own values with those of most large corporations?*

A—Stop looking... in the wrong place for the wrong thing. The majority of companies operating in the Compete paradigm are experiencing enormous challenges as they transition to the Create and Collaborate paradigms. They are constantly restructuring, because they are in long-term decline. Would you rather work for a well-known company where the underlying mood is fearful—

worried when the next restructuring is coming—or for an unknown company where the underlying mood is always upbeat? If it's the second, then why focus on the first? Your values don't resonate with these companies, because you are operating from a different level of consciousness or energy than they are—so you will always feel frustrated and "trapped." Forget the idea that you need to gain experience working with these companies. Why would you want to gain experience working for a company that reinforces the archaic man-made system? Instead, I would encourage you to look at companies in ecosystems that are growing rapidly—for instance, wellbeing, technology and personal development. Rather than look for a "job," consider instead how you can create one. Entrepreneurialism is exploding all over the world. Even if you're not ready to create your own business, find an entrepreneur whose values resonate with yours and then work out how you can add value to them. That's exactly what participants in my cohorts are doing with me all the time.

Q—*I have been solving problems for years. Right now, I see blockages everywhere... what can I do?*

A—I understand. You are not alone though. Many others are in a similar situation. As we transition from one paradigm to another, many of us will appear to face an insurmountable wall. So, imagine that wall is in front of you now. Imagine it's so high, you can't see over it. But somehow you know, there is something behind it—a different world, the world you always dreamed of living in—one where you love what you do and are valued for who you are. What do you do? If you push the wall, nothing happens. If you hit the wall, nothing happens. If you try to get around the wall, nothing happens. You feel like you're constantly hitting your head against the wall. Still, nothing happens. What would happen if you accepted that the wall exists and you simply elevated your perspective? If you elevated your perspective high enough, you would be able to see over the wall. You haven't changed the wall, you have changed your perspective of the wall. So, how do you elevate your perspective? By elevating your energy—by changing your beliefs—by reclaiming your resistance to the wall—by reclaiming the walls within you. The wall doesn't disappear, but your resistance to it does. It no longer bothers you. And if it no longer bothers you, even if you are still on one side of the wall physically, you are on the other side metaphysically. Isn't this exactly what Nelson Mandela and Alexander Solzhenitsyn did in jail? Others who were kept in captivity for that long went out of their mind. So, did Mandela and Solzhenitsyn. The difference is, while they were out of the mind, they realized no wall, bars or body could imprison them. And that's true freedom. You can free yourself too. Try the techniques in this book and allow yourself to be surprised.

> *"As I walked out the door toward the gate that would lead to my freedom, I knew if I didn't leave my bitterness and hatred behind, I'd still be in prison."*
>
> **Nelson Mandela**

Join The Masterpiece Movement

Create your Masterpiece

I'm looking for the misfits, the crazy ones, the artists with wild ideas—anyone who has been rejected—to create their Masterpiece. We think different. Together we can change our worlds.

The original purpose of this book was to help you create the Masterpiece you were born to create. As you are now at the end of this book, you may find you have all the information you need to do this. In this case, I'm delighted. Enjoy the journey of creation and please let me know what you create by sending me an email at hello@alexander-inchbald.com

Alternatively, you may feel your journey is just starting and you would value support as you articulate your Purpose, define your Mission, reclaim what you have suppressed, create your Masterpiece and bring it to life through a Communications Flow and Money Flow System. I know from personal experience how difficult it is to do this work on your own. If this is the case, you may like to apply for one of the following programs:

#Masterpiece | Online

Every quarter we accept a limited cohort of new participants to our online program. During this online program, we help you:

- Articulate your Personal Purpose
- Define your Mission
- Discover what your Masterpiece is ...and bring it to life!

You will have a chance to work with many of the characters you have come across in this book: Peter Koenig, Kari Aina Eik, Jean-Philippe Challandes, Gabriel Uribe and more who are joining this band of misfits and rejects every day.

The program starts with four modules in four days:

1. Purpose and Power
2. Mission and Money
3. Your Artist Profile
4. Your Masterpiece.

Then, over the next ten weeks, we support you on your journey to create your Masterpiece. Woven throughout the program is reclamation work—Peter's tool—as described in this book, and other tools, including working directly with your unconscious mind through guided journeys as I described in Chapter 7.

In addition, you have access to background videos on WorldClass.Academy which explain each of the main concepts and two one-to-one 60-minute bonus sessions.

This program isn't for everyone. It is a deep dive into yourself. You can find out more information about this program online at https://WorldClass.Academy.

#Masterpiece 1:1

You may prefer to work on a 1:1 basis for whatever reason. I work with a limited number of people each year to help them create their Masterpiece. This program consists of:

- Four ninety-minute sessions with me via Zoom.

It covers exactly the same material as in the group program and you have access to all the background material on WorldClass.Academy. The only difference is I personalize it to you so you can accelerate your journey. I only have one condition for this program: our energy should resonate. If not, we are wasting each other's time. If you feel you might meet this condition, please book fifteen minutes in my online diary by following the link to Book a Call on my website: https://alexander-inchbald.com

About the Author

Alexander Inchbald helps Changemakers, misfits, the crazy ones, the artists with wild ideas—anyone who has been rejected—love what they do all the time by bringing the Masterpiece they were born to create to life. Over the last few years, he has helped thousands of leaders articulate their Purpose and create their Masterpiece. He has worked on all of the United Nations Sustainable Development Goals for organizations like The United Nations, World Health Organization, UNICEF and the International Committee of The Red Cross. He is founder of WorldClass Academy and the Masterpiece Movement, Creative Director of the largest Congress on reinventing the money system, a sought-after Creation Coach and an Extreme Artist. He lives with his family above Lake Geneva in Switzerland.

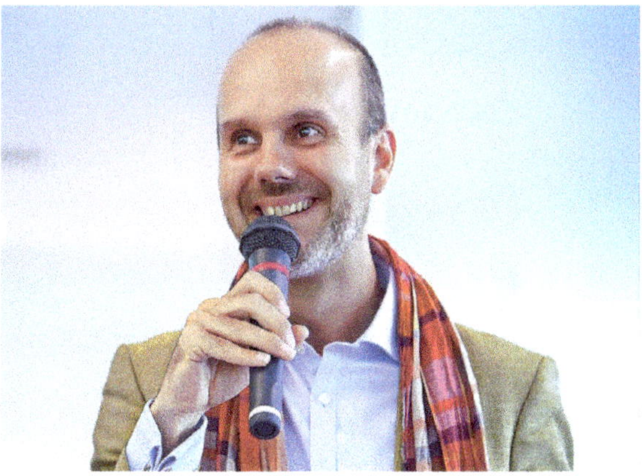

https://alexander-inchbald.com

Acknowledgments

What is manifesting around me is deeply humbling—an ecosystem of extraordinary individuals united by a shared mission—we can create a better world for ourselves and our children—one in which I ski with my grandchildren and you love what you do too. I truly believe a better world will transpire despite the media headlines and what you may read on social media. In fact, it is inevitable. You may think I'm crazy for saying this and I'm fine with that.

I'm eternally grateful to each of you—the "Rejects United"—who are on the same journey and have helped me bring #Masterpiece to life. Each of you is creating your own Masterpiece: a center of the forest we are growing together. It stretches around the globe. Let me start by thanking Natalie Deane, who encouraged me to write this book. She is an accomplished author in her own right and generously offered her skills, with her friend, Jacqueline Cripps. It took Michelangelo four years to create his first Masterpiece—the statue of *David*, because he polished and polished and polished it. Natalie worked tirelessly to polish this book. I am forever grateful. Two Aussies helping a Brit—I did say impossible is nothing! Let me also thank Edwin Hassink, the best designer I have ever come across, and Mark Harrison, the best communications executive I have ever come across, for bringing the book to life visually and through communications. I'd also like to thank Erika Pahk, Riccardo Giacometti and Nyaima Taylor for their support with the communications.

Let's get to the heart of the matter. The content of this book is inspired by conversations with the greatest thinkers, coaches and visionaries I have met. I'm privileged to call you my partners: Peter Koenig, the Money Master, who wrote the Foreword and freely shares his wisdom including reclamation work with the world. I am constantly inspired by your example; Kari Aina Eik, who is changing the world with her Masterpiece, United Cities—I'm just grateful for our friendship; Jean-Philippe Challandes, the Swiss surgeon of consciousness—what a journey you're on; Gabriel Uribe—the crazy Mexican, who always comes up with new idea. Special thanks to Jason Bernhardt-Lanier, who has supported me in bringing the Legacy NOW Test and Personal Purpose app to life—thank you for your love and friendship. Without your belief in me, this wouldn't have happened. The same goes for Tamami Ushiki, my partner in Japan—I can't wait to bring #Masterpiece to the Land of the Rising Sun so I can eat some more divine sushi.

Then, there are my clients—without you, I wouldn't have been able to test the models in this book. I'm particularly grateful to Riccardo Bellini at Richemont, Michelle Crossan-Matos at Samsung and Nate Hurst, previously at HP Inc. If my work has touched you in any way, I am grateful to you too. Each of you has helped to shape this book. You are too numerous to mention here, but you know who you are. You hold a very special place in my heart—thank you.

Let me finish by thanking the three people to who this book is dedicated—my wife Anna, who told me to never write another book—thank you for your love, patience and eternal support. Marrying you was the second-best moment of my life. The best was bringing Sasha and Daniel into this world. I have no idea how to thank the two of you. You're the greatest teachers in the world. Thank you for choosing me as your father. Keep being you—the best you you can be. This book is my gift to you—my dream for a better world that one day you will inherit. I can't wait to ski with your children. I love you.

Lightning Source UK Ltd.
Milton Keynes UK
UKHW021648110123
415157UK00012B/190

9 782839 931878